Economic Restructuring
AND
Emerging Patterns
OF
Industrial Relations

Stephen R. Sleigh
Editor

1993

W.E. UPJOHN INSTITUTE for Employment Research
Kalamazoo, Michigan 49007

Library of Congress Cataloging-in-Publication Data

Economic restructuring and emerging patterns of industrial relations /
Stephen R. Sleigh, editor.
  p. cm.
  Includes bibliographical references.
  ISBN 0-88099-131-3 (pbk.) — ISBN 0-88099-132-1 (cloth)
  1. Industrial relations—United States—Case studies.
  2. Industrial relations—Europe—Case studies.   I. Sleigh, Stephen R.
HD8072.5.E37   1992
331—dc20   92-36997
                                                                     CIP

Copyright © 1993
W.E. Upjohn Institute for Employment Research
300 S. Westnedge Avenue
Kalamazoo, Michigan 49007

Cover design by J.R. Underhill.
Index prepared by Shirley Kessel.
Printed in the United States of America.

PREFACE

The Center for Labor-Management Policy Studies at the City University of New York hosted a year-long series of seminars during the academic year 1989-90 that brought together academics, union leaders, government officials, business executives, and graduate fellows at the Center to discuss and analyze the relationship between economic restructuring and industrial relations. In the fall of 1990 the Center hosted a conference at Princeton University, which included all of the seminar participants and an array of scholars and practitioners who have worked on understanding and shaping the highly competitive economic environment in which most organizations find themselves. Complete lists of seminar presenters and conference participants are included in Appendix I and Appendix II, respectively. This volume grew out of the seminars and conference sponsored by the Center.

Bruce Herman and I, both graduate fellows at the Center during this period, organized the seminar series and conference under the guidance of Professor Seamus O'Cleireacain, then Assistant Director of the Center now at the Ford Foundation. We received financial, intellectual, and editing assistance from Susan Houseman, Allan Hunt, and Judy Gentry of the W.E. Upjohn Institute for Employment Research. We were also supported in our efforts by the Centers director, Victor Gotbaum, and deputy director, Richard Styskal. Richard died tragically in the summer of 1990. All of us at the Center miss Richard's guidance and good humor.

In early 1991 Bruce Herman became President of the Garment Industry Development Corporation (GIDC) of New York, where he has put into practice many of the ideas that he writes about in the chapter on the Emilia-Romagna region of Italy. I assumed Richard Styskal's position as deputy director of the Center.

In any edited collection of works there inevitably are differences in writing styles and practice. To the greatest extent possible, we have sought to smooth them out so that the reader can extract the greatest amount of information from each of the cases. In the introduction I have briefly summarized the case studies and analyses, and have provided an executive summary of the key conclusions that follow from the papers. A bibliography is provided for readers interested in following up on the many subjects that are raised in this collection.

THE AUTHOR

Stephen R. Sleigh is the Deputy Director of the Center for Labor-Management Policy Studies at the City University of New York. He received his PhD in Sociology from the Graduate School and University Center of City University of New York in January 1991, and a Masters of Public Administration at Harvard University's Kennedy School of Government in 1987. He was formerly employed with the Economic Policy Council of the United Nations Association, where he was the director of research activities. Prior to his policy and research work, Dr. Sleigh was a printing press erector and machinist from 1974 to 1985, work which took him to over fifty newspapers in seven countries.

Dr. Sleigh's current research topics include labor-management relations in the American newspaper industry, labor's role in technological development, and the social dimensions of global economic activity.

CONTENTS

1
Introduction

Stephen R. Sleigh
City University of New York

Over the last 20 years, global competition, product obsolescence, and excess capacity in traditional industries have brought about pronounced changes in the structure of the world economy. In response to these changes, unions, corporations, and governments have struggled to develop economic policies that will ensure adequate returns on investment, create or save jobs, and anchor industries within national borders. The purpose of this book is to review innovative responses to economic restructuring that have involved the joint efforts of unions, corporations, and government.

The record of these initiatives forms a mosaic of varied responses and results. Through a year-long series of seminars conducted by the Center for Labor Management Policy Studies of the City University of New York, culminating in a conference in the fall of 1990, analyses of efforts were presented where workers and their unions, businesses and government at the local, regional, or state level, have worked together to develop economic restructuring processes. These efforts include case studies from Western Europe, as well as detailed examination of U.S. examples, particularly state-level efforts from Michigan, Massachusetts, and Pennsylvania. The analyses emphasize the role of industrial relations in these processes. Detailing the seminars and the conference, this book serves as a resource for unions, businesses, and government on current economic restructuring activities and as a survey of current thinking about the process of economic restructuring, particularly the often neglected role workers and their unions play in this process.[1]

The wide-ranging economic shocks of technological change and global competition have produced fundamental changes in the past two decades. In the steel industry alone, 460,000 American jobs were lost during the 1980s, cutting the membership of the United Steelworkers of America in half. In the automobile industry, General Motors, Ford, and Chrysler all experienced reductions in the workforce and market share throughout the 1980s, and judging by recent announcements by GM that another 74,000 jobs will be cut over the next three years, the trend will continue. These changes have altered the respective roles of workers and their uniors, management, and government in economic development. As the response time to these continuing changes shortens, considerable experimentation is underway in Western Europe and the United States to find the proper mix of employee involvement in managerial decisionmaking and government support for restructuring efforts. No clear paradigm has yet emerged that would replace the traditional adversarial relationships between labor, management, and government which in many respects have been institutionalized.[2]

In the United States, the importance of developing a coherent national economic restructuring strategy is becoming increasingly clear. President Bush's trip to Japan in January 1992 with a cadre of influential American CEOs highlighted the lack of a national strategy beyond the need to open up Asian markets to American products. The cases in this book point to a general direction for plotting a policy that is responsive to the highly competitive global economy in which enterprises large and small now operate.[3]

The 1989-90 seminar series brought together practitioners to report on and critically assess the reciprocal relationships among technological change, economic restructuring, and industrial relations. During the course of the project, three main issues were examined: the extent to which work organization and market share or competitive position are influenced by technical innovation; how these changes are conditioned by government policies; and the role collective bargaining relationships between unions and companies play in the economic restructuring process. The answers provided in these case studies are essentially qualitative judgments for which the analysis of cross-national experiences is of considerable value. The comparative perspective allows one to identify those patterns that are specific to particular conditions within and between nations and regions, and those that form a more universal set of relationships. The case studies from Western Europe and the United States provide a context for two "thought" pieces, one by Wolfgang Streeck and one by Charles Sabel, on the implications these efforts have for industrial relations.

While the exact mix of the respective roles of labor, management, and government varied in the cases examined, the project concentrated on efforts in which these three sectors are working cooperatively to address economic restructuring. More specifically, the project focused on collaborative efforts to expand and deepen market share through more diversified, higher value-added and customized products, and the reorganization strategies initiated to achieve these goals. The seminars primarily, though not exclusively, dealt with unionized workforces in manufacturing industries.

In both pieces by Charles Sabel and by Wolfgang Streeck the emphasis is on the importance of taking into account an institutional perspective of the labor market. The social dimension of economic restructuring is in part based upon the collection of institutional competencies that make, in specific conditions, positive contributions to competitive market performance. The case studies, which are briefly described below, sought to identify what specific conditions and institutional mechanisms facilitated successful economic restructuring.

Case Studies of Economic
Restructuring—European Experience

The first three case studies are from Western Europe. They were selected for their diversity of experience and for their emphasis on different aspects of the economic restructuring process. The three cases, from the Emilia-Romagna region of Italy, from Andalusia, Spain, and of the Auroux laws in France, are similar to the United States in that in each case unions at the national level are relatively weak.

Making transnational comparisons is always a difficult task, but we believe that the cases selected have important lessons for American policymakers because the problems faced in each case were roughly comparable. During the course of the seminar series we also hosted sessions on German codetermination and Swedish social democracy. We elected to include the less well-known examples from Italy, Spain, and France even though many people, particularly those in the labor movement, aspire to the high level of coordination that has prevailed between business, labor, and government in Germany and Sweden. It bears noting, however, that the paper by Wolfgang Streeck on training as a strategic variable in economic restructuring borrows heavily from his experience and understanding of the German system.

The first case study, by Bruce Herman, analyzes the successful economic development of Emilia-Romagna, Italy. As explained by Herman, Emilia-Romagna has undergone a dramatic transformation in the past 50 years, moving from fascist domination and civil war to a situation of broad economic well-being and 40 years of government by the Italian left in the region.

In the 1950s, the Emilian economy was based primarily on agricultural production. What manufacturing did exist was concentrated in a small number of very large, vertically integrated firms. As manufacturing grew, there was a decline in large firms and a proliferation of small firms. Initially, the small firms of Emilia-Romagna served large enterprises as dependent subcontractors. To overcome the negative consequences of this situation, small shops learned to diversify their client base through horizontal linkages to other firms. Stronger commercial linkages reinforced the tendency of industry sectors to cluster, further stimulating the consolidation of industrial districts comprised of firms involved in different stages of production.

Supporting industrial restructuring in Emilia-Romagna is a system of business services rooted in public/private cooperation. At first, industry experts were provided by trade associations to take advantage of appropriate economies of scale and cut overhead costs for member firms. Following the lead of the trade associations, regional and local governments became actively involved in economic restructuring, as has the trade union movement in Emilia-Romagna.

Local unions, particularly the FIOM (the metalworkers union), have concentrated on using the collective bargaining process to broaden participation and gain more autonomy within the process of production. Beginning in 1987 the FIOM began to sign a series of agreements aimed at establishing more participatory cooperation through group-oriented work organization. Still in its initial stages, the FIOM is making sure that the shop floor is not overlooked. The Emilian case shows the importance of strategic alliances between firms and the role that government and organized labor can play in fostering these connections.

The second European case, by Michael Barzelay, is from Andalusia, Spain. The focus of this paper is entirely different from any of the others in this collection in that the role workers or their unions play is tangential to the economic restructuring process. What Barzelay does develop is a detailed rendering of the difficulties one public sector manager encounters as he tries to bring about a shift in the organization of an entire industry in his region. The role of a dedicated public administrator is clearly critical to success in this case, and a component that is often overlooked when policymakers think up economic development strategy.

The case of Andalusia's attempts to revitalize the declining marble industry in this poor southeastern state in Spain starts with the end of the Franco era in the mid-1970s and the dawning of democracy in Spain. As a result of the reconfiguration of political boundaries after Franco, a series of autonomous states was created. Without a history of local self-government, the patterns of government assistance and regulation remained to be defined in Andalusia. The principal activities Barzelay recorded from 1983 to 1988 were those of the director of the Institute of Industrial Promotion of Andalusia (IPIA), which was charged with instigating planning efforts, identifying the activities and tasks that must be carried out for planning to be productive, inducing participants to understand the competitive environment, insisting that joint actions which create common competitive advantages be conceived and undertaken, and mobilizing resources for these individual and joint actions that fit the mutually agreed upon plan. The industry most in need of IPIA's assistance was the centuries old marble quarrying in Andalusia.

In 1983 nearly 70 percent of the marble extracted from the industry's quarries was sold in unfinished or semifinished form to manufacturers in other regions. The marble industry was characterized at that time by small, family-owned quarries that typically employed only a handful of workers, and those often only on a seasonal basis. Lacking modern technology and equipment, miners relied on the same techniques of extraction that had been used for generations, and local fabricators produced only artisanal goods.

The marble industry of the communities of Macael County, which employed 7,000, was in need of strategic realignment: jobs were being lost to more sophisticated operations; existing jobs were unsteady and, for the most part, poorly paid. After initiating an action plan in 1985 with the support of the mine owners and workers, the industry began to turn around. By 1987, only 30 percent of the marble extracted was sold in unfinished form, while the remainder was processed locally into higher value-added finished products.

Barzelay's case shows how social change and strategic planning, instigated and coordinated by a regional governmental institution, can dramatically improve the performance and competitive capacities of a traditional industry, even in one of Europe's most underdeveloped regions. While the case does not focus on industrial relations as such, it does offer a richly detailed analysis of the kinds of problems that a public administrator can expect to face when taking on the process of economic restructuring.

The third European case is also distinctive. In this piece Bernard Brown looks at the Auroux laws in France. Working from a new-found position of strength after the election of Mitterrand, the French labor movement worked closely with Socialist Minister of Labor, Jean Auroux, to develop "new rights for workers." These efforts culminated in a series of four laws enacted in 1982 that were intended to give workers a direct say in the decisionmaking process of all enterprises employing more than 200 people. The intentions of the Socialist government and French labor movement, to create a new form of labor-management relations system through public action, were not realized, according to Brown. The most fundamental change seems to have occurred within management, described by Brown as a "cultural revolution that has taken place within the enterprise" in support of participatory programs.

Brown's brief analysis of the Auroux laws points to an ongoing debate among scholars of industrial relations in the United States as to the benefit of employee participation schemes. As one part of competitiveness strategy, employee participation in decisionmaking has gained widespread support in both unionized and nonunion organizations in the United States. In 1978, the United States went so far as to adopt the Labor-Management Cooperation Act, whose main goal is "to improve communication between representatives of labor and management." Other steps along the same lines have included the creation of the Bureau of Labor Management Relations and Cooperative Programs within the Department of Labor and various efforts at improving quality service through cooperation in federal programs such as at the Federal Aviation Administration. Brown's analysis of the French experience casts doubt on the way in which the participatory process was conceived and operationalized in France, a country with a relatively weak labor movement. The implications for unions in the United States are sobering and are reflected in the lack of a participation policy at the AFL-CIO.

Case Studies of Economic Restructuring—U.S. Experience

The first case study from the United States, by Peter Lazes, describes the collaborative efforts of New York State and Cornell University's Program for Employment and Workplace Systems (PEWS) to keep a Buffalo windshield wiper blade company operating. Lazes worked closely with the company, Trico Products, and the union, United Automobile Workers, from 1985 to 1987 in trying to find innovative solutions to the competitive challenge posed by the option to produce Trico's main product in Mexico at a fraction of the labor cost in the Buffalo plant.

The odds were long that the difference between costs in the Mexican plant—a "maquiladora," or assembly plant, on the U.S.-Mexico border and the Buffalo plant could be significantly reduced: the prevailing wage in Mexico was $1.20 an hour versus $12.50 in Trico's Buffalo plant. An independent analysis by a well-known management consulting firm showed that labor costs in Buffalo would have to be cut 30 percent in order to remain competitive with the cost of producing in Mexico. In early 1985 the state's Urban Development Corporation agreed with Trico's management that the advantages of producing in Mexico were too great to overcome. But Lazes and the UAW regional director persuaded the skeptics to give PEWS and the workers in the plant some time to do their own analysis of possible cost savings from restructuring the work process.

Working together with Rensselaer Polytechnic Institute and PEWS, union members and production management came up with a plan that exceeded the cost savings projected for the Mexican plant. The in-plant cost study teams, according to Lazes, created a new sense of togetherness among workers and between labor and management. While Trico's original projections were to close the Buffalo production facility—and in the process eliminate between 1,400 and 2,000 well-paid union jobs—the in-plant teams projected that half of the workforce could be saved. In what Lazes described as a bittersweet outcome, despite the concerted efforts to keep all production based in Buffalo, Trico's management still moved some production to Mexico. The Trico case presented by Lazes shows both what is possible through joint labor, business, and state efforts, and the limitations of these efforts. The inability of the state or the union to persuade Trico to approve their proposed improvements was an agonizing difficulty that could not be overcome.

Robert Coy, director of the Office of Policy Planning and Evaluation for the Commonwealth of Pennsylvania, along with Saul Rubenstein and Mike Shay, present the second U.S. case study by describing the state's Manufacturing Innovation Network Initiatives (MAIN) projects in the Lehigh Valley. At present the MAIN projects involve four different industries: the plastics industry in northwestern Pennsylvania; the metalworking and machine tool industries in the southwestern part of the state; and the apparel industry in the Lehigh Valley. The basic approach of the MAIN projects is to work with clusters or groups of firms rather than trying to provide assistance in a piecemeal one-on-one fashion.

In order to develop the appropriate response, all MAIN projects begin with a strategic audit of the industry, which is used to gather information and to begin to define a constituency of firms. In turn, steering committees are established to organize the projects, while the specific industry needs identified are used to form working groups charged with coordinating and developing programs to address restructuring problems. Within the Lehigh Valley there are over 200 apparel firms with over 15,000 employees. Pursuing a participatory restructuring approach, which included representatives from business, labor, and government, the Lehigh Valley Project Steering Committee identified issues ranging from labor force problems, training, management systems and technology, industrial structure and linkages, and marketing and sourcing concerns. While these initiatives have not reached the implementation stage, this case stresses that the MAIN projects bode well for continued cooperative efforts.

In the third case study from the United States, Mike Schippani gives an inside account of the Michigan Modernization Project, which was created by Governor Blanchard in 1984 to bring together labor, business, and the state in reversing the declining competitiveness of Michigan's industrial base. The state's plan, writes Schippani, was threefold.

The first part of Michigan's modernization strategy was a vision of Michigan as an international center for the development of manufacturing technology. The goal was to build institutions that would be in the business of developing and applying technology to the manufacturing base of Michigan. Two institutions were created to achieve this goal: the Industrial Technology Institute and the Michigan Modernization Service—a sort of industrial extension program.

The second part of the strategy was the creation of innovation capital to fill the gaps in financing available to newer firms or nontraditional projects. To accomplish this goal the state created the Michigan Strategic Fund.

The third part of the strategy centered around workforce learning and workplace relations. The keys to this aspect of the strategy, Schippani argues, were the education and training of the workforce and innovations in labor-management relations. Bringing together resources from the state's Department of Education and Department of Labor, the Michigan Modernization Plan was able to provide technical services to hundreds of firms.

While evidence on the program's effectiveness is still under evaluation, Schippani notes the importance of involving business, organized labor, and the government in joint collaborative efforts. As the three-part Michigan strategy grew and matured, it became clearer that early, proactive union involvement was critical to the success of maintaining industrial competitiveness. The elections in the fall of 1990, which displaced Governor Blanchard, occasioned a fundamental shift in direction in economic development strategy in Michigan described by Schippani.

The final case study from the United States, presented by Frank Emspak, then director of the Massachusetts Center for Applied Technology, further emphasizes the need for inclusive, participatory restructuring. Emspak writes that the Center for Applied Technology concentrates on skills-based automation (user-driven design) as a key component of shop-floor reorganization. Utilizing the skills-based approach, the Center for Applied Technology has sought to involve blue-collar workers in technology development and deployment strategies. To date the Center's efforts have been modest, impacting only a handful of firms. Nonetheless, Emspak stresses that worker-inclusive needs assessment creates a situation whereby the analysis of the problem helps build consensus for possible solutions. As in Michigan, the defeat of a liberal Democratic governor in the 1990 elections brought about significant changes in policy direction away from collaborative efforts involving business, unions, and government as equal partners to the traditional model of direct aid on an *ad hoc* basis from government to industry.

Economic Restructuring
and Industrial Relations: Two Views

The two papers that conclude the volume provide provocative analyses of economic restructuring and the emerging patterns of industrial relations. The two authors have written extensively on these and related topics during the 1980s and open up the debate on future economic restructuring policy.

Charles Sabel writes of the relationship between international competition, the organization of production, and labor-management relations. Pointing out that changing interfirm relationships are driving an ongoing industrial restructuring, Sabel examines how the reorganization of production challenges the labor movement by creating new demands on behalf of both management and the rank-and-file.

Sabel links the development of unstable market conditions, and the subsequent need to respond through more flexible production, with the difficulties national unions are having in maintaining cohesion and membership. He argues that economic restructuring is creating a new set of production relations as the demise of stable mass markets undermines industrial organization based on the mass production of standardized commodities. The mass production regime, predicated on mass consumer markets, dedicated machinery, and semiskilled workers and dependent on captive subsuppliers, is being superseded by a more fluid, increasingly differentiated, system of production, according to Sabel.

In this economic environment, firms are forced to establish more interdependent relationships with subsuppliers and seek cooperative joint ventures with other firms to keep pace with changes in key technologies. This type of industrial configuration requires considerable workforce reskilling as rigid, long-run, standard product technologies are replaced by more flexible, short-run, computer-enhanced equipment. Also present is the potential for a more decentralized system of control, within the chain of production, between the various units contributing to the final product, and in labor-management relations.

In terms of labor-management relations, the demands for increased flexibility have led to a situation where local agreements are circumventing national contracts. Across Europe and the United States Sabel notes the emergence of local-level agreements, which he characterizes as the establishment of "jointness" rather than cooperation. That is, the responsibilities of labor and management became more intertwined, blurring the distinction between roles that requires joint action. Moreover, there is evidence of a shift toward decentralized bargaining, even where it is not officially sanctioned by national unions. As the cases show, these developments are rooted in the changing system of production.

Wolfgang Streeck's paper concludes the book by specifying an institutional mechanism of the sort that Sabel is describing in a more general fashion. Streeck focuses primarily on the value of union involvement in vocational training. In his view, skill formation is the key to enhancing productivity, and unions are well positioned to provide common linkage across firms to promote high standards of training. Streeck is clearly influenced by the successful German model of apprenticeship training, but he makes the case that the same logic that has brought business, labor, and government together in Germany may apply to other industrial countries as well. Supported by public policies that help reduce the incentive for employers to look for a free ride from someone else's training, unions may develop an active commitment to enforce high standards of training stringently, in the interest of high wages, secure employment, and a non-Taylorist organization of work.

Conclusions and Policy Implications

"If we don't develop a national program in the next five years, it's going to be impossible for us to be serious industrial contenders by the year 2000. I'm advocating for us collectively—government and industry—to accept that there is a problem and that we have to come up with responsible solutions." So said Andrew Grove, president and chief executive officer of silicone chip manufacturer Intel Corporation in 1990.[4] We concur with this sentiment. The cases presented show, in varied ways, how the third social partner—workers and their unions—can contribute to the economic restructuring process.

In the absence of a national industrial policy in the United States, state governments have taken the initiative by setting the agenda, providing funding, and establishing technical support programs for cooperative restructuring efforts. Throughout the 1980s, individual states started a wide variety of programs that responded to declining economic competitiveness—particularly in the industrialized states of the Northeast and Midwest. These efforts were not strictly partisan, as evidenced by the innovative programs developed by Republican Governors Thornburgh of Pennsylvania, Kean of New Jersey, and Orr of Indiana. These Republican governors had no problem with seeking out governmental responses to declining competitiveness in the 1980s, often with the assistance of organized labor. The states examined in this book, along with the cases from Western Europe, point towards a common direction supporting an economic restructuring process that integrates social goal-setting while retaining the efficiency of market competition.

State efforts were developed out of pragmatic assessments of the need to remain competitive, not out of ideological commitment. What the cases show is that the ability of governments to positively influence economic development is limited when they go it alone. The question these states faced was not which industries are worth saving (the sunrise versus sunset debate that characterized the discussion of industrial policy in the late 1970s and early 1980s), but rather how can government bring resources to promote joint efforts between businesses, workers, and unions who are trying to adapt to a profoundly changed operating environment.

Still, the failure of "industrial policy" as a political idea in the United States, and the apparent success of various models of market economies the world over, would seem to indicate that rethinking the role of collaborative efforts between business, labor, and government is unnecessary. Transnational alliances, and direct foreign investment, blur the national identity of corporate identities, making life more difficult for interventionist policymakers not convinced of the benefits of trade liberalization. Policymakers long accustomed to a world in which they could identify and support "national champions," increasingly find that national champions have foreign alliances. The growth and diversity of these strategic alliances complicates the established relationships between policymakers and national champions. In some instances, the contributions of national champions to national employment, Gross National Product, and tax revenue may be little different from those of competitors who have opened production facilities in the national champion's home market.

Indeed, recent efforts emanating from Washington at coordinating business and governmental activities in economic development have been, by and large, spectacular flops. The much-publicized U.S. Memories project, a ground-breaking attempt by American computer companies to cooperate in producing memory chips with federal government backing, was officially declared dead in early 1990. Similarly, the Defense Advanced Research Projects Agency's attempts to fund basic research and development of commercial technology for high-definition television, a project that enjoyed almost universal support on Capitol Hill in the spring of 1989, was effectively ended in the spring of 1990.

Given these failures, why is the idea of joint business, labor, and governmental coordination in economic restructuring being promoted in this book? The answer, as it emerges in the case studies in this volume, is that joint efforts work when the right conditions and well thought out policies prevail. This is not an ideological or moral argument—it is a pragmatic assessment that follows from and supports basic values of democratic participation. The lessons of how best to pursue economic restructuring are being learned piece by piece, and place by place. The importance of this volume is that it takes a step toward synthesizing these lessons into a coherent policy that is of use to workers and their unions, business, and government.

A number of common themes which emerged from the case studies are useful for policymakers from business, labor, or government trying to fashion a coherent response to economic restructuring. We identified three.

1. Intrafirm organization, or workplace organization. As the case studies from Michigan, Massachusetts, and Italy clearly show, shop-floor organization and reorganization involve questions of employee participation in areas traditionally reserved for managerial decisionmaking and control over the decisionmaking process. Shortening product life cycles, doing away with rigid distinctions between jobs and departments in order to speed new product development, and just-in-time sourcing demand higher levels of coordination and cooperation within firms. Many of the firms discussed in the case studies have moved toward group, or team-based, work organization in an attempt to manage the growing complexity of production. The French example, however, serves as a cautionary note that the benefits of participation may work against a weakened labor movement.

2. Interfirm linkages. The cases of Michigan, Pennsylvania, Italy, and Spain show that the improved competitive position of an individual firm, or semiautonomous unit of a larger corporation, is often the result of the quality of interfirm relations. The example of the increased interdependence of suppliers and original equipment manufacturers in the auto industry, whether in the United States, Germany, or Japan, is a case in point. The importance of interfirm relations is in turn compounded by the need for access to technical specialization which is often prohibitively expensive to maintain, or by market uncertainty, both of which demand more flexible production. Increasingly, as these cases show, the competitive position of any individual firm is rooted in a web of forward and backward linkages with other suppliers and client firms.

3. Industry policy. Distinct from the focus of debates about industrial policy in the past, these cases suggest that when discussing the competitive situation of an industry sector, a subnational or regional focus tends to be the proper reference point. While the U.S. case studies showed that lack of a coherent federal policy was often the driving force behind the development of a state-level economic restructuring strategy, a more regional approach often made more sense for the states anyway. The competitive position of an industry sector, our cases indicated, is increasingly determined by the health of mutually reinforcing networks within regions.[5]

In conclusion, the essays in this book demonstrate the challenges and opportunities that exist for forging alliances between business, organized labor, and government that can create economic value. The diversity of cases also indicates that developing a coherent and effective federal-level industrial policy is problematic. Perhaps the best role the federal government can play in the United States is to help coordinate and facilitate the activities undertaken at the local, regional, or state level. Providing a clearinghouse of information on such activities would perform a valuable service for local government officials, business executives, and labor leaders. More comprehensive data on the effectiveness of differing approaches to economic restructuring would also assist researchers in assessing these new models.

Four observations follow from Sabel's essay and the case studies that involved the active participation of unions. Unions can influence restructuring, either positively through active participation in the process or negatively by clinging to outdated work rules or practices, but union participation is neither necessary nor sufficient to insure a beneficial outcome for labor. Weak unions in Japan, for example, seem quite compatible with international competitiveness, while strong unions and a management sheltered from market competition in the United States has in some instances led to mutual stagnation. Second, strong unions may well be undermined by successful corporate restructuring. Skilled workers, for example, may lose their position as skills get transferred to automated processes or professional employees.

An additional point raised by Sabel, and evidenced in the case studies of Italy and Michigan, is that labor organizations need substantial internal reforms in order to face the challenges of economic restructuring. Because of the rapid integration of firms with their suppliers, the unit of organization of the union can no longer be the firm or corporation, but must be regional or national. The whipsawing of plants against one another within General Motors, pitting UAW members in New York against UAW members in Michigan, is an example of this problem. Finally, the point was made that even in Europe, where unions are generally stronger and more politically influential than in the United States, workers and their unions often get hurt by restructuring. While firms require more commitment from workers in high value-added operations, they often provide less job security. Moreover, the pressures for continuous learning in these firms has the effect of empowering workers but also of separating workers who have skills from those who do not. The subsequent stress and insecurity of workers are areas that unions are only beginning to address.

Perhaps the most important lesson of all, however, is made clear in Wolfgang Streeck's concluding essay. Without an institutional base for supporting economic restructuring, the short-term pressures on politicians will overwhelm the longer-term needs of economics. The cases of Michigan and Massachusetts provide ample testimony to this— without a strong institutional base, the changing of political parties governing the state led to significant retrenchment of economic restructuring programs. By institutionalizing the processes or policies described in the case studies, an economic restructuring process that pays attention to the emerging patterns of industrial relations can help address the difficulties of adapting to a highly competitive global marketplace. Putting the pieces together is a critical challenge for policymakers in business, labor, and government throughout the industrial democracies in the 1990s.

NOTES

1. All too often unions and workers are considered the cause of lagging competitiveness rather than part of the solution. A recent attempt to correct this view can be found in Lawrence Mishel and Paula Voos, editors, *Unions and Economic Competitiveness*. Armonk, NY: M.E. Sharpe, 1992.

2. Many studies have looked at the competitiveness of American industry over the last several years. Notable among these works are: Bruce Scott and George C. Lodge, editors, *U.S. Competitiveness in the World Economy*. Boston: Harvard Business School Press, 1985; Martin K. Starr, editor, *Global Competitiveness: Getting the U.S. Back on Track*. NY: W.W. Norton, 1988; and Anthony Carnevale, *America and the New Economy*. San Francisco: Jossey-Bass, 1991. A number of studies have also looked at the effect of technological change on competitiveness and workplace relations. Among these are: Richard Hyman and Wolfgang Streeck, editors, *New Technology and Industrial Relations*. Oxford: Basil Blackwell, 1988; and Richard Cyert and David Mowery, editors, *Technology and Employment*. Washington, DC: National Academy Press, 1987. All the data presented are from the U.S. Bureau of Labor Statistics, various publications.

3. From a policy perspective, some authors have argued for a more entrepreneurial state. See for example, Peter Eisinger, *The Rise of the Entrepreneurial State*. Madison: University of Wisconsin Press, 1988; Ted Gabler and David Osborne, *Reinventing Government: How the Entrepreneurial Spirit is Transforming the Public Sector*. Reading, MA: Addison-Wesley, 1992; and David Osborne, *Laboratories of Democracy*. Boston: Harvard Business School Press, 1988.

4. Larry Hicks, "Intel Chief Urges U.S. Industrial Policy," *Sacramento Bee*, May 3, 1990, E1.

5. Along similar lines of thought see, Robert Beauregard, editor, *Economic Restructuring and Political Response*, in *Urban Affairs Annual Reviews*, vol. 34. London: Sage, 1989; and Michael Storper and Allen Scott, editors, *Pathways to Industrialization and Regional Development in the 1990s*. Boston: Unwin and Hyman, 1991.

2
Economic Development and Industrial Relations in a Small-Firm Economy

The Experience of Metalworkers in Emilia-Romagna, Italy

Bruce Herman
Garment Industry Development Corporation

One example often referred to in discussions of successful economic restructuring is the "Third Italy," particularly the Emilia-Romagna region of north-central Italy. And yet in the growing literature on Emilia-Romagna there is often little mention of the role of industrial relations in this predominantly small-firm economy. This chapter seeks to explain the history and results of a proactive collective bargaining strategy developed by the Federazione Impiegati Operai Metallurgici (FIOM), the metal-mechanical union affiliated with the Confederazione Generale Italiana del Lavoro (CGIL), in the context of the successful industrial restructuring of the Emilian economy.

The FIOM, with almost 70,000 members in the region (Catholic and Republican affiliates have 16,000 members), in an industry sector with a 55 percent unionization rate, has used its strength to pursue a proactive collective bargaining strategy designed to increase worker participation and control.[1] Leveraging needed organizational change within the firm to gain greater autonomy and an expanded role in the restructuring process, the FIOM is trying to "regain" control of work layout and job design. The goal of the FIOM approach is to establish an ongoing, autonomous union role in what are often referred to as areas of management prerogative (such as work layout and staffing) inside individual firms (intrafirm). Yet, given the complex web of relations between firms (interfirm) in Emilia-Romagna, the FIOM strategy is also clearly intended to promote an active union role in defining inter-firm relations as well.

The initial objective of the FIOM strategy is to expand the scope of collective bargaining to establish interdisciplinary (cutting horizontally across existing vertical hierarchies), autonomous work groups, thereby bilaterally determining job design and layout. Once established, these work groups will pursue productivity improvements and be rewarded based upon the results achieved. However, because of the autonomy of the work groups, management does not automatically gain access to the methods whereby the productivity improvements were achieved. Therefore, by attempting to establish ongoing autonomy and control over production decisions, the FIOM of Emilia-Romagna is redefining the boundaries of collective bargaining and industrial relations.

Background

Industrial relations have been in a state of flux for the past few decades, with the Italian situation exhibiting considerable volatility.[2] Twenty-five years ago the Italian labor movement found itself with for-mal recognition guaranteed by the Italian constitution, but with very little real power and almost no presence inside the factory.[3] The union federations—Communist/Socialist (CGIL), Catholic (CISL), Republi-can (UIL)—were numerically significant, yet they lacked effective power both on the shop floor and at the national policymaking level. This situation of formal recognition but *de facto* exclusion was swept away by the social unrest of the late 1960s and the "Italian Hot Autumn" of 1969. Throughout this phase of rapid ascendancy on the part of labor and the working class, the union movement played a var-ied role, from that of catalyst to reactive captive, attempting to "ride the tiger."[4] Nonetheless, despite a somewhat contradictory approach, by the mid-1970s the Italian labor movement was considerably strengthened and therefore had much to lose in the subsequent period of resurgent capital.

During the late 1960s and early 1970s, the Italian labor movement succeeded in establishing, or co-opting, factory-based workers coun-cils (consigli di fabbrica) while simultaneously achieving a national role in setting macroeconomic policy. Utilizing a process of political exchange, the Italian union federations were able to insert themselves into a tripartite, neo-corporatist bargaining process involving government and industry.[5] Once having gained a seat at the national policy-making table, the union federations used their ability to control the political activities of their members (e.g., strikes, job actions, and broader demonstrations) in exchange for favored macroeconomic and social policy. The passage of the Italian Labor Bill of Rights (Statuto di Lavoro) in 1970, the legislative response to the unrest of 1968-69, proved to be the most enduring result of this period of tripartite bargaining.

Relations between the three national trade union federations— CGIL, CISL, and UIL—also improved dramatically during the 1970s. Increased cooperation among them led to the adoption in February 1978 of a common platform, the EUR Accord, and it appeared as though a new era of industrial relations was beginning.[6] The post-EUR optimism proved to be short-lived.

Union solidarity ruptured when CISL, UIL, and part of the CGIL supported the Craxi government plan to limit the wage indexing system (scala mobile) in 1984. The metalworkers union, the Federazione Lavoratori Metalmeccanici (FLM), officially broke apart in February 1984, although the crisis had been in the making since 1979-80. In particular, the failed 35-day strike at FIAT in 1980 was emblematic, marking a significant shift in power away from unions and toward management initiative.[7] After the 35-day strike, FIAT management moved quickly to reassert complete control over the organization of the factory by using technology to unilaterally restructure the firm.[8]

Throughout Italy firms followed FIAT's lead as industry restructured to the detriment of organized labor. Management began to outsource components, followed by whole subassemblies, in order to circumvent large unionized firms.[9] Growing decentralization, fueled by outsourcing, contributed substantially to the proliferation of small firms; and as some of these firms increased their sophistication and capacity to meet market demand, local industrial agglomerations began to coalesce.[10] The development of a broad range of business services, including market, financial, and production assistance, by trade associations and some local governments assisted small firms in achieving certain "external" economies of scale. Shaped by the decentralization process and the subsequent interventions on behalf of trade associations and government, Emilia-Romagna evolved into one of the most advanced examples of a small-firm economy. Today, while some large, vertically integrated firms continue to operate in the region (FIAT's tractor factory in Modena is one example), the Emilian reality is predominantly one of small and medium-sized firms.

Located in the heart of what has come to be known as the Third Italy (an area stretching from the Veneto to Tuscany), the Emilia-Romagna region of north-central Italy provides a useful example of dynamic economic development.[11] This region has undergone a dramatic transformation in the past 50 years, moving from fascist domination and civil war to a situation of broad economic well-being and political domination by the Italian Communist Party (PCI).[12] The present, unquestionably fluid situation in which the PCI is attempting to "refound" itself does not negate over 40 years of the PCI's rule.

The PCI's historic Bologna Congress of March 1990 confirmed the initiative to reconstitute the party, and at the Rimini Congress in early 1991, the PCI officially became the Partito Democratico della Sinistra (Democratic Party of the Left—PdS). Different interpretations of the new course remain and the divisions could well be destabilizing for the PdS. PdS Secretary, Achille Ochetto, the architect of the transformation, was himself rebuffed at the Rimini Congress by not being reelected Secretary on the first ballot, although he was reelected on the second ballot. Still, Ochetto, his cadre of quarantenne (40-year-olds, a reference to youth and an acknowledgment that the post-World War II generation has taken the lead within the party apparatus), and the normally allied reformist "miglioristi" wing of the party appear to have mustered a somewhat unstable majority.

Long-term PCI control over local governments has made Emilia-Romagna a center of activity for both the miglioristi and the postwar militants. Often in conflict in the past, many members of these two groups found themselves united in the "si" (promajoritarian/Ochetto platform) coalition during the heated internal debate that led to the demise of the PCI and the simultaneous birth of the PdS.[13] Perhaps more important, the transformation of the PCI into the PdS is, according to the majoritarian position, an attempt to broaden the party to include other progressive forces. In this respect, Emilia-Romagna has been a leading example of inclusive politics based on the dominant electoral position of the PCI.

Coalition politics and government are familiar situations in Emilia-Romagna where the PCI has usually preferred to govern with the Italian Socialist Party (PSI). Recent, exclusively PCI, "monocolore" governments appeared to challenge the norm of coalition, but the municipal elections of May 1990, in which the PCI continued to lose votes, led to a return of coalition government.

Since July 1990, Bologna (the capital of Emilia-Romagna) has been governed by a PCI, PSI and Psdi (Italian Social-Democratic Party) coalition headed by Renato Imbeni of the PdS, member of the European Parliament and mayor since 1983. At the regional level, the numerical impossibility of a local equivalent to the ruling national coalition (the pentapartito or five-party coalition comprised of the Christian Democrats, PSI, Psdi, Republicans and Liberals) led to a regional agreement between the PCI, PSI, Psdi and the Republican Party. These recent political changes have resulted in the election of Socialist Enrico Boselli as President of the region.[14]

In terms of industrial policy, the Regional Ministry of Industry, traditionally the domain of the PCI, is now in the hands of the Republican Party. The Republican Party is not a formal member of the governing coalition, but the Republicans agreed to support the new government and were given the Regional Ministry of Industry as part of that agreement. Whether or not these political changes will lead to any significant shifts in industrial policy remains to be seen.

The Emilian Economy

At the end of World War II, the local economy of Emilia-Romagna was primarily agricultural, with the manufacturing that did exist being concentrated in a small number of large, vertically integrated firms.[15] This situation changed drastically during the 1950s and 1960s as agriculture was replaced by manufacturing as the dominant economic activity in the region.

It was also during the immediate post-World War II period that an active cooperative sector began to reassert itself.[16] Originally, the co-op movement was based in the agricultural sector, but it quickly spread to construction, food processing and distribution, light manufacturing, and transportation. Today, many Emilian co-ops have become large enterprises, dominating some industry sectors (construction, food processing and distribution) and active in all economic areas.[17]

As industry grew, there was a concomitant deterioration of the dominance of a few sizable manufacturing firms and a proliferation of flexible, specialized small firms. Today, Emilia-Romagna, with a population of almost 4 million, has over 325,000 individual firms. More than 90 percent employ fewer than 50 people, and almost 40 percent of the workforce is engaged in manufacturing. The results of this decentralized, yet integrated, system of firms are striking.

•Wage rates arc almost double the Italian average.

•Productivity is among Europe's highest.

•Exports are increasing (7.9 percent of Italian exports originated in Emilia-Romagna in 1973; 10.2 percent in 1986).

•*Per capita* income grew faster than the Italian average between 1970 and 1979; by 1979 *per capita* income in the region was 127 percent of the national average. During the same 1970-79 period, the provinces of Modena and Reggio moved from seventeenth and twelfth in national income rankings to second and fourth, respectively (Brusco 1982).

•From 1971 to the present, Gross Regional Product has increased over 50 percent.[18]

Overall, the economy of Emilia-Romagna has proved to be both resilient, specializing in high value-added products, and adaptable, adjusting quickly to market fluctuations. A system of auxiliary industry services that operate through pooled resources, accessible programs, and accountable member organizations has directly contributed to the high level of technical expertise attained by individual firms.

Decentralized Production and Flexible Manufacturing

Initially, the small firms of Emilia-Romagna served large enterprises as dependent subcontractors, and some of those relationships continue today. For example, many of the Modena artisans continue to supply components, or specialized manufacturing services such as grinding and heat treating, to FIAT's tractor factory, one of the remaining large, vertically integrated firms in Emilia-Romagna. Still, to overcome the negative consequences of being dependent subcontractors, many small shops learned to diversify their client base through horizontal linkages to other small firms. This process was accelerated as small firms decided to pursue discrete specializations in order to differentiate their activities and expertise from that of other small firms.

Relationships of trust grew as firms subcontracted among themselves rather than refusing to take on contracts too large for the individual shop. Informal networks developed, especially in the tightly knit industrial districts in and around Bologna, Modena, and north along the via Emilia (Carpi, Reggio-Emilia, Piacenza) to Milan.[19]

Commercial linkages were also encouraged by the diversification, fragmentation, and customization of market demand, which led firms to adapt flexible production techniques, both internally and externally, through outsourcing. Specialization strengthened commercial linkages, and as the small firms became increasingly independent of large enterprises, they began to coordinate their respective expertise, thereby developing value-adding partnerships.[20]

Cooperation between firms made it feasible to bid on larger, more valuable contracts, and this in turn stimulated the growth of value-adding chains which could be coordinated to create complete products. Stronger commercial relationships reinforced the tendency of industry sectors to cluster, further stimulating the consolidation of industrial districts comprised of firms involved in different stages of production.[21] These developments were facilitated by the growth of industry services which helped overcome the traditional limits of small business.

Informal relations between firms have become more structured as some medium-sized local firms have begun to acquire outright, or take a minority equity position in smaller, generally more specialized satellite firms. For example, Corazza, a medium-sized company producing food packaging equipment located outside Bologna, recently bought one of its more sophisticated subcontractors and acquired equity positions in other small suppliers. Similar relations are being established throughout the Emilian economy.

Many of the larger co-ops have grown by merging with other co-ops.[22] Recent studies have also identified significant merger and acquisition activity as many of the Emilian firms are increasingly integrated into the global economy through large multinational corporations.[23]

Industry Services

In Emilia-Romagna, industry services are used not only to support individual firms, but to stimulate shared solutions to what appear at first to be individual problems.[24] At the outset, industry services were provided by trade associations to take advantage of appropriate economies of scale and cut overhead costs for member firms. Because resources could be pooled by trade associations, shared accounting, payroll, and business planning services were available for reduced user fees. Easy access to these services (available to nonmember firms as well, though at a higher price) allows firms to cut costs while concentrating on producing high quality products.

The National Confederation of Artisans (CNA) is the most notable example of a small-firm trade association aggressively involved in providing an array of business services.[25] Formed in the immediate post-World War II period, the CNA has grown to include 340,000 member firms (80,000 in Emilia-Romagna). Nationally, the organization has 2,300 offices and 7,000 employees and is financed through annual membership dues of $100, plus 1 percent of payroll. As with most Italian trade associations, the CNA is organized both geographically and by industry sector. Local CNA chapters are organized at the provincial level and governed by an elected board of directors who must themselves be artisans. Sector-specific trade federations are organized nationally in 27 categories (i.e., metalworking, woodworking, clothing). Thus, artisan firms normally belong to a sector-specific trade federation within provincial chapters of the CNA.

The sector-specific focus allows the CNA and its federations to develop considerable expertise and sophisticated, tailored business services. Sector-specific expertise, channeled into geographically proximal clusters of related firms, allows the CNA staff to maximize its outreach for minimal cost. The democratic and participatory nature of the CNA also facilitates an ongoing process of interaction and exchange of information among member firms. As the CNA began to develop more sophisticated types of business services, member firms grew to expect and therefore demand increased levels of service.

Following the lead of trade associations, the regional and local governments became actively involved in enterprise creation and development. Promoting a system of industry services that facilitates economic development, public planners opted for an "incubator without walls" strategy. Economic development activities focused on:

•assistance in business expansion and new enterprise creation by developing targeted industrial parks for small firms and supporting trade associations and cooperatives to foster new enterprises;

•sectoral technology transfer programs and research services to aid innovation;

•market information, export assistance and support for trade fairs;

•upgrading the entire vocational and technical training system;

•financial assistance for an array of needs including training, group procurement, and purchasing new equipment.

To implement this strategy, a public-private partnership, ERVET, was created by the regional government with the support of local banks and trade associations in 1974. ERVET's industrial policy is geared towards sectors rather than individual firms and designed to provide both vertical (sector-specific) and horizontal (across industries) assistance through technology transfer and marketing service centers located in their respective industrial districts. Established centers include:

Vertical (sector-specific)	CITER (1980) for knitwear and fashion
	CESMA (1983) for agricultural machinery
	CERCAL (1983) for shoe firms

	QUASCO (1985) for the construction industry
Horizontal (cutting across sector)	CERMET (1985) for the metal mechanical and related industries
	ASTER (1985) technology transfer and R&D center
	RESFOR (1986) promotes subcontracting arrangements among firms located in the region
	SVEX (1989) export assistance for small firms

Labor's Role

The success of the broad, highly articulated economic development infrastructure of Emilia-Romagna is generally acknowledged. Less discussed is the role of industrial relations and organized labor in the Emilian economy.[26] To date, trade unions play no direct role in the established service centers, and unlike local banks, trade associations and educational institutions, labor unions do not sit on the advisory boards of ERVET or the established centers.

The fact that organized labor plays little direct role in the service centers is criticized by the unions, although the criticism is somewhat muted given the leading role of the PCI-PdS and its historic alliance with the trade union movement (especially the CGIL). Still, organized labor's demand to be part of the governing board for a long-anticipated regional research complex, Polo Tecnologica, was the principal impediment that delayed the start of the project for almost three years. Recently, the controversy was settled in labor's favor and the unions will be represented on the governing board of Polo Tecnologica.[27] This in itself is an interesting prospect, since few unions share a similar role in the world's increasingly numerous science parks.

FIOM's Strategy

While the FIOM supports efforts to gain access to the region's economic development apparatus, it has concentrated on using the collective bargaining process to broaden participation and gain more autonomy on the shop floor and increased control over the process of production. As explained by the FIOM's Regional General Secretary, Francesco Garibaldo:

> Since the end of the sixties a specific characteristic of the Bolognese metal-mechanical workers' experience is the enduring interest in the organization of work considered as the meeting point of every strategic problem: wage, work environment, pace and intensity of production and career development.[28]

Focusing on work organization assisted the FIOM in successfully contesting management's efforts during the 1970s to improve productivity by simply speeding up production rather than exploring a more efficient organization of production.

The success of FIOM's bargaining position influenced management's decision to initiate a new investment cycle through the introduction of computer-numerically-controlled equipment. During this phase of technological change and reorganization, the FIOM pursued a policy designed "to contest the capitalistic work organization and to build up the power of the workers over their work conditions." Overall, the strategy was quite successful and workers gained significant power within the firm; piecework was done away with, "the whole wage was a bargained wage" with wage differentials based on skill, and a 35-hour workweek was established.

Management attempts to divide craft activities, such as those of machine tool workers or design engineers, into many unskilled jobs was also resisted. Instead, the FIOM insisted upon an open career for each craft-like activity. Career mobility would be encouraged by requiring that rotation and recomposition schemes be linked to broad-based education courses, rather than more limited task-specific training. These achievements may seem modest, yet when compared to counterparts in the rest of the industrialized world, the FIOM has clearly succeeded where many others have failed.

The FIOM's organizational presence and power inside the firm compelled management to bargain and, in exchange for performance, to increase wages as well as allow for growing self-management over work conditions. However, by 1977 this strategy had reached an impasse; the expansion of outsourcing and supply firms, coupled with the introduction of new computer-based technologies and new organizational criteria combined to erode the gains derived from the FIOM's policies.[29]

Searching for a new approach, FIOM concentrated on building up craft-based professional areas (technicians, design engineers, operators and fitters) but strong management pressure for increased flexibility limited the FIOM strategy to "a few small experiments."[30] Given these unsatisfactory results, FIOM continued to search for a viable alternative.

The Search for an Alternative

The conceptual basis for FIOM's new approach is the belief that the world economy is in the midst of a new industrial revolution. In the emerging industrial order there is a growing tension between the "integration needs" inherent in the increasingly complex organizational and technical aspects of production and the model of social relations. In the "old" social model, employee cooperation was bargained for in a rigid, mechanical (Tayloristic) fashion, resulting in complex, hierarchical work rules. Within the emerging system of production, employee cooperation needs to be of an organic (flexible) nature, involving more interactive problemsolving than was previously the case.

To better comprehend the transition from mechanical to flexible cooperation, the FIOM initiated two research projects. The first aimed at understanding the impact of emerging economic conditions on the structure of the firm and work organization, while the second project concentrated on identifying and comprehending the subjective feelings of the workers about their work experience.[31] The results of these two projects were widely discussed as the FIOM debated a new strategy.

From 1985 to 1987, the FIOM began to pull together the methodology needed to pursue an "alternative strategy." The starting point was a new educational scheme for unionists designed not to rely upon a pre-fabricated set of solutions, but rather promote an interdisciplinary understanding of the new technological and organizational revolution currently underway. This new educational program was in turn linked to a participatory design process geared toward a radical reform of work organization and industrial relations.

Acknowledging that there are diverse strategies to achieve a more "organic cooperation," the FIOM decided to pursue a "democratic alternative" based on interactive work groups.[32] The decision to promote work organization based on group activities was itself a risky one. As pointed out by the FIOM's chief consultant on the project:

> Work organized by groups, like work carried out individually, is marked by contradiction. On the one hand, such groups can be manipulated by the mechanisms of management; on the other, they can use the bargaining process to reclaim the ability to manage themselves.
>
> Embracing the dynamic of group experience does not mean adhering strictly to approaches which favor workers alone. Indeed, such an approach can only be subordinate to corporate goals. The issue is rather one of distinguishing between the work organization "produced" by the group in the framework of a given firm, and the group's relationship to worker identity—an equally critical process.[33]

Beginning in 1987, the FIOM began to sign a series of agreements aimed at establishing more participatory cooperation through group-oriented work organization. Briefly, two broad categories of agreements have been signed. The first, and more limited set of agreements, established procedures whereby the unions and factory council delegates would receive advance information on new technologies and/or changes in work organization. Once informed, the union and the delegates can propose an alternative plan which management must review and discuss. The weakness of this first approach is that there is no obligation to come to a mutually acceptable agreement.

The second approach includes the procedures of the first but goes further by establishing bargained patterns of work organization with considerable autonomy from management intrusion for some areas of the firm. In these agreements there are provisions which establish diverse, autonomous work groups. For example, certain agreements established "unified production groups." The main characteristics of these groups are:

1. The group has autonomy to decide its own task assignments, maintenance, and educational courses for skill development.

2. The group has a coordinator (usually a skilled worker) who coordinates the management of the group. The position of coordinator rotates from every four to six months depending on the agreement.

3. The group workload is bargained for once a year and production beyond the agreed upon amount is rewarded. Other types of groups have been established in specific functional segments of the firm (e.g., design department groups), or for systems integration/assembly (e.g., the "fitting group," which assembles a complex automatic machine).

The specifics vary from firm to firm and agreement to agreement, but the overall approach is consistent; the focus remains the control over the organization of production, autonomy from what is viewed as rigid, hierarchical management control, and "bargained results" where management agrees to reward productivity improvements but, because of the autonomy of the work groups, does not automatically obtain ownership of the method by which the productivity improvements were obtained.

The FIOM is also quick to point out the importance of how the group is established and its role in shaping the worker's identity.

> The group planning phase is not a technical one, but is rather one of the processes by which workers' identity is formed in relation to both the company and the socio-political context. Hence the benefits of this reorganization of work are continuously channeled in two directions: towards the company and towards the workers. On the one hand, this approach results in the reduction of lead time and the improvement of product quality; on the other, it tends to strengthen the relationship between professional experience and identity.[34]

The importance of the group's autonomy from management is paramount for the FIOM. According to FIOM strategists, autonomy within the firm (intrafirm) could eventually be used to establish contact across firms (interfirm) without having to go through the normal channels of management hierarchy. The FIOM believes the results would be a more efficient and flexible system of production that acknowledges and rewards the efforts of members.

To date the FIOM of Emilia-Romagna has successfully signed dozens of contracts which, to varying degrees, create autonomous work groups within the firm (see appendix).[35] Still very much in the experimental stage, the strategy did nevertheless receive a sympathetic hearing at the FIOM's 1988 National Congress, but no formal endorsement was forthcoming.

The success at the intrafirm level has not yet been expanded to entail interfirm linkages; informally, however, on a problemsolving basis, work groups have begun to communicate across firms. At the Ferrari factory in Maranello, a suburb of Modena, the installation of a sophisticated flexible machining system(FMS) to machine engine blocks presented a complex set of problems that needed to be resolved quickly to bring the system on-line.

The FMS, a complex series of computer-integrated machining centers, is made by Mandelli in nearby Piacenza. Communication through the respective Ferrari and Mandelli management hierarchies proved to be a time consuming, inefficient way to debug the FMS. Therefore, the work group installing the system found it necessary to circumvent management hierarchies and establish direct contact with the Mandelli team that built the FMS. In this case, a telephone link from one shop floor to the other proved more effective than the established corporate channels of communication.[36]

Although the contracts signed so far have involved mostly medium-sized firms, the metalworkers have not neglected the artisan firm sector, signing their first contract (involving all three metalworkers unions) with the National Confederation of Artisans (CNA) in 1984. Efforts to expand this precedent to other sectors have been slow to show results. A modest breakthrough occurred in 1989 when the textile workers unions signed a contract with the Emilia-Romagna CNA and continued to pressure the other small-firm associations.

At the national level, recent legislation extended employee protection from arbitrary dismissal to include the artisan firms, further incorporating the small-firm sector into the national industrial relations system. Still, much remains to be done within both the Italian and overall European contexts to bring small firms into a more regulated system.

The innovative bargaining approach developed by the FIOM of Emilia-Romagna, and the results achieved, argue well for the possibility of a more democratic alternative to hierarchical, rigid production systems. However, the limited role of organized labor in many of the economic development agencies in Emilia-Romagna may prove to be an impediment to continued successful economic restructuring.

NOTES

1. In the 1970s, combined support for the metalworkers unions was 110,000. The 55 percent unionization rate is an aggregate figure; roughly 75 percent of the production workers are organized, but only 20 percent of the clerical/white-collar staff. (Figures supplied by the FIOM.)

2. See, among others, Gian Primo Cella and Tiziano Treu, *Relazioni industriali: manuale per l'analisi della esperienza italiana* (Bologna: Il Mulino, 1982); Peter Lange, George Ross and Maurizio Vannicelli, *Union, Change and Crisis: French and Italian Union Strategy and the Political Economy, 1945-1980* (London: Allen & Unwin, 1982); Umberto Romagnoli and Tiziano Treu, *I sindacati in Italia dal '45 a oggi: storia di una strategia* (Bologna: Il Mulino, 1981); Richard Locke, "The Resurgence of the Local Union: Industrial Restructuring and Industrial Relations in Italy," *Politics & Society* 18, no. 3 (1990): 347-379.

3. For the immediate post-World War II period, see, Aris Accornero, *Gli anni' 50 in fabbrica* (Bari: De Donato, 1973).

4. The literature on this period is extensive. See, John Lowe-Beer, *Protest and Participation: The New Working Class in Italy* (Cambridge: Cambridge University Press, 1978); Alessandro Pizzorno, Emilio Reyneri, Marino Regini and Ida Regalia, *Lotte operaie e sindacato: il ciclo 1968-1972 in Italia* (Bologna: Il Mulino, 1978).

5. See, Gino Giugni, *Il sindacato fra contratti e riforme, 1969-1973* (Bari: De Donato, 1973); on political exchange see, Alessandro Pizzorno, "Political Exchange and Collective Identity in Industrial Conflict," in Crouch and Pizzorno, eds. *The Resurgence of Class Conflict in Western Europe*, vol. 2 (New York: Holmes and Meier, 1978) 277-299; A. Pizzorno, *I soggetti del pluralismo* (Bologna: Il Mulino, 1980).

6. See, Luciano Lama (intervista di Fabrizio D'Agostini), *Il potere del sindacato* (Roma: Riuniti, 1978); and K. Robert Nilsson, "The EUR Accords & the Historic Compromise: Italian Labor & Eurocommunism," *Polity* (Fall) 1981; for a good overview of this period see, Marino Regini, *I dilemmi del sindacato* (Bologna: Il Mulino, 1981); focusing on Turin metalworkers and the rank-and-file resistance to the austerity policies accepted by the national federations, see Miriam Golden, "Austerity and its Opposition: Italian Working Class Politics in the 1970's," PhD dissertation, Cornell University, 1983.

7. FIAT proposed that 24,000 workers be placed in Casa Integrazione, a state-financed redundancy/layoff fund. The union rejected this proposal and broke off relations. FIAT responded by declaring its intention to fire 15,000 workers. The ensuing strike lasted 35 days until FIAT foremen and supervisors organized a successful demonstration when 40,000 people marched silently through Turin protesting for a return to work. For more see, Alberto Baldissera, "Alle origini della politica della disuguaglianza nell'Italia degli anni '80: la marcia dei quarantamila," *Quaderni di*

Sociologia 31, 1984; Giuseppe Bonazzi, "La lotta dei 35 giorni alla FIAT: un'analisi sociologica," and Fabrizio Carmignini, "Il sindacato di classe nella lotta dei 35 giorni alla FIAT," both in *Politica ed Economia*, no. 11 (1984); on FIAT in transition see, Ada Becchi Collida and Serafino Negrelli, *La transizione nell'industria e nelle relazioni industriali: l'auto e il caso FIAT* (Milan: Franco Angeli, 1977).

8. For an analysis of this process see, Richard Locke and Serafino Negrelli, "Il caso FIAT AUTO," in Marino Regini and Charles Sabel, eds., *Strategie di riaggiustamento industriale* (Bologna: Il Mulino, 1989); for FIAT management's perspective, see, G. Fardin, M. Casoli and L. Cerato, *Come cambia la fabbrica: Nuovi sistemi produttivi e professionalità* (Turin: Fondazione Giovanni Agnelli, 1986).

9. For the Italian restructuring experience see, Gilberto Antonelli, *Innovazioni tecnologiche e struttura produttiva: la posizione dell'Italia* (Bologna: Il Mulino, 1984); Valeriano Balloni, ed., *Esperienze di ristrutturazione industriale* (Bologna: Il Mulino, 1985); Federico Butera, *L'orologio e l'organismo* (Milan: Franco Angeli, 1985); Laura Pennacchi, ed., *L'industria italiana: trasformazioni strutturali e possibilità di governo politico* (Milan: Franco Angeli, 1981); Marino Regini, ed., *La sfida della flessibilità* (Milan: Franco Angeli, 1988); Marino Regini and Charles Sabel, *Strategie di riaggiustamento industriale* (Bologna: Il Mulino, 1989).

10. The causes and significance of the decentralization of production are widely debated. Among those who make reference to Emilia-Romagna, or Italian Industrial Districts, see, Giacomo Becattini, "The Development of Light Industry in Tuscany: An Interpretation," *Economic Notes* 3, 1978; Becattini, ed., *Mercato e forze locali: il distretto industriale* (Bologna: Il Mulino, 1987); Edward Goodman, Julia Bamford and Peter Saynor, *Small Firms and Industrial Districts in Italy* (London: Routledge, 1989); Michael Piore and Charles Sabel, *The Second Industrial Divide* (New York: Basic Books, 1984); Marino Regini, ed., *op. cit.*; Marino Regini and Charles Sabel, eds., *op. cit.*; Charles Sabel, *Work and Politics* (Cambridge: Cambridge University Press, 1982); C. Sabel, "Flexible Specialization and the Re-emergence of Regional Economies," in Paul Hirst and Jonathan Zeitlin, eds., *Reversing Industrial Decline?* (Oxford: Berg Publishers, 1989), pp. 17-70; for a critical perspective, see, Ash Amin, "Flexible Specialization and Small Firms in Italy: Myths and Realities," *Antipode* 21, 1, 1989, pp. 13-34; and Richard Hyman, "Flexible Specialization: Miracle or Myth?" in R. Hyman and W. Streeck, eds., *New Technology and Industrial Relations* (Oxford: Basil Blackwell, 1988). For a labor perspective, see Robert Garvini, Franco Calistri, Ornella Cilora, *A quatra Italia: il lavoro e la politica industriale nei distretti e nelle aree integrate in Italia* (Rome: Edlesse, 1988).

11. There is a growing body of literature on the Third Italy and the Emilian economy. See, among others, Arnaldo Bagnasco, *Tre Italie* (Bologna: Il Mulino, 1977); Sebastiano Brusco, "The Emilian Model: Productive Decentralization and Social Integration," *Cambridge Journal of Economics* 6, 2, 1982; Brusco, *Piccole imprese e distretti industriali: una raccolta di saggi* (Turin: Rosenberg & Sellier, 1989); Giorgio Tassinari, *Il sistema industriale dell' 'Emilia-Romagna* (Bologna: Il Mulino, 1986).

12. For an analysis of the interrelationship between small firms and dominant political parties (both red and white regions), see, Carlo Trigilia, *Grandi partiti e piccole imprese* (Bologna: Il Mulino, 1986); a shorter English version, Trigilia, "Small-firm development and political subcultures in Italy," *European Sociological Review* 2, 3, December 1986. For an excellent overview of social mobility, see, Marizio Barbagli, Vittorio Capecchi and Antonio Cobalti, *La mobilità sociale in Emilia-Romagna* (Bologna: Il Mulino, 1988).

13. Local leaders from very diverse perspectives, such as Irene Rubini, Regional Secretary of the Confederazione Nazionale dell'Artigianato (the artisan/small-firm trade association) and Lanfranco Turci, President of Emilia-Romagna for most of the 1980s and recent head of the national "red" co-op league, all long-standing miglioristi, found themselves aligned with Francesco Garib-

aldo, Regional Secretary of the FIOM trade union and Antonio LaForgia, a former Bologna City Council Member, individuals traditionally associated with Pietro Ingrao (historic leader of the left-wing of the PCI and prominent spokesperson for the "no" coalition).

14. *La Republica,* 7/17/90.

15. See, among others, Stefania Conti, Raffaele Lungarella and Franco Piro, *L'economia emiliana nel dopoguerra* (Bologna: Marsilio, 1979).

16. The Italian cooperative movement began through the agitation of the agrarian wing of the Italian Socialist Party, especially early leaders such as Massarenti who was particularly active in Romagna. For a good history describing 19th Century roots, see, Giulio Sapelli, ed., *Il movimento cooperativo in Italia* (Turin: Einaudi, 1981).

17. In 1988 the Lega Emilia-Romagna ("red" co-op league), comprised 1,750 individual co-ops, with 60,580 employees and 916,762 soci (co-op members). The largest categories remain the agriculture and consumer sectors but there are over 250,000 soci and 30,000 employees in the production and services sectors. For complete details, see, *I bilanci delle imprese cooperative 1988* (Bologna: Lega Emilia-Romagna, 1989); for labor relations in the co-ops, see Marco Biagi, *Cooperative e rapporti di lavoro* (Milan: Franco Angeli, 1983).

18. Information provided by the Regional Government of Emilia-Romagna, Regional Ministry of Industry.

19. For a description of this process, see, Sebastiano Brusco, "Flessibilitá e solidità del sistema: l'esperienza Emiliana," in Fiorgio Fuá and Carlo Zacchia, eds., *Industrializzazione senza frattura* (Bologna: Il Mulino, 1983); S. Brusco, "Small Firms and Industrial Districts: The Experience of Italy," in *New Firms and Regional Development in Europe,* David Keeble and Egbert Werer, eds. (London: Croom Helm, 1986); S. Brusco and Charles Sabel, "Artisan Production and Economic Growth," in Frank Wilkinson, ed., *The Dynamics of Labour Market Segmentation* (New York: Academic Press, 1981).

20. See, Russell Johnston and Paul Lawrence, "Beyond Vertical Integration: The Rise of the Value-Adding Partnership," *Harvard Business Review* (July-August, 1988).

21. Interfirm linkages within industrial districts have been labeled by some observers as "manufacturing networks." See especially C. Richard Hatch, "Learning From Italy's Industrial Renaissance," *The Entrepreneurial Economy* 6, no. 1 (July/August), 1987. The network concept has in turn been criticized by Bennett Harrison because: "In one degree or another, industrial (like all social) organization has always entailed 'networking.'...Most seriously, the concept of the 'network' lends itself to silence on the question of relations of *power* and *control.*" See, Bennett Harrison, "Concentration Without Centralization: The Changing Morphology of the Small Firm Industrial Districts of the Third Italy," paper presented to the International Symposium on Local Employment (National Institute of Employment and Vocational Research, Tokyo, Japan, September 12-14, 1989), p. 22.

22. Almost all of the large construction co-ops were formed through mergers between smaller co-ops. For example Co-op Sette, a firm engaged in construction and furniture production, was formed by the merger of six different co-ops, hence its name. At a more international level there is Co-op COM, a furniture producer headquartered near Bologna, with a complex set of joint ventures and strategic alliances stretching around the globe.

23. See, Giuseppina Gualtieri, ed., *Acquisizioni, fusioni, concorrenza* (Bologna: NOMISMA, 1988); Bennett Harrison, Ibid.; Michael Storper and Bennett Harrison, "Flexibility, Hierarchy and Regional Development: The Changing Structure of Industrial Production Systems and Their Forms of Governance in the 1990's," paper presented at the International Conference on Industrial Policy: New Issues and New Models, the Regional Experience, Bologna, November 16-17, 1989.

24. Patrizio Bianchi, "Servizi reali e politica industriale a livello locale," in *Stato e Mercato* 16 (1986), pp. 123-146; Massimo D'Angelillo, *Servizi reali: politiche industriali e servizi alle imprese in Italia e in Europa* (Bologna: I Quaderni di Quarantacinque, 1987); *Politica industriale e servizi reali: riflessioni su alcune esperienze ERVET e sulle prospettive degli anni '90* (Bologna: ERVET, 1989); *Politica industriale, servizi reali e opportunità di sviluppo a livello locale* (Bologna: NOMISMA, 1985); *I centri di servizio reali alle imprese: stato dell'arte e repertorio delle esperienze italiane* (Bologna: NOMISMA, 1988); for an analysis of the situation in Lombardy, see, Angelo Lassini, *Gli interventi regionali per i servizi alle imprese* (Milan: Franco Angeli, 1985); for a general overview of the Italian system of regional governments and economic development, see, Raffaella Nanetti, *Growth and Territorial Policies: The Italian Model of Social Capitalism* (New York: Pinter, 1988); and, Robert Putnam, Robert Leonardi, and Raffaella Nanetti, *La pianta e le radici* (Bologna: Il Mulino, 1985).

25. For a history of the CNA in Modena see, Andrea Tosi, *Il ruolo di una associazione sindacale artigiana nello sviluppo modenese: la CNA dal dopoguerra ad oggi*, Tesi di Laurea, Facoltà di Economia e Commercio, Università di Modena, 1986; for Bologna, see, Maurizio Angelini, "Rapporti fra organizzazioni artigiane ed enti locali nell' esperienza della CNA di Bologna," in Andrea Tosi, ed., *La politica industriale delle regione* (Milan: CLUP, 1983). The CNA is the largest and most significant of four national artisan associations. "Artisan" is a legal category in Italy referring to firms with fewer than 20 employees (excluding family members and apprentices). Owners of artisan firms must also be directly engaged in production work and the firm cannot be structured as a limited liability entity.

26. In the broader Italian context see, Marino Regini and Charles Sabel, eds., *op. cit.*; for the Province of Modena see, Paolo Perulli, "Il distretto industriale di Modena," *Ibid.*, pp. 249-282.

27. *Il Polo Scientifico e Tecnologico Bolognese* (Bologna: ERVET, 1987).

28. Francesco Garibaldo, "Problemi di politica rivendicativa: la natura dei rapporti cooperativi tra i laboratori rispetto alla struttura dell'impresa. Esperienze e problemi di progettazione organizzativa nei metalmeccanici bolognesi," p. 13, in Oscar Marchisio, ed., *Frammenti di innovazione* (Milan: Franco Angeli, 1988); see also, F. Garibaldo, *Lavoro, innovazione, sindacato* (Genoa: Costa & Nolan, 1988).

29. For a brief overview of these events in English, see, Francesco Garibaldo, "The crisis of the demanding model and the search for an alternative in the experience of the metalworkers union in Emilia-Romagna," paper presented at Bielefeld University, March 30, 1989.

30. *Ibid.*

31. For an analysis of the second project, see, Alberto Merini and Emilio Rebecchi, *L'altra faccia della luna* (Bologna: CLUEB, 1986).

32. The planning process itself is crucial, as explained by the FIOM consultant:

> Whenever we discuss the planning of an area, we necessarily take into consideration the informal roles in the factory, not the structure of job titles and grades, which is the explicit instrument used to redesign different occupational roles, but a much more important structure: the informal statuses created by the interaction of professional, political and cultural experiences and histories.
>
> This explains why, when planning an area, we encounter not the risk, but the certainty of modifying the geography of the work relationship in that particular corporate structure.

See, O. Marchisio, "Groups and project planning: a bargaining procedure," Mimeo, 1989, p. 3.

33. Oscar Marchisio, *Ibid.*, p. 1; see also, O. Marchisio, "La progettazione organizzativa fra negoziazione ed identitá: i casi della regione Emilia-Romagna," in Michele La Rosa, ed., *Il modello giapponeses* (Milan: Franco Angeli, 1988).

34. O. Marchisio, Mimeo, *op. cit.*, p. 2.

35. For a description of some of the various agreements, see, S. Bassi, R. Bennati, CdF. Biotec, O. Marchisio, M. Melotti, S. Pinazzi and M. Ruffino, "Strumenti di lavoro: i casi," the second part of, O. Marchisio, ed., *Frammenti di innovazione, op. cit.*

36. The Ferrari-Mandelli case study was presented by Oscar Marchisio at the Conference on Economic Restructuring in Princeton, NJ, October 5-6, 1990. The conference was organized by the Center for Labor-Management Policy Studies.

Appendix to Chapter 2
Composition of Work Groups by Individual Firm

Firms	Areas of Activity and Composition
Biotec	Analysis (125) Design (1235) Production (25) Bargaining (1235) Supervision (12)
Pai Demm	Education (1238) Analysis (12358) Design (1235) Production (123568)
Mectrak	Analysis (238) Design (1238)
Cima	Education (128) Analysis (238) Design (1238)
Giuliani	Analysis (235) Design (235)
G.D.	Education (2358) Analysis (1234568) Design (1234568) Bargaining (236) Supervision (12)
Ima	Education (23) Analysis (12345) Design (2345)
Sasib	Education (238) Analysis (1234568) Design (23568)
Co-op Cam	Education (23) Analysis (12358) Design (1235) Production (123568)
Sabiem	Education (12) Analysis (735) Design (1235)

Participants
1 - Department workers
2 - Worker's Council delegates
3 - Education Department of the metalworkers union
4 - Bargaining Department of the metalworkers union
5 - Organizational Department of the metalworkers union
6 - Metalworkers union secretary
7 - Representative from Bologna Camera di Lavoro
8 - Consultant

Adopted from: O. Marchisio, "La progettazione organizzativa fra negoziazione ed identitá: i casi della regione Emilia-Romagna," in M. La Rosa, ed., *Il modello giapponese* (Milan: Franco Angeli, 1988).

3
Managing Local Development

Lessons from Spain

Michael Barzelay
Harvard University

In the democratizing societies of Europe and Latin America, political officials of many subnational jurisdictions are likely to be elected on platforms of promoting economic development. As they formulate their policies, many such officials will predictably face similar institutional and substantive constraints: few conventional economic policy instruments under their control; administrators inexperienced in managing government agencies in a democratic context; few business owners or managers with an adequate conception of how their industries can create and capture value in highly integrated market-oriented economies; innovation or entrepreneurship in business activity unlikely to be a cultural tradition; and government intervention through "planning" discredited in the public mind.

The search for effective combinations of policies, agency mandates, organizational strategies, and operational methods in such settings might be significantly aided by examining how the challenge of promoting economic development was handled in one of Spain's poorest regions—Andalusia—after the nation consolidated its transition to democracy. The goal of improving the economic well-being of this region was codified in the Statute of Autonomy, which became law in 1981.[1] The same commitment was embodied in the electoral program of the party winning an absolute majority in the 1982 regional parliamentary elections. Once in power, the region's first political executives faced the institutional and substantive constraints listed above.

After a policymaking process described as an act of democratic planning, top regional officials announced a policy of achieving development-from-within.[2] Concurrently, the regional parliament created the Institute of Industrial Promotion of Andalusia (IPIA), whose mandate was to promote small and medium-sized locally owned industrial enterprises.[3] IPIA's organizational strategy sought to involve the stakeholders of a handful of industries in formulating and implementing a common competitive strategy[4] and to persuade public and private financial institutions to extend credit and subsidies to participating firms.[5] IPIA's operational method was to instigate an interactive planning process that focused stakeholders' attention on the need to improve natural resource utilization, product quality, marketing strategy, infrastructure, plant and equipment, access to financing, procurement, working conditions, and training. In addition, the planning process intended to identify a large number of actions that would permit the region's firms to create and capture more value as a result of their work.[6] This process entailed negotiating what was termed a comprehensive and dynamic action plan.[7]

IPIA's most successful action plan—given the policy of development-from-within and the agency's mission and strategy—involved Andalusia's white marble mining and fabrication industry, which is clustered around the mountain communities of Macael (pronounced Mahk-eye-el) County in Almería province. During the first phase of the Macael Action Plan (1983-87), the industry's sales revenues expanded fivefold. The Macael firms' new ability to compete in the growing market for quality finished marble construction materials accounts for the prodigious growth in revenues. Analysis of this case shows that IPIA's operational method—championing the formulation and implementation of a negotiated, comprehensive, and dynamic action plan—enabled Macael firms to compete in the marble construction materials industry.

The skills needed to employ IPIA's operational method successfully—in Andalusia as elsewhere—include leadership, negotiation, and political management. Skilled leaders can mobilize people to face their problems, search for solutions, make informed decisions, and accept change. Skilled negotiators can forge networks of value-creating agreements, often involving significant degrees of cooperation among people and institutions. Skilled political managers can influence the policy and operational decisions of people and institutions without the aid of formal authority.

Arguably, officials responsible for agencies such as IPIA can only develop the skills of leadership, negotiation, and political management through practice and coaching. It is conceivable, however, that a prior skillful performance in one setting may leave a residue of clinical knowledge, which, if identified and utilized, would improve the skill displayed by officials subsequently using the same operational method in other settings. In an effort to begin cumulating clinical knowledge relevant for operating in policy contexts bearing a family resemblance to Andalusia in the mid-1980s, this paper offers a series of narrative accounts and interpretations of how the successful Macael Action Plan gradually unfolded.

Initial Conditions

When the Macael Action Plan was initiated in 1983, some 150 family-owned firms employing an average of seven workers were engaged in marble mining and/or fabrication. Business owners followed the production and marketing practices of their forebears, resulting in technological backwardness. Dynamite, rather than precision saws, was the principal means by which marble was loosened from hillsides. Few fabricating shops were equipped with mechanical cutting and polishing devices. Even fewer firms were able to establish brand name recognition and none had the capacity to fill a major construction order. As a result, 70 percent of extracted marble was sold to manufacturers in other regions in Spain, who produced quality goods for the huge national construction industry, while Macael fabricators limited their production to a narrow line of artisanal goods. This pattern of economic activity had characterized the marble industry in Macael for decades, resulting in static revenues and ingrained resistance to change. Overcoming such impediments would have required some degree of collaboration among firms. However, for Macael's individualistic business owners, collaboration was anathema.

The Joining-Up Process

Events at Macael

IPIA's first contact with Macael business owners took place in their own quarries and fabricating shops. Accompanied by the local mayor, IPIA's director general spent two days touring these sites before the idea of holding a meeting was broached with business owners. The director used this opportunity to learn about the industry's work and Macael's deteriorating economy. Through his presence, manner, and line of questioning, IPIA's director also sought to demonstrate his genuine concern for the industry and to spark curiosity about why IPIA had come to Macael.

By then, it had become common knowledge that a man from IPIA was in town. When the mayor called an impromptu meeting of the employers association and trade unions, their leaders came. The director, Ricardo Sánchez de la Morena, explained that IPIA's aim was to build on the strengths of Andalusia's land and people to promote entrepreneurship in the region. He noted that those he had spoken with during the previous two days felt the local marble industry was in crisis and that a solution was not evident. He did not offer a diagnosis, though he mentioned that deficiencies in infrastructure and equipment were clear. He invited the people in attendance to work with IPIA in developing an action plan to "totally modernize" the local industry.

The Macael Action Plan, the director explained, would be unlike most development plans. It would deal with all issues concerning the marble industry, including technology, products, finance, infrastructure, and working conditions; it would be dynamic, beginning with a diagnosis of the problems and opportunities of the local marble industry; and it would focus on changing the reality of the industry. The Macael Action Plan would not be formulated by IPIA, but rather would be negotiated by the assembled group, with IPIA serving as general coordinator. Sánchez de la Morena also promised that IPIA would use its influence to mobilize resources from banks, utilities, and government agencies—so long as the group agreed *unanimously* on every element of the Action Plan.

Knowing that the audience's aspirations for economic betterment were checked by anxieties about participating in such a group process, IPIA's director wanted to build immediate commitment to an action plan. He gave them a stark choice: either agree unanimously at that moment to work with IPIA on a comprehensive, negotiated, and dynamic action plan, or forfeit the chance to enlist his support for modernizing the Macael marble industry.[8] After some discussion, a vote was taken. It demonstrated that the balance of sentiments had tipped uniformly in favor of initiating the process.

Clinical Interpretations

The initial meeting must include the active participation of the industry's professional associations. No one would be in a better institutional position to speak on behalf of business owners than top officials of the employers association. The participation of local governmental officials and union leaders may also be essential for substantive and political reasons.

How the regional government frames the problem and describes an action plan is of paramount importance. While it is valuable to leave open the question of substance to the industry's own sense of its situation and potential, it is equally important to emphasize the defining characteristics of an action plan: that it is negotiated, comprehensive, and dynamic, and that all decisions must be unanimous. These features ensure that each component of the local industry will be a full partner in the action plan and that the interests and concerns of all participants will be addressed during the planning process.

Whether IPIA's brinkmanship during the first meeting at Macael was generally appropriate can be debated. The chief merit of this approach is that it frames as sharply as possible the question of whether to continue sliding into crisis or to work together towards a common solution, drawing to some degree on outside help. Putting the issue to an immediate vote serves other purposes as well. It forces the attendees to make a public commitment to the agency and to each other. If the vote is positive, some of the anxieties about the process will likely be suppressed. Imposing the unanimity rule also serves to embed this important process norm in the group's experience from the start.

Negotiating the Action Plan

Events at Macael

In advance of the first official meeting of the planning committee, which took place in September 1983, IPIA wrote and distributed a draft document that enumerated what it regarded as the key issues and problems of the local marble industry. The broad categories of issues were production, commercialization, and personnel. IPIA's director general began the meeting by presenting the draft outline. As the discussion developed, it became apparent that opinions differed sharply on factual premises as well as on what should be done. Before closing the session, IPIA urged the committee to adopt a work plan for preparing its next meeting. The employers association said it would survey the industry to count the number of firms and workers belonging to each branch of activity and to gauge each firm's level of technological development. In addition, subcommittees on production, commercialization, and personnel were formed. These groups were charged with the task of drafting preliminary reports about their respective areas of interest, to be presented to the full committee at its October meeting. Each report was to identify problems, proposed solutions, and suggest who would be responsible for followup.

The director came away from the meeting convinced that IPIA needed to be in constant, if informal, contact with the subcommittees during this critical phase in the process. Since travel time between Macael and the Institute's headquarters in Sevilla exceeded eight hours, he could not play this role himself. Sánchez de la Morena therefore asked a consultant in whom he had complete confidence to spend the following weeks or months in Macael.

While the work plan did not allow time for formal studies to be done, the subcommittees did have access to advice from knowledgeable individuals. As an example, the production subcommittee interviewed on several occasions the chief of the mining section of the central government's provincial delegation. The expert, Rafael Escribano, shared with the committee the limited information that was known about Macael's white marble deposits and suggested a number of specific studies that he believed would be valuable.

The full committee debated the draft reports during two days of meetings in October. While many disagreements persisted, they were muted by three factors: some disputes about facts were resolved by investigation or expert opinion, committee members had experienced working together, and every participant felt ownership of at least one subcommittee's draft report. By the end of the second day, IPIA's director believed that agreement on the issues was sufficient to support the formalization of an action plan. He promised that IPIA would use the subcommittee reports in preparing a full draft of the plan, which would serve as the basis for discussion at the meeting scheduled for November.

Apart from summarizing the problems, the draft identified a number of lines of action, including revising contractual mining rights, commissioning geological and engineering studies of the area's marble deposits, establishing an office for technological support, contracting with designers for assistance in gauging the artisanal goods market, setting standards for product quality, improving roads, expanding electrical networks, planning industrial sites, creating a purchasing cooperative, conducting market research, founding a marketing cooperative, improving occupational health and safety, sponsoring educational programs, and seeking official financing. Each line of action identified the problem it addressed, conceptualized distinct phases, set a time frame for each phase, and assigned responsibility for implementation to specific subcommittees. A slightly modified version of IPIA's proposal was unanimously adopted by the full committee in November 1983 and became the official "Comprehensive Action Plan of the Area of Marble of Macael."

Clinical Interpretations

When the planning process begins, knowledge about the environment mostly reflects each committee member's respective experience. Intense conflict is to be expected when people whose perceptions of reality are untested interact for the first time.

Conflict can be productive if it motivates committee members to inquire into questions that they had considered settled. In striving towards this ideal, the action plan coordinator must be willing to play a leadership role in the planning committee. This role entails taking responsibility for structuring the initial discussions, as well as ensuring that diverse viewpoints are heard. Offering a roster of key issues is one way to focus attention. In managing the ensuing discussion, the regional promotion agency should not suppress differences of opinion, but rather should seek to help stakeholders to work through their disagreements.

Subcommittees can bear much of the burden of detailing definitions of problematic issues, proposing lines of action, and fostering the participants' sense of ownership of the planning process. An action plan coordinator can influence the pace of the subcommittees' work by asking them to report by a certain date to the full group. The coordinator also can influence the substance of this work through ongoing informal contacts, which may require establishing a personal presence in the community during this phase of the process.

The realities of the planning process suggest it is incumbent on the coordinator to press for unanimous agreement on the action plan before the industry's problems are systematically studied. It might be thought that this approach is tantamount to putting the cart before the horse. However, the coordinator has to be concerned with building a cohesive planning committee, with creating a sense of momentum and accomplishment, with expressing respect for what the industry believed was true, and with projecting a unified image to agencies that would be asked to fund the studies recommended by the committee. Negotiating the first official version of the action plan before the research phase can place an industry in a better position both to obtain resources for high quality studies and to make effective use of what can be learned from expert inquiry. An additional advantage of this seemingly "inverted sequence" is that it embeds deeply into the fabric of the planning group's experience the norm that an action plan is negotiated and dynamic.[9]

Envisioning the Future

Events at Macael

IPIA's first major task in implementing the Action Plan was to arrange for studies of the area's geological structure and mining practices. Preliminary contacts with a state-owned research enterprise, ADARO, indicated that the proposed studies would cost more than 100 million pesetas (roughly, $US 700,000) to complete. Under the national mining promotion law, the Ministry of Industry's General Direction for Mines could fund three-quarters of such costs. Since neither IPIA nor Macael could afford to make up the difference, Sánchez de la Morena decided to ask the Ministry to fund the full project. He invited Macael's mayor and the president of the employers association to accompany him at a meeting with Ministry of Industry officials in Madrid. In making their case, the trio claimed that Macael was fully committed to finding common solutions to its current crisis, as evidenced by its ability to reach unanimous agreement on its comprehensive Action Plan. Studies of Macael's geological structure and mining practices were, they argued, crucial to the further development and success of the Action Plan. In the end, the Ministry agreed to fund 100 percent of the ADARO studies.

Thanks to the active role played in formulating the plan by Rafael Escribano, the provincial mining official, participants on the planning committee knew from the outset what information they wanted to obtain through the geological and mining studies. They were looking for an authoritative measure of the magnitude of Macael's marble deposits. They wanted to know how the quality of the area's marble compared with that of other regions in Spain and with that of Carrara, Italy's premier white marble-producing area. They hoped to learn how to reduce the debris generated in huge quantities by the technique of blasting marble blocks and boulders out of quarry frontages. They sought ways to prevent landslides in the mines. In addition, they were curious about how the spatial distribution of the area's various marble formations related to the boundaries of their respective quarries. Some committee members were also interested to know how this information might be used in planning the industry's development.

Since much of ADARO's work took place in the field, many business owners came into direct contact with the activities of the Action Plan. Some business owners gained additional familiarity with the geological and mining research studies by attending periodic meetings, called by the employers association, at which interim results were discussed. At one event, for instance, Rafael Escribano and ADARO researchers explained the significance of detailed aerial photographs that had been taken of Macael's surroundings. At a subsequent meeting, it was announced that Macael possessed Spain's largest endowment of white marble, which ADARO said would likely remain plentiful for at least a few generations, and that Macael's marble was more durable than Carrara's.

With the aid of science, IPIA was able to draw out the competitive implications of these facts about nature: If Macael's white marble was the most plentiful in Spain and more durable than Carrara's, then the area should strive to become a formidable competitor in the national and European marble industry. As to why Macael was suffering an economic crisis, despite its potential competitive advantages, scientific studies provided an alternative answer to a lack of subsidies: the boundaries of the existing quarries did not correspond to rock formations and the use of dynamite reduced the yield of valuable marble blocks. This analysis implied that Macael needed to seek solutions to its problems, such as restructuring property rights and introducing major technological change, that were not part of the industry's usual way of looking at itself. These conclusions did ring true for a sizable number of Macael business owners, as indicated by their eventual enthusiasm for both kinds of changes.

Sensing that business owners were emboldened by the news that Macael was richly endowed with marble of the highest quality, yet anxious about the recommendation that mining rights be restructured and technology updated, IPIA created an opportunity for members of the employers association, along with a few other planning committee participants, to travel to Carrara. IPIA and the employers association agreed to share the projected travel expenses of 3 million pesetas ($US 25,000). The trip to Italy by bus was an important experience for those who went along, most of whom had yet to travel beyond Spain. In Carrara, they toured quarries, fabricating shops, and residential areas, finding little resemblance between the world of Macael and the one they were coming to know. In many quarries, for example, they saw fully automated machines, equipped with industrial diamonds, cut huge blocks out of marble veins. In the fabricating shops, they observed the operation of automatic saws that sliced marble blocks into thin sheets, which were then mechanically polished into finished floor tiles and steps. During the stay, the visitors from Macael also had a chance to meet with their local counterparts and representatives of Italian equipment manufacturers. Some members of the delegation came away from this experience saying to themselves, "We are nobodies in this business." The term "total modernization," which had been bandied about by IPIA even since Sánchez de la Morena first proposed the idea of working on an action plan for Macael, suddenly had a fuller meaning.

Clinical Interpretations

An important task at this stage in the process is to draw out the competitive implications of objective knowledge about the physical and economic environment of the industry. Once business owners become accustomed to thinking that the operating environment can be understood with some degree of objectivity and that the local industry is a valid unit of analysis, action plan coordinators should help work out a detailed, shared vision that expresses what the industry as a whole wants to achieve. A vision is not so much a statement of objectives as a shared cognitive and affecting image of a state of affairs that individuals sense is worth striving toward. Shared visions motivate individual and collective action and foster agreement on what operational steps should be taken.

When most people reflect upon what they want to achieve, they look for role models. It is reasonable to infer by analogy that a traditional industry's effort to envision an attractive future will be aided if its stakeholders are familiar with traditional industries which overcame the competitive disadvantages of fragmentation. Bringing action plan participants into contact with potential role models could well be the most cost-effective investment a coordinator can make.

Building Institutions and Planning Investments

Events at Macael

During 1984, while the ADARO studies were in progress, members of the planning committee began to explore ways to solve certain problems common to all firms in the area. Almost everyone felt, for example, that the dirt roads leading into the quarries were a problem. They were dusty in summer, muddy in winter, and generally unsafe for the large trucks that drove along them hauling away marble stones and boulders. The narrow, winding paved roads that connected the several municipalities of the Macael area to one another and to the major provincial roads were also considered inadequate. Knowing that the regional government, which was responsible for roads, was short on funds, the employers association proposed that its members and the government share the costs: if the regional government would pay for the asphalt, the firms would supply the labor to lay it on the roadbed. After some delay, the initiative succeeded. This event set the stage for a more comprehensive agreement in mid-1985 for road improvements, signed by Macael and two departments of the regional government.[10]

A second major problem upon which all could agree was the need to improve the availability of electricity in the industrial and mining areas. Solving this problem required the cooperation of the privately owned electric power utility of Andalusia, the Compañía Sevillana de Electricidad. IPIA took the lead in pressuring the utility to invest in Macael. As a result, the company invested about 74 million pesetas ($US 500,000) in the area in 1984, up from 13 million pesetas the previous year.[11]

The Macael Action Plan called for studying the feasibility of creating several industrywide institutions, which were strongly favored by IPIA and the local government. One of these proposed institutions was a purchasing cooperative, which would take title to inputs it acquired in bulk and stored in its own warehouse until they were repurchased by Macael firms. The proposal did not spark much resistance since interfirm rivalry focused on sales, and business owners recognized that they could purchase supplies at lower prices by concentrating their buying power. Moreover, a similar arrangement among extraction firms for the production and delivery of compressed air—a key blasting input—was already in place. Once the industry agreed in November 1984 to create the purchasing cooperative, plans were made for constructing the warehouse and a former local priest was hired to manage the operation. The issue that generated the most conflict was the proposed joint sales and marketing cooperative. Both Macael's mayor and IPIA expected this institution to solve such key problems as small firms' inability to fill the large orders of major construction firms, field a sales organization, and fund promotional campaigns. They also hoped that it would mitigate tendencies of local firms to compete with each other for sales principally on the basis of price. Business owners, however, viewed this proposal as a threat to their individual autonomy. The firms whose commercial connections were better developed, furthermore, did not see how they would be advantaged by the marketing cooperative. Despite stiff resistance from the employers association, both IPIA and the mayor pressed ahead with the feasibility study called for by the Action Plan. The opposition of the employers association relented in mid-1985, when agreement on a relatively weak marketing cooperative was hammered out.[12]

In early 1985, IPIA shifted attention to the idea of creating a corporation whose principal asset would initially be the brand name, "Marble of Macael." This corporation, at a minimum, would prepare audiovisual materials on the industry's products, represent the industry at trade fairs, and promote the name of Marble of Macael in the media. A more ambitious conception was to give the corporation the power to prohibit local firms from using the brand name if they failed to meet specific quality standards. This latter suggestion, however, foundered on business owners' unwillingness to have the quality of their products judged by such an organization. IPIA and the mayor believed it was more important to launch the brand name corporation, the "Sociedad de la Marca 'Mármol de Macael,' S.A.," than to hold out for more restrictive bylaws. The two camps reached an agreement in November 1985.[13]

A second major objective of the Action Plan in 1985—in addition to building institutions—was to translate the general vision of Macael's modernization into a plan for investing in plant and equipment. Such a plan was to be used in attracting financing from official and private institutions and in inducing changes in the operations of individual firms. Formulating the industrial restructuring model required detailed knowledge of firms' existing product lines, scale, output quality, access to raw materials, plant, equipment, production management, sales capacity, administrative skill, and the like. This information was collected by a consulting firm hired by IPIA and the employers association. The interim product of this effort was a classification of Macael firms by product line, based on their existing capacities and what their future role in the industry might be.

This formulation of the industrywide plan for firm-level investments generated some controversy at meetings of business owners convened by the employers association. The consulting firm modified the proposed model somewhat before recommending investments for each category of firms.

In November 1985, the planning committee made the industrial restructuring model and its investment plan part of the official Macael Action Plan.[14] Shortly thereafter, IPIA announced that it would cover 9 percent of the investment costs of the larger firms and 18 percent of those of smaller firms, so long as these firms' proposed projects were consistent with the industrial restructuring model.

By the beginning of 1986, about two years into the implementation of the Action Plan, Macael was thus well positioned to respond to the rising domestic demand for marble construction materials. Some infrastructural improvements were complete and many more were planned, including the development of industrial sites equipped with electrical lines, telephone circuits, and water supplies. Business owners were beginning to collaborate with one another, as long as their autonomy was not genuinely threatened. As a symbol of this new willingness to cooperate, a centrally located building containing the offices of the employers association and the warehouse of the buyers cooperative was about to be inaugurated. The Sociedad de la Marca was gearing up to promote the brand name, *Mármol de Macael.* Many business owners were primed to invest in new plant and equipment; a few had already begun to do so by reinvesting whatever profits they had been earning. The idea of a comprehensive and negotiated action plan for the modernization of Macael's marble industry, furthermore, had been given a detailed, logical expression in the industrial restructuring model. But IPIA and the industry knew that even the best laid plans for Macael could founder on the absence of external financial support.

Clinical Interpretations

An action plan should eventually offer a clear conception of how the industry as a whole intends to compete in the national and international marketplace. It should also embody specific plans for designing, producing, and selling products. And it should offer a framework for planning and evaluating the array of firm-level and collective investments that would make it possible to carry out the strategic business plan.

At the time a shared vision begins to form, such a detailed plan can only be a distant objective. In deciding what issues to take up, in what order, and with what duration of inquiry, an action plan coordinator, therefore, should also seek to achieve some interim process objectives. One such objective is to sustain industry leaders' newly generated optimism about the prospects for meaningful change and to help their respective constituencies share this attitude.

An action plan committee may create a sense of momentum by initially working on issues that tend to generate modest conflict (e.g., road paving and the purchasing cooperative in Macael). When commitment to the action plan concept is strong and a specific vision is beginning to form, the planning process can handle intense conflict (such as that generated by the marketing and sales cooperative issue).

In managing intensely conflictual issues, an action plan coordinator might best take a long-term view of its goals. The critical short-term interest includes educating business owners about the prospects of their industry and demonstrating to the outside world that the industry is overcoming the effects of fragmentation. In the short run, it may be less important to enforce common standards of quality, for instance, than to enlarge business owners' experience with collaborative institutions.

Handling controversial issues sequentially is useful in containing conflict, building decisionmaking capacity, and distributing the planning committee's workload over time. Yet, dealing simultaneously with a range of issues, such as infrastructure, plant and equipment, and collaborative institutions is necessary for planning to result in a competitive strategy before too long.

In advancing simultaneously along these lines without overtaxing the planning committee, it is almost certainly necessary to use the services of consulting firms. Action plan coordinators can reduce the risks of involving consultants by educating them about the premises and precepts of the process. In addition, it is advisable to arrange for at least one of the other planning committee members to share the costs of the consulting work. This arrangement strengthens the norm that the planning committee is responsible for making the decisions that shape the local industry's future. It also facilitates the interactive relationship among experts and decisionmakers essential to a successful action plan.

Mobilizing Resources

Events at Macael

IPIA's early fund-raising efforts on behalf of the Macael Action Plan met with considerable success. As discussed above, the Ministry of Industry agreed to cover the entire cost of ADARO's scientific and engineering studies. The Compañía Sevillana de Electricidad and Telefónica were persuaded to greatly increase their rate of investment in Macael. The regional government, as well, invested $3.5 million during 1984-85 in roads, market research, warehousing facilities for the buyers and marketing cooperatives, office space for the employers association, and a medical clinic for Macael's workers.

Despite these early successes in channeling funds towards research and infrastructure projects, IPIA was extremely anxious about delivering on its commitment to help firms finance investments in plant and equipment. The pressures on the Institute to fulfill business owners' expectations became especially acute in late 1985, when the planning committee approved the industrial restructuring model.[15] This detailed plan called for investments of more than 3 billion pesetas ($US 25 million) in Macael's fabricating shops (i.e., seven times the amount generated by the Action Plan so far).

IPIA's anxiety about delivering on its promise to mobilize resources was further heightened by several facts. IPIA knew that most Macael firms had never obtained subsidies from the central government. Andalusia's regional government, moreover, remained short on funds while the fiscal system for Spain's 17 Autonomous Communities evolved. And Macael firms could not yet finance a high proportion of these investments from operating profits.

IPIA also entered into discussions with the Ministry of Industry, which managed the national industrialization fund for Andalusia, to reduce the bureaucratic obstacles that had impeded Macael firms' access to this funding source. In early 1986, the Ministry agreed to provide the highest degree of financial support it could, namely, up to 25 percent of those planned outlays for plant and equipment judged by IPIA to be consistent with the restructuring model. It was also agreed that IPIA would serve as a conduit for subsidy proposals.

IPIA also sought to make it easier for Macael firms to borrow funds from private sources. Commercial banks in Andalusia were historically wary of loaning funds to small enterprises. In the years immediately preceding the Action Plan, banks practically refused to extend credit to Macael firms, including Banco Popular, which had maintained a branch office in Macael for 30 years. As the result of negotiations that began in January 1986, this bank agreed to extend five-year loans instead of its usual short-term loans for industrialization projects. The regional government, in turn, agreed to provide an interest rate subsidy of 2 percent for projects that implemented the Action Plan. A similar agreement was reached later in the year with the quasi-public savings bank of Almería (Caja de Ahorros).[16]

When meeting with banks and agencies, IPIA usually noted that Macael's proven marble reserves were plentiful and that the demand for the area's products would grow markedly. The ADARO studies and the sharp upturn in demand that occurred in 1985—as construction activity revived along Andalusia's Costa del Sol—gave credibility to these points. Citing investments in infrastructure, IPIA also sought to demonstrate the public sector's commitment to eliminating bottlenecks. At such meetings, the president of the employers association argued that the area's business owners were committed to making Macael a major force in the national and European marble industry.

In mobilizing resources for Macael, the Institute anticipated that social and political arguments would be as persuasive to some audiences as economic ones. Andalusia's weak industrialization was widely considered to be a pressing social problem. Many institutions, moreover, were extremely sensitive to the fact that the socialist party had won an absolute majority in the regional parliament after campaigning on a platform of social and economic development.[17] Sánchez de la Morena explained that IPIA's specific mission was to find ways of manufacturing valuable products from Andalusia's rich endowment of natural resources and to stitch together the region's economic fabric. He pointed out that Almería province was otherwise virtually bereft of industrial activity. By implication, financing investments at Macael represented an excellent way to advance the industrial development goals of the regional government and of the Andalusian public.

The Macael planning committee promoted this concept through a variety of means. For example, the employers association in 1985 invented the *Premio de Mármol*, a prize to be awarded annually to an individual or institution who made a significant contribution to the local industry. The association's leadership chose the award recipients carefully. In 1987, for instance, *a Premio de Mármol* was given to the editor of a national news magazine, *Cambio 16*, who had previously worked for a prominent newspaper in Almería; to the director of a major provincial bank, Caja Almería; and to the trade association of eastern Andalusia's architects. In this way, special ties were fostered with national media, banking, and customer organizations. Members of the planning committee found additional ways to draw influential outsiders to Macael. As just one example, the regional government's president came to inaugurate the warehouses for the buyers and marketing cooperatives in March 1986. Apart from these special events, planning committee leaders created hundreds of opportunities to project Macael's image as an industry and community on the move.[18]

The combined efforts of IPIA and the Macael Action Plan leaders succeeded in generating about 700 million pesetas ($US 5 million) in government grants and about 1,850 million pesetas ($US 15 million) in loans for investments in plant and equipment during 1986-88. The goals for aggregate investment in plant and equipment, set out in the industrial restructuring model, were practically reached before the end of 1988, thanks in large part to an extremely high rate of profit reinvestment. The total investment in Macael, including infrastructure, research, and institution-building, exceeded 5 billion pesetas ($US 42 million) during the first five years of the Action Plan.

Clinical Interpretations

Once the coordinator votes in favor of an action plan proposal requiring external financial resources, it is obligated to use its institutional muscle with banks, government agencies, and utilities in order to implement the agreed upon plan. In many cases, banks and government agencies are reluctant to invest in industries of the past. When decisionmakers are naturally skeptical of investing resources in traditional industries, it is advantageous to expose them to the action plan process. One way to do so is for the coordinator to be joined by other key planning committee members at negotiating sessions; another is to invite decisionmakers to make site visits. The action plan's numerous diagnostic and prescriptive studies are another important tool for explaining how implementing the plan will enable the local industry to compete.

If agencies are seeking to make their programs visible in the public eye, it makes sense to intimate that a formal agreement will be publicized and that credit for the overall success of the action plan will be shared. If funding agencies and banks are looking for ways to serve small and medium-sized firms efficiently, it is advantageous to explain how the framework of the action plan will reduce the transaction costs of evaluating individual project proposals. To underscore this advantage, action plan coordinators might serve as a conduit between particular firms and these large institutions.

Outcomes

While total quarry output increased 33 percent between 1983 and 1987, the production of marble suited for construction materials rose by 75 percent.[19] As a result of improvements in mining and fabrication, some 20 firms became major suppliers of building materials. By 1987, only 30 percent of sales were accounted for by unprocessed marble, while annual revenues reached 15 billion pesetas ($US 125 million).[20]

The industrial restructuring study recommended that firms that could not produce raw materials economically focus on the fabrication of decorative objects. The extent to which firms have followed this recommendation cannot be estimated with available data. It is, however, clear that some shops have purchased equipment to mechanize this production process.

The number of firms that complied with the Action Plan and received subsidies from the regional government increased from 16 to 64 between 1985, when the industrial restructuring study was completed, and 1987.[21] Total investment in plant and equipment during 1984-88 reached $US 30.6 million.[22]

The Sociedad de la Marca has been extremely active in promoting the brand name *"Mármol de Macael."* Between 1986 and 1987, it administered an advertising promotion budget of more than 70 million pesetas (about $US 600,000). Its activities, along with the objective improvements in product quality, have made the name "Macael" a potent signal of value in the national marble industry.

Macael firms have utilized their purchasing cooperative. It is difficult to estimate, however, the magnitude of the cost savings it generated. The sales and marketing cooperative has not been utilized by firms catering to the construction industry. Most firms have been selling directly all they can produce, thanks to a boom in luxury construction activity in Spain.

Conclusion

The use of the operational method of coordinating a negotiated, comprehensive, and dynamic Action Plan helped to achieve results in Macael that were congruent with the political platform of Andalusia's elected leaders and public policies, as well as with IPIA's mandate and organizational strategy during the 1982-87 period. These results were achieved despite such constraints as distrust of governmental economic or regional planning, a weak enterprising tradition, and the regional government's minimal direct control over economic policy instruments. The Macael case shows that this combination of policies, mandates, organizational strategies, and operational methods can be remarkably effective in contexts such as Andalusia, where subnational governmental officials were committed to promoting economic development in the aftermath of a transition to democracy.

An action plan is an operational method whose effectiveness in promoting the aims of public policy depends significantly on the skill with which it is managed. While some skilled performances may be based *solely* on personal and inarticulate knowledge,[23] coordinating an action plan is not one of them. Practitioners' skill in using this method may be enhanced by expanding their clinical knowledge.[24] This paper expands clinical knowledge about the use of this operational method by interpreting why specific actions in Macael helped achieve the public policy aim of developing locally based industries in Andalusia.[25]

To be skilled practitioners, coordinators of action plans also need a way to conceptualize or frame the role they play. Role frames "determine practitioners' strategies of attention and thereby set the directions in which they try to shape the problematic situations they confront."[26] Judging from the Macael case, an appropriate role frame for action plan coordinators may be grounded in conceptual networks such as service management, issue framing, leadership, social learning, negotiation, and political management.[27] The literature about these conceptual networks—which structure an emerging American conception of public management—is a useful source of precepts for developing the role frame of action plan coordinators, as indicated below.

1. *Service Management.* Treat the stakeholders in an industry as customers. Imagine how customers are likely to experience initial contacts with agency personnel. Assure stakeholders that the agency wants to provide a service rather than to exercise administrative control. Indicate that if stakeholders reach agreement on an action plan, the agency would champion it in contacts with government agencies, banks, and other resource providers.[28]

2. *Issue Framing.* Choose carefully the categories employed to define the situation.[29] Identify goals that are attractive to all stakeholders, given the dominant ideology of the period.[30] Indicate that the problem is multifaceted, involving production, marketing, finance, and working conditions.

3. *Leadership.* Develop a transactive relationship with the stakeholders conducive to mutual learning.[31] Explain that the action plan should be *theirs,* not the government's. Insist that the purpose of an action plan is to achieve change, not just to study problems. Provide a certain amount of structure for stakeholders' involvement in the planning activity.[32]

Empower stakeholders to perform leadership functions.[33] Modulate conflict among stakeholders so that they are stimulated to master the situation they are facing, while not overwhelmed by the task.[34] Generate small wins and celebrate successes.[35]

4. *Social Learning.* Create an experiential and institutional basis for joint inquiry and action. Use formal inquiry and analysis to create movement in the group process.[36] Ensure that expert knowledge is collected or developed in response to stakeholders' perception of a need for it.[37] Give stakeholders an opportunity to accept, amend, or reject the results. Help stakeholders fashion an attractive and realistic vision of the future. Focus attention on how the local industry fits into the broader environment.[38] Let specific objectives emerge in the course of ongoing inquiry and action.[39]

5. *Negotiation.* Negotiate networks of linked agreements consistent with public policy and the agency's strategy.[40] Provide incentives for firms to collaborate when it is beneficial for the local industry as a whole.[41] Seek firms' compliance with the action plan by making it the basis for allocating subsidies and credit.

6. *Political Management.* Publicize the planning process and results. Use analysis as an instrument of persuasion.[42] Highlight stakeholders' commitment to achieving their vision for the local industry. Remind audiences of the relationship between public policy and the operational method of action plans.[43]

The conceptual networks within which these precepts are embedded emerged in the mainstream literature about public administration as the result of decades of criticism of a vision of good government as centralized, hierarchical, and staffed by experts. They reflect many contemporary American beliefs about social problemsolving and governance in a decentralized liberal democracy. As elected officials and managers in Eastern Europe and Latin America look for role frames appropriate to both their positions in democratic institutions and the substantive problems of postauthoritarian situations, they may find the experientially grounded conceptual networks of public management attractive.

NOTES

•A version of this paper appeared under the same title in *Policy Sciences* 24 (1991): 271-290. It appears here with permission of the publisher, Kluwer Academic Publishers. Earlier versions were presented at an OECD Conference on Regional Policies in the Europe of the Nineties, at the 1989 Annual Research Conference of the Association for Public Policy Analysis and Management, and at the Graduate Center of the City University of New York. Funding for the research was provided by the German Marshall Fund of the United States. The assistance of Catherine Moukheibir is gratefully acknowledged. The author has benefited from comments by Mark Moore, Raymond Vernon, Scott Pearson, José M. O'Kean, Charles E. Lindblom, Michael Reich, Larry Wortzel, Lee Friedman, Robert Putnam, Ronald Ferguson, Andrew Stone, Alasdair Roberts, William Ascher, and two anonymous referees.

1. Estatuto de Autonomía, Art. 12, §3, 10, *Legislación Sobre Comunidades Autónomas, Vol. 1* (Madrid: Tecnos, 1982). The Autonomy Statute was granted by the national parliament in 1981 in accordance with Title VIII of the 1978 Spanish Constitution.

2. See Michael Barzelay, "Andalusian Socialism: Political Ideology and Economic Policy in an Autonomous Community in Spain," paper presented at the American Political Science Meetings, Washington, DC, August 1986. Development-from-within, or endogenous development, is a programmatic concept arising from sustained critiques of European regional policies of the 1950s and 1960s as well as of industrial recruitment strategies in the Third World and U.S. contexts.

3. See Michael Barzelay, "Ricardo Sánchez de la Morena and the Institute for Industrial Promotion of Andalusia," Case Program, John F. Kennedy School of Government, Harvard University, Number C16-90-974; and Javier Pérez Royo and Antonio Porras Nadales (eds.), *El Parlamento de Andalucía: Análisis de la Primera Legislatura (1982-1986)* (Madrid: Tecnos, 1987), pp. 240-264.

4. See Michael Porter, *Competitive Strategy* (New York: The Free Press, 1980), *Competitive Advantage* (New York: The Free Press, 1985), and *The Competitive Advantage of Nations* (New York: The Free Press, 1990).

5. Much of the literature on the mandates and strategies of regional agencies is very general. See, e.g., OECD, *Agencies for Industrial Adaptation and Development* (Paris: OECD, 1978), p. 49: "There appears to be a fairly general tendency for agencies to develop counselling and technical assistance functions. This would seem to be a normal tendency for small-scale agencies, which do not want to immobilise too large a proportion of their resources in particular operations. They thus look, jointly with enterprise managements, for outside financial, technical, and industrial support....It appears that, in general, the agencies are looking for action across the whole front, with financial operations associated with technological and occasionally with regional aspects of adaptation." Some studies recommend that policymakers combine three "policy options," namely, mobilizing funding, providing information, and fostering an individual and collective enterprising spirit (termed social animation). See William J. Coffey and Mario Polese, "Local Development: Conceptual Bases and Policy Implications," *Regional Studies*, April 1985.

6. On creating and claiming value, see David A. Lax and James K. Sebenius, *The Manager as Negotiator: Bargaining for Cooperation and Competitive Gain* (New York: The Free Press, 1986), pp. 29-45; and Michael Porter, *Competitive Advantage* (New York: The Free Press, 1985), pp. 4-10.

7. See Ricardo Sánchez de la Morena and José María Bueno, "El Instituto de Promoción Industrial de Andalucía," *Boletín Económico de Andalucía*, No. 4, 1984, pp. 88-94.

8. The expression Sánchez de la Morena recalls using to frame the choice was, *"O jugamos juntos o pinchamos la pelota,"* roughly translated as "either we play together or we puncture the ball." Interviewed in Sevilla, July 1988.

9. Albert O. Hirschman, "Introduction: Political Economics and Possibilism," in his *Bias For Hope* (New Haven: Yale University Press, 1971), pp. 26-37.

10. "Se gestiona la celebración de la I Feria del Mármol," *La Crónica de Almería,* August 4, 1985.

11. Data supplied by the provincial office of the Instituto de Fomento de Andalucía, the successor organization to IPIA.

12. *La Crónica de Almería,* July 7, 1985.

13. The thorny question of how to assess Macael firms for their use of the brand name was sidestepped by the municipality's offer to give the corporation one-tenth of the mining fees it collected. "Firmado el compromiso de constitución de la sociedad 'Mármol de Macael'," *La Crónica de Almería,* November 23, 1985.

14. "Los objetivos del plan están cumplidos en un 90 por ciento." *La Crónica de Almería,* November 28, 1984.

15. Pressures started becoming more intense in mid-1985, as indicated by such provincial newspaper headlines as, "The reindustrialization is still up in the air." *La Cronica de Almería,* July 19, 1985.

16. *La Voz de Almería,* May 8, 1986.

17. Some audiences may also have been sensitive to the fact that the PSOE held an absolute majority in the national parliament, as well.

18. To provide just one illustration, a provincial newspaper on the same day published an interview with Macael's mayor, entitled, "The economic objectives have been accomplished," and another with the employers association president, entitled, "The industrial planning of Macael: White marble is competitive in Europe." *La Cronica de Almería,* October 5, 1986.

19. These data were collected by the local government of Macael and reported to the Instituto de Fomento de Andalucía.

20. In 1983, total sales were 3 billion pesetas. Inflation during 1983-87 averaged about 5 percent.

21. Instituto de Fomento de Andalucía, "Inversiones Derivadas del Plan de Actuación Global de la Zona del Mármol de Macael," March 1989.

22. Idem.

23. Michael Polanyi, *Personal Knowledge* (Chicago: University of Chicago Press, 1958), pp. 49-53.

24. Stuart Hart decries the lack of development of clinical knowledge about how to manage interactive planning processes such as the operational method studied here. "The complexity of problems [like economic development] places the planner at the crossroads between analysis and politics, as a facilitator of a strategic social process. Planning in this mode requires a gentle blend of targeted, strategic analysis and structured interaction among stakeholders with different perspectives and varying kinds of knowledge and information....[But] while analysts and commentators on such matters have been long on description of such problems and the broad characteristics of the integrative approach [to planning], *there has been little in the way of practical prescription or method development. Few writers have wrestled with the down-to-earth realities of operationalizing the integrative approach"* (emphasis added). See, "Steering the Path Between Ambiguity and Overload: Planning as a Strategic Social Process," in *Interdisciplinary Planning: A Perspective for the Future,* edited by Milan Dluhy and Kan Chen (New York: Center for Urban Policy Research, 1986), pp. 117-121.

25. Donald A. Schön, *The Reflective Practitioner: How Professionals Think in Action* (New York: Basic Books, 1983), p. 315, refers to such case analysis as repertoire-building research.

26. Schön, *The Reflective Practitioner*, p. 309.

27. See, Michael Barzelay and Linda Kaboolian, "Structural Metaphors and Public Management Education," *Journal of Policy Analysis and Management*, Fall 1990, and literature cited therein.

28. On service management, see Michael Barzelay and Babak Armajani, "Breaking Through Bureaucracy," book manuscript, Chapter 1; Barzelay and Kaboolian, "Structural Metaphors and Public Management Education"; James Heskett, *Managing in the Service Economy* (Boston: Harvard Business School Press, 1986); and Karl Albrecht, *At America's Service* (Homewood, IL: Dow-Jones Irwin, 1988).

29. John W. Kingdon, *Agendas, Alternatives, and Public Policies* (Boston: Little Brown, 1984), pp. 117-121.

30. "Goals are carrots and problems are sticks; both are inducements to support measures people might otherwise find painful, unwise, or irrelevant to their lives." See, Murray Edelman, *Constructing the Political Spectacle* (Chicago: University of Chicago Press, 1988), p. 22.

31. See, John Friedmann, *Planning in the Public Domain* (Princeton: Princeton University Press, 1987), pp. 181-187.

32. See, J. Richard Hackman and Richard E. Walton, "Leading Groups in Organizations," in *Designing Effective Work Groups*, edited by Paul S. Goodman (San Francisco: Jossey-Bass, 1986); and Ronald A. Heifetz and Riley M. Sinder, "Political Leadership: Managing the Public's Problem Solving," in *The Power of Public Ideas*, edited by Robert Reich (Cambridge: Ballinger, 1988).

33. Rosabeth Moss Kanter, *The Change Masters* (New York: Simon and Schuster, 1983).

34. Ronald A. Heifetz, et al., "Teaching and Assessing Leadership Courses at the John F. Kennedy School of Government," *Journal of Policy Analysis and Management*, Summer 1989, p. 542.

35. Thomas J. Peters and Robert H. Waterman, Jr., *In Search of Excellence* (New York: Harper & Row, 1982), pp. 67-74; and Robert Behn, "Management By Groping Along," *Journal of Policy Analysis and Management*, Fall 1988, p. 646.

36. K.K. Smith and David Berg, *Paradoxes of Group Life: Understanding Conflict, Paralysis and Movement in Groups* (San Francisco: Jossey-Bass, 1987).

37. Hart, "Planning as a Strategic Social Process," p. 117; Charles E. Lindblom and David K. Cohen, *Usable Knowledge: Social Science and Social Problem-Solving* (New Haven: Yale University Press, 1979), pp. 72-85; Mark H. Moore, "What Sort of Ideas Become Public Ideas?" in *The Power of Public Ideas*, edited by Robert B. Reich (Cambridge: Harvard University Press, 1990), p. 83.

38. Warren Bennis and Burt Nanus, *Leaders: Strategies for Taking Charge* (New York: Harper & Row, 1985).

39. Friedmann, *Planning in the Public Domain*, p. 187.

40. Lax and Sebenius, *The Manager as Negotiator*, pp. 261-268.

41. The need for both individual and joint action in the context of fragmented industries is apparent in the industrial districts literature. On the Italian case, see Sebastiano Brusco and Charles Sabel, "Artisan Production and Economic Growth," in *The Dynamics of Labor Market Segmentation*, edited by Frank Wilkinson (London: Academic Press, 1981).

42. Charles E. Lindblom, *The Policy-Making Process*, 2d edition (Englewood Cliffs: Prentice-Hall, 1980), pp. 28-31.

43. Philip Heymann, *The Politics of Public Management* (New Haven: Yale University Press, 1987), pp. 74-75, 90-92, notes that democratic mandates are a source of the legitimacy of managerial actions and a basis for negotiating with other organizations in the policy environment.

4
Worker Democracy in Socialist France

Bernard E. Brown
City University of New York

Worker participation hardly existed in French enterprise before the victory of the Left in 1981. Enterprise committees ("comités d'entreprise"), created after World War II, were concerned almost entirely with external activities (travel, holiday, cultural and educational programs). Trade unions competed vigorously for control of enterprise committees, whose sizable budgets offered opportunities for employment of union militants and shaping of working-class attitudes. But enterprise committees did not share meaningfully in management.

It was the intention of the Left government in 1981 to transform authority relations within enterprises. The stated goal was eventually to achieve economic democracy, summed up in the slogan "autogestion" (literally, self-management). Roundly condemning both capitalism (Socialists agreed with Communists on the need to break with this evil system) and Russian-style communism (Communists agreed with Socialists that the Soviet Union represented a form of authoritarian socialism that had to be transcended), the united Left pledged to enable workers to become masters and shapers of their own destinies.[1]

In the summer and fall of 1982 a series of four laws was enacted by the National Assembly creating "new rights for workers," known popularly thereafter by the name of the Socialist Minister of Labor, Jean Auroux. The lois Auroux, or Auroux laws, mandated the creation in all enterprises employing over 200 people of "groupes d'expression directe" (expression groups), in which workers would be able to speak up directly and collectively on any aspect of their workday life. Important new powers were also devolved upon the enterprise committees, whose members are elected only by workers. Management was required to inform enterprise committees ahead of time concerning any important decisions—including production and pricing strategy, intro-

67

duction of new technology, and investment policies. And enterprises were also required to bargain collectively with unions every year. What happened? Did the French Left find a "third way" between grasping capitalism and authoritarian socialism?

To judge by the accounts that have appeared so far outside of France, very little of consequence has happened.[2] Foreign observers have tended to downgrade the changes introduced by the Auroux laws. W. Rand Smith demonstrates convincingly that the laws have not enabled workers to challenge the basic power of private (and, we may add, public) employers to make decisions. Hence, autogestion (defined as the exercise of control over workplace decisions), he says, has not been achieved. Indeed, employers have turned the Auroux laws to their advantage, so that worker control is farther away than ever. The laws are an attempt to "modernize" labor-management relations, Smith concludes, "by giving workers an opportunity to express themselves and by encouraging collective bargaining."[3] Hence, French practice has merely been brought into line with practice elsewhere.

Bernard Moss affirms also that the Auroux laws have failed to bring about a change in the balance of power. He sees continuity in labor-management relations as the major feature of the modern period in France, described as "the cycle of managerial supremacy interrupted by waves of radical protest which have characterized its industrial past."[4] Similarly, Duncan Gallie concludes that the laws did little to modify the traditional structure of French industrial relations.[5] A slight difference of emphasis may be noted in the appraisals of these observers. "Modernized" managerial supremacy presumably is not the same as an immutable traditional structure.

Why didn't the French Left break with capitalism? The reasons mentioned by Smith and Moss include: the inherent ambiguity of the notion of autogestion, the rivalry between Socialists and Communists, divisions among the unions, and government-sponsored austerity measures. "Under these conditions," Moss observes, "it was not surprising that managerial adversaries rather than union supporters derived the greatest satisfaction from the application of the new laws."[6] In addition to the unfavorable circumstances, Smith adds, the Socialist party was not able to adopt a program capable of translating its aspirations into reality. The implication is that under favorable conditions—unity of the Left parties and of the working class, a period of economic growth and prosperity, and a firm political will to break with capitalism—the goal of autogestion would be within reach. As the French would say, "Vouloir, c'est pouvoir" (where there is a will, there is a way).

These critics are thoroughly familiar with labor-management relations in France, and with the excellent studies by French labor sociologists on the implementation of the Auroux laws.[7] Each point in their argument is well taken. But they have underestimated the importance of changes in the climate of labor-management relations and have drawn partial conclusions. The purpose of this essay is to call attention to new developments in industrial relations in France since the adoption of the Auroux laws, and to show that the failure to achieve the stated goal of the French Left sheds precious light on the theory of economic democracy.

Managerial Supremacy—But Why?

Agreement may be registered at the outset on one key point: the participative structures created by the Auroux laws have come under the domination of management. To understand why, let us take a closer look at these structures. Between 1983 and 1985, when the Auroux laws were reviewed, amended, and reenacted by the National Assembly, some 6,000 agreements were reached between management and the representatives of workers (either unions or enterprise committees), leading to the creation of about 100,000 expression groups. Typically, an expression group consists of 15 to 20 people who meet two or three times a year and have the right to "express" themselves on any aspect of their working conditions.

Some major trends were immediately evident. Better educated workers tended to speak up and monopolize the time of most groups; only skilled leadership was able to prevent this from happening. As predicted by the skeptics, apathy set in after the initial period of enthusiasm. Workers generally lost interest in attending meetings, even though they were on company time. Within two years, about one-third of the expression groups had ceased to meet altogether, and another one-third met only intermittently.

Expression groups that meet regularly share a crucial characteristic: their worker-members are mobilized and actively supported by management. As one French sociologist put it, successful expression groups have been a creation of "the Prince."[8] This development resulted from a turnaround of business policy on workforce participation. Immediately after the adoption of the Auroux laws, the Conseil National du Patronat Français (CNPF)—which had fought their adoption tooth and nail—encouraged its members to play the game according to the changed rules in order to prevent the Communist-led Confédération Générale du Travail (CGT) from taking over. An Estates-General of the CNPF in 1983 urged managers to train foremen and supervisory employees (cadres) as discussion leaders and to throw their resources and energies into the struggle to control the new groups.

Managers were advised through the business press to take the following steps: set up training courses for cadres; reward cadres for taking the lead in groups; make sure that questions and criticism receive the attention of the hierarchy; rapidly resolve problems thus called to the attention of superiors; and communicate this information to the groups. When managers were reluctant to take these measures (either because they were unconvinced of the need, had too much difficulty with cadres who wished to preserve their traditional prerogatives, or were harassed by a strong union leadership), expression groups faded away or were easily contained.

It was virtually impossible for the CGT or Confédération Française Démocratique du Travail (CFDT) to displace management in giving a firm lead to the groups. Most militants were formed in the school of class conflict, and were not ready for instant conversion into apostles of class cooperation. Nor did their training prepare them to be adept at two-way communication between rank-and-file at one end and management at the other. In rare cases where unions were able to mobilize and guide workers, management was able to contain unruly expression groups by ignoring them. After a while, discouraged workers simply gave up.

An unforeseen development after 1982 was the phenomenal expansion, not of expression groups but rather of all things, quality circles. A handful of French businessmen, inspired by Japanese production methods during an Asian tour, had founded the Association Française des Cercles de Qualité (AFCERQ) a year before the passage of the Auroux laws. The attempt to introduce Japanese-style quality circles was a failure—considered by workers to be the latest of many business-sponsored schemes to intensify class exploitation. It was only after the passage of the Auroux laws that the quality circle movement took off. As of 1988, AFCERQ had presided over the creation of some 40,000 quality circles, and the principle was extended by the Chirac government to the civil service.

How did it happen? Managers were advised to consider the expression group as a useful technique for involving workers in their enterprise and identifying problems. In a second step, workers were to be encouraged to help resolve problems—through quality circles. AFCERQ consultants warned that quality circles would wither unless substantial resources, time, and energy were invested in them. Successful quality circles, according to AFCERQ, would require: commitment from top management; organization of study groups for travel to the United States or Japan; weekend seminars for all managers and cadres in order to consider the recommendations of the consultants; discussion by all employees of the new procedures; and, finally and only then, creation and constant care of the quality circles.

The pressure on workers to enter and participate in the quality movement was irresistible. The unions, including even the CGT, gave up their boycott. Alas (for management), quality circles are subject to the same trends of apathy that wreaked such havoc with expression groups. The most recent development is to make emphasis on quality part of the productive process through work teams, suggestion boxes, and collective participation in definition of goals for the enterprise, along with expression groups and quality circles.[9]

Equally disappointing to advocates of worker control has been the performance of enterprise committees. In the original conception, delegates elected by workers are to give an opinion on all important decisions by management before they are taken. Management is also required to submit annual reports to enterprise committees, which are permitted to hire specialists (such as accountants, lawyers, or engineers)—at company expense—to help them understand these reports. Great hopes were placed in enterprise committees, suitably aided by outside experts, union headquarters, and political parties, to counter management proposals with their own. Enterprise committees were to constitute a rival power within the structure of enterprise, and perhaps prepare the way for the assumption of managerial prerogatives by workers. The Communist party planned to use enterprise committees to impose its celebrated "new criteria of management"— production for use rather than for profit—throughout the economy.

Enterprise committees suffered the same fate as expression groups, and for much the same reasons. Management could ignore recommendations from hostile enterprise committees with relative ease. More positively, management made the agreeable discovery that it could communicate more effectively with workers through their elected delegates, and with delegates through their hired experts. Instead of challenging capitalism, enterprise committees and expression groups for the most part were enrolled in a vast campaign to strengthen it—in order to protect jobs and raise salaries.

The fate of participative structures thus points up the inherent difficulty of maintaining worker autonomy against the formidable pressure that can be brought to bear by the concentrated power of management. Only one effective counterforce can be envisaged: the unions. But worker autonomy has meant, in France, independence of workers from all external constraints, including that of unions, which are bureaucratized and linked to potentially domineering political parties and the State. Worker control is not the same as control by unions and parties in the name of workers.[10]

The failure of enterprise committees to offer a feasible alternative to management policies is highly instructive. Almost immediately after the passage of the Auroux laws, the CFDT found that its resources were stretched too thin to be able to take on managerial functions as well, and it stopped submitting counterproposals. The CGT, on the other hand, drew up a number of counterproposals, particularly in industries threatened by layoffs or plant closings.

Invariably, the CGT counterproposal consisted of a detailed inventory of customer needs, and of functions performed by each work post, all leading to the triumphant conclusion that the enterprise is viable and not a single job need be lost. What if there is no longer a market? That is because management is thinking in terms of short-term profit instead of social use. Plenty of customers are out there, in the Third World and in Eastern Europe. How those customers would be able to pay for goods without subsidies from French taxpayers is never explained. Part of the standard counterproposal was also elimination of bothersome imports, while foreigners presumably would be happy to go on buying French goods without any thought of retaliation. CGT proposals were considered unconnected to reality, not only by management of private enterprises, but also (perhaps even more forcefully) by the Socialist State responsible for the nationalized industries.[11]

Why has it been impossible to maintain worker autonomy against bureaucratic pressure? For Edmond Maire, perhaps the most important advocate of autogestion in the 1970s, the reasons go beyond the contingent factors mentioned by Smith and Moss (unemployment, austerity, lack of political will). It is the very notion of worker autonomy that he calls into question. For a long time, Maire concedes, the labor movement contrasted monarchical enterprise (where the boss wields absolute power) with models reflecting the belief that workers can decide everything. But now we must go further, declares the former general secretary of the CFDT, and recognize the specificity and legitimacy of the managerial function, which cannot be the result of collective deliberation. Autogestion, he concludes, remains a valid ideal, but is not a model for enterprise. The need today is not for a "break with capitalism" (termed by Maire "a dangerous illusion and nonoperative") but vigorous defense of workers' interests and "logic" within enterprises. In effect, virtually every plank of the CFDT's radical program of the 1970s has been discarded since the adoption of the Auroux laws.[12]

"Capitalism Ain't What It Used to Be"

A new model of enterprise has emerged in France, and it has become dominant within the large, professionally managed sector of the economy (both public and private). Before 1981, it was taken for granted that management made all decisions, which were then transmitted downward to employees. Negotiations with unions took place mainly at the branch or industry level (not within individual enterprises), following guidelines set by the State. In turn, business was expected to follow the lead of the State, whose top functionaries were presumed to have a sense of national interest. This patriarchal model reflected the prevailing belief within the French political class after the

Liberation that French capitalism was backward, and that only a dynamic State, served by specially trained civil servants, could accomplish the task of rapid modernization.

"Le capitalisme n'est plus ce qu'il était," exclaimed Edmond Maire, who can hardly be accused of special sympathy for the profit motive. Capitalism has undergone a "cultural revolution," observes Pierre Rosanvallon, not an admirer of capitalism in the past. And Henri Weber, former Trotskyist and now close collaborator of Laurent Fabius, speaks of a "mutation" of French capitalism.[13] What they all refer to is the new model of the dynamic sector, based on a freer flow of information throughout enterprises oriented to the market rather than to the State. A significant portion of the budget of a modern French enterprise (about 5 percent of the total payroll) is now devoted to securing information from the base, circulating it through the hierarchy, and ensuring collaboration of employees, cadres, and managers in the achievement of agreed-upon goals. This emphasis on permanent dialogue, two-way communication, and service to customers rather than carrying out the commands of the State is a break with past practice.

However, management's very success in creating participative structures opens the way for a possible counterattack by unions and workers from within the citadel. The process of dialogue changes attitudes and affects power relationships. In an enterprise fully committed to participation, managers must eventually recognize the legitimacy of a "workers' logic," to use Edmond Maire's term, and the importance of workers' contribution to production. Absolute monarchy is converted into at least a *rechtstaat*, or rule of law, with democracy perhaps in the offing. But industrial democracy in this sense means interaction between managers (who retain their prerogatives) and workers, not the absorption of elites into a self-governing community.

The new model enterprise poses a formidable problem for unions, which lost half of their members between 1976 and 1988. Pierre Rosanvallon estimates union membership as of 1988 as follows: 600,000 for the CGT; 400,000 each for the CFDT and the Force-Ouvrière (FO); and 200,000 for the teachers' union.[14] The virtual collapse of unions, says Rosanvallon, is due to their inability so far to cope with the cultural revolution that has taken place in enterprise. Unions traditionally represent workers in negotiations with business and the State, and also in social security and welfare councils. They have not been oriented towards participation in an "informational" enterprise in which workers, cadres, and managers are in direct communication with each other and collectively regulate daily life. To meet this immense challenge, unions must recast their structures and create a new culture based on communication rather than either confrontation or meek submission. Only CFDT leaders have thought through the problem, but so far they have not been able to gain the support of their own militants in bringing about the necessary reforms.

Primacy of the Political

Political factors have been and remain crucial determinants of the nature of labor-management relations in France. Paradoxically, it was the victory of the Left that led to an expansion of managerial power. Before 1981 all attempts by business and parties of the Right to integrate workers into enterprise were rejected by unions and the parties of the Left. But when the Left, in power, vowed to "break with capitalism," workers and unions were carried into new structures of participation on a wave of enthusiasm. Radicalization of the Socialist party was a deliberate tactic by François Mitterrand to outflank the Communist party on its Left, and to demonstrate to workers that they could have socialism of a democratic rather than an authoritarian variety. Autogestion was an integral part of a Socialist program designed to reduce the Communist party's appeal; it was a useful fiction. But, as it turned out, once workers entered into the structures created by the Auroux laws they could not resist domination by cadres and managers.

When the Socialists returned to power after the legislative elections of 1988, they did not revive the ideological battle cries of 1981. On the contrary, Prime Minister Michel Rocard fully accepted the principle of worker participation and free flow of information within enterprise. He embraced quality circles, instructed every ministry to draw up plans for improving quality, and called for constant dialogue between workers and managers as a top *Socialist* priority—thus trying to appropriate the quality movement for the Left. The Socialists are seeking ways to push the balance of power back in the direction of workers and unions—an extraordinarily difficult task. The experience of the Auroux laws so far demonstrates that management enjoys an inherent advantage in the contest for control of decisionmaking within enterprise.

To further complicate matters, the Socialist party did not have an absolute majority in the National Assembly. The Communist party made a slight comeback, gaining enough representation in the National Assembly to command respect. The strategy of both the Communist party and the CGT was to take a militant line, resort to confrontational tactics, and compel the Socialists to turn toward the Left instead of opening to the Center. Class collaboration may prove to be as elusive as the Socialist commonwealth.

Were the Auroux laws, in the final analysis, a failure? I suggest that this attempt to create a worker democracy was actually an extraordinary success, because it permitted François Mitterrand to attain his supreme goal: to reduce the influence of both the Communist party and the CGT. Many workers were now persuaded that the Socialist party indeed had their interests at heart. They responded by turning away from the Communists, enabling Socialists to dominate the Left; the way was thus cleared for genuine alternation in power between the Right and a now respectable Left. As a result, the climate of labor-management relations in France has changed significantly.

Worker democracy was always an unrealistic goal; but giving workers a say in enterprise is a major progressive development. Only the victory of the Left in 1981 and the Auroux laws made it possible to break down working-class and trade union resistance to participation in enterprise. Management was able to dominate participatory structures easily enough in a first step. But French business is beginning to realize that there is a distinctive and valuable workers' logic (as Edmond Maire put it). For French enterprises to compete effectively, it is now currently accepted, they must convert to models in which information flow is circular rather than merely from the top down. The battle between labor and management, and between Left and Right, is now being redefined within a transformed economy.

The social base of French politics is no longer what it was before the passage of the Auroux laws. The major actors within the system—business and labor—have in the past decade undergone at least the beginning of a mutation. Labor-management relations in France have not reverted to their pre-1981 status; nor have they become a copy of foreign models. Traditions of Jacobinism, business paternalism, revolutionary syndicalism, and mass communism have produced unique conditions for the ongoing experiment in workforce participation. Industrial relations surely will continue to evolve and to reflect a distinctively French political culture somewhere this side of Utopia.

NOTES

1. I have dealt with the conversion of the Parti Socialiste and the Parti Communiste Français into parties of "autogestion" in *Socialism of a Different Kind: The Reshaping of the French Left* (Westport, CT: Greenwood Press, 1982), chaps. 4 and 5.
2. Note especially two full-length articles on the Auroux laws: W. Rand Smith, "Towards Autogestion in Socialist France? The Impact of Industrial Relations Reform," *West European Politics* 10, no. 1 (January 1987), pp. 46-62; and Bernard H. Moss, "After the Auroux Laws: Employers, Industrial Relations, and the Right in France," *ibid.*, 11, no. 1 (January 1988), pp. 68-80. See also the earlier study by Duncan Gallie, "Les Lois Auroux: The Reform of French Industrial Relations?" in Howard Machin and Vincent Wright, eds., *Economic Policy and Policy-Making Under the Mitterrand Presidency, 1981-1984* (London: Frances Pinter, 1985), pp. 205-21. For a fuller statement of my views on the Auroux laws, see Bernard E. Brown, "Worker Participation in France," in M. Donald Hancock and John Logue, eds., *Managing Modern Capitalism* (Westport, CT: Praeger-Greenwood, 1992).
3. Smith, *op. cit.*, p. 47.
4. Moss, *op. cit.*, p. 78.
5. Duncan Gallie, *op. cit.*, p. 218.
6. Moss, *op. cit.*, p. 75.
7. The literature on the implementation of the Auroux laws is a treasure trove for students of workforce participation. See in particular: Annie Borzeix, Danièle Linhart, and Denis Segrestin, *Sur les traces du droit d'expression*, 2 vols. (Paris: CNAM, 1985); Philippe Bernoux et al., *De l'expression à la négotiation* (Ministère de la Recherche et de l'Industrie, 1985); Jean Bunel, *Le triangle de l'entreprise* (Ministère de la Recherche et de l'Industrie, 1985); and Daniel Mothé-Gautrat, *Pour une nouvelle culture de l'entreprise* (Editions de la Découverte, 1986).
8. Daniel Mothé-Gautrat, *op. cit.*, p. 145.
9. AFCERQ, apparently in need of expert advice itself, declared bankruptcy in August 1989. But support for the quality circle movement is continuing through management, government, and other consulting firms.
10. A point well made by Jacques Julliard, *Autonomie ouvrière: études sur le syndicalisme d'action directe* (Gallimard, 1988), pp. 30, 32.
11. See Elie Cohen, "Le 'moment lois Auroux' ou la désublimation de l'économie," *Sociologie du Travail* 28, no. 3 (1986), especially pp. 277-79.
12. Edmond Maire, *Nouvelles frontières pour le syndicalisme* (Paris: Syros, 1987), pp. 131-49. See also Jean-Paul Jacquier, *Les cow-boys ne meurent jamais, l'aventure syndicale continue* (Paris: Syros 1986).
13. See Edmond Maire, *Nouvelles frontières, op. cit.*, p. 138; Pierre Rosanvallon, "Participation et syndicats," *Management et Qualité* 25 (Mars 1988), pp. 14-16; *La question syndicale*. (Paris: Calmann-Lévy, 1988); and Henri Weber, *Le parti des patrons* (Paris: Seuil, 1986), p. 420.
14. Rosanvallon, *La question syndicale, op. cit.*, p. 15.

5
International Competition and the Organization of Production

The Study Action Team Process at Trico Products

Peter Lazes
Cornell University

After losing $28 million over a four-year period, and faced with increasing pressure from OEMs (Original Equipment Manufacturers) demanding that Trico Products reduce their product costs, Dick Wolf, the president of the company, announced his plan to lay off 1,400 out of 2,000 workers in November 1985. The "Big Three" automakers were forcing Trico to reduce their costs by 30 percent in three years in order to retain their contracts. Trico decided, with the encouragement of Ford executives, to move the bulk of plant operations to Mexico and Texas in order to remain competitive, as this move would result in significant wage reductions. Little was done to investigate the feasibility of cutting operating costs in order to remain in Buffalo; it seemed that these costs were accepted as a given that could not be changed.

The projected plant closing and move from Buffalo was a major departure from the company's traditions. Trico Products had been founded in Buffalo in 1917 and was still controlled by a Board of Directors mainly based in the city. For years, a basic concern of this board was to keep jobs and manufacturing in their area, yet the plan to set up plants in Mexico and Texas seemed to them to be the only practical way to remain profitable.

Soon after hearing of the relocation plan, I contacted both Dick Wolf and Tom Monaghan, the regional director of the United Auto Workers (UAW), to explore an alternate approach. I suggested that they consider the possibility of restructuring the existing Trico plants in order to reduce manufacturing costs and improve production quality, thereby obviating the need to relocate. The proposal included the development of small groups of workers and managers as Study Action Teams (SATs) who would work full time on analyzing manufacturing procedures and the costs of production, and then propose alternative cost-cutting methods. This approach was based on a process that I had helped to establish at the Xerox Corporation in 1982-84, which eliminated the need for substantial layoffs by reducing production costs by 30 percent.[1] In my work with the PEWS (Programs for Employment and Workplace Systems) group at the Cornell School of Industrial and Labor Relations, I had continued to refine this method successfully in working with several other companies and unions.[2]

Wolf was initially reluctant to discuss the possibility of a Study Action Team process at Trico, because he had already given up on the attempt to make the Buffalo operation profitable. However, he finally agreed, after six weeks of discussions, to meet with local 2100 of the UAW and with Vincent Tese, director of the New York State Department of Economic Development, to at least consider the proposal. At this meeting, he was persuaded to set up Study Action Teams with three purposes: to examine ways to improve efficiency in Trico's manufacturing operations, to identify specific methods to reduce yearly costs, and to improve the quality and timeliness of product delivery. The Department of Economic Development would share the costs with Trico for Cornell consultants who would help to establish and guide the SAT process. While Wolf agreed to establish the Study Action Teams, he refused to set targets for each SAT, or to commit the company to a reversal of its relocation plan if the SATs were in fact successful. Despite this, the UAW informally set a 30 percent cost reduction target for the teams, which was the amount of the cost reduction required by Ford. It was decided by Wolf and the union that three SATs would be established and have 18 weeks to work on this project. Two teams would each study a different area of the plant—the toolroom and linkage assembly areas—and the third would analyze the possibility of constructing a new plant to replace current obsolete facilities and compare the costs of this with constructing new plants in Mexico and Texas.

Method of Analysis and Action

The Trico Study Action Teams for the toolroom and linkage assembly areas consisted of two workers (union representatives) and two managers from each of the departments. Each team was assisted by the Cornell staff and by a manufacturing engineer from Rensselaer Polytechnic Institute (RPI). The third SAT consisted of members of the executive committee of UAW local 2100, the manufacturing engineer from RPI, and an architect from Boston to study new plant construction. In addition, a joint Labor-Management Steering Committee of middle and upper management of the company and the executive committee of the union was established to meet with the three teams every two weeks.

The role of the Steering Committee was to provide overall guidance to each team, help link and integrate their work, and remove roadblocks to obtaining technical assistance and production/customer information. It would also help judge the value of projects and implement solutions.

All three SATs worked full time on their respective tasks. Technical and financial assistance was obtained from Trico employees upon the written request of the teams. However, towards the end of the SAT process, access to accounting staff became hard to obtain, so the consulting manufacturing engineer from RPI was asked to analyze and evaluate many of the final proposals.

In addition to the three SAT projects, Cornell conducted a study analyzing the successes and problems of firms that had relocated to the Texas-Mexico border where Trico planned to move. This study, which was included in the final report to Trico, examined the type of work performed, the skills and wages of workers in the area, and the availability of technical specialists.

Training for Study Action Teams

Study Action Team and Steering Committee members took part in an intensive four-day training program which included exercises in problemsolving and team building; cost-accounting procedures (cost-benefit analysis); presentation methods; team meeting skills; techniques to obtain technical and financial information; breakdowns of the cost structure of the toolroom and linkage departments; methods for conducting surveys and questionnaires; methods for involving employees in changes within their departments; and methods of evaluating the workflow of production. Former SAT members from the Xerox Corporation participated in two training sessions and presented techniques they had found successful for identifying, analyzing, and implementing solutions.

Plant visits were also arranged for the SAT members to meet with labor and management of Packard Electric, a major supplier of parts for General Motors, and Harley Davidson. At Harley Davidson, workers and managers are engaged in cost reductions, product improvement, and restructuring of the decisionmaking roles of labor and management. Meeting and observing other teams in action provided the Trico SAT members with suggestions for changes and specific areas to investigate, and helped them better understand their roles.

Initial Outcomes

At the end of 18 weeks, the two in-plant SATs presented their recommendations for changes to the Trico management, regional UAW representatives, local 2100 executives, and New York State government officials. All of the recommendations had been analyzed by the appropriate production areas prior to this meeting and had received the approval of line operators.

The toolroom SAT proposals included: a new layout of equipment, a comprehensive training program for all employees in CAD/CAM to improve their capacity for insourcing work, improved workflow within the department, a gainsharing compensation plan, and a flexible time schedule for workers. The most controversial recommendation was a wage increase, which was suggested because 38 skilled workers had quit during the past 18 months due to the low pay in comparison to other companies in Buffalo.

The linkage SAT presented over 60 cost-saving projects. Savings amounted to over $9 million per year for this department—considerably more than the $8 million (30 percent cost reduction) target originally set by the team. Included in this proposal were suggestions for a substantial redesign of almost all jobs and a new layout of equipment and material storage. Recommendations by this team focused on the elimination of production supervisors: all operators would be trained and have responsibility for the quality of each stage of the production process. An investment in high-speed presses and modification of old equipment were recommended to enable the assembly area to reduce set-up time, improve servicing of equipment, and increase their ability to make quick die changeovers. New equipment and accessible areas for storing component parts were to be integrated into a just-in-time inventory control system. These changes would eliminate the need for their expensive computerized Materials Information System. As a result of these restructuring activities, extensive amounts of in-process inventory would also be eliminated. Inventory would consist only of what was immediately needed. Adjustments in compensation were also suggested by this team, including the elimination of the piece-rate system and the development of a plantwide gainsharing process.

Final Outcomes and Agreements

A final meeting was held at the Department of Economic Development office in New York City on October 8, 1986 to review all of the recommendations of the SATs. This meeting was held with Dick Wolf, Vincent Tese, the manufacturing engineer consultant, the shop chairman of the UAW, and myself. Our final report summarized the total cost savings based on the findings of the two in-plant SATs, and the work of the third SAT, which had analyzed the cost savings as a result of consolidating all operations in Buffalo and constructing a new plant at square footage costs equal to those in Brownsville, Texas. The combined work of the three SATs amounted to the identification of cost savings of $37.5 million per year, amounting to 30 percent of operating costs—the initial target. Although the consolidation into one plant would result in a loss of 250 direct and 100 indirect jobs, most of these reductions would be achieved by retirement and attrition. The UAW agreed to these reductions as part of the total proposal.

Our report also concluded that, no matter where the plants were located, it would be critical for Trico to change its production philosophy and not just chase low wages if it wanted to achieve a just-in-time, flexible, high-performance work system. The report also stressed the need for technological breakthroughs by acquiring modular assembly parts such as electric motors, since the Big Three were moving towards modular assembly units. The report maintained that although competitors might find it easy to manufacture where wage rates are low, they would not have the skilled workforce and technical resources of New York to continue to improve their production system.

In summary, the report stated that the lack of a skilled workforce and technical resources in Brownsville and Matamoros, coupled with the cost-saving analysis of the three SATs, proved that the strategy to move south was "economically unsound" and, further, would eventually erode Trico's technological superiority. It also concluded that going forward with the plan to move would likely result in the loss of all manufacturing jobs in Buffalo. Vincent Tese offered Dick Wolf funds to help pay for release time for training employees in the new work systems and in how to use new equipment, R&D funds to assist in acquiring the new motor for modular assembly, and the development of a high-tech training center to be located adjacent to the new factory.

In February 1987, after months of meetings between Trico and the UAW, a final agreement on the SAT proposal was reached between Trico Products and UAW Local 2100. Although Trico decided not to reverse their decision to move, the company did decide to keep an additional 300 jobs in Buffalo over what they had originally planned. (Left behind was to have been a skeleton staff of 600 employees to do basic engineering, research and development, and low-volume work.) The 300 additional jobs resulted from productivity improvements suggested by the linkage SAT in several of their low-volume areas. A strong severance package was established for all workers to be laid off, which included continued medical insurance for several months, creation of an outplacement center, and additional pay for years of service.

The toolroom suggestions were implemented by Trico, except for the proposed wage increase, which was tabled for future discussion. The linkage assembly proposal to enable operators to inspect their own work and eliminate the need for final inspectors was also implemented, and several joint labor-management committees became a permanent part of this department for training and to investigate the best use of equipment.

A significant focus of the union during negotiations, aside from the number of jobs that would remain in Buffalo, was the need to establish a new production system with appropriate compensation. It had become apparent to the leaders of UAW local 2100 during the SAT process that significant changes would be needed in the production system in order to save the jobs of Trico workers in the future.

General Risks and Benefits
of the Process for Participants

The entire SAT process was a risk for the union, management, and the state. For management, the possibility of reversing their decision to relocate involved losing approximately $5 million of construction costs already committed to building a new plant. If it were not for the fact that they were locally owned and that there was considerable community pressure to reduce the continued erosion of manufacturing jobs, they would probably never even have considered the SAT proposal.

The union took a risk in getting involved in the SAT process because they had no guarantee from Trico that the plan to move would be changed. However, they were facing a no-win situation anyway, at best being able to bargain for keeping only a few hundred jobs. The gamble paid off as the Study Action Team process evolved into a constructive method which saved an additional 300 jobs.

The SAT process provided union representatives with extensive access to financial and production information, giving them skills for evaluating financial balance sheets and production accounting, and giving them valuable information about advanced manufacturing methods. The experience gained in these areas proved to be useful during the final negotiations for severance pay and benefits and for keeping more jobs in Buffalo.

Risks and Benefits of the SAT Approach

There are several questions raised concerning the Trico project, some of them related to the SAT process itself. How effective is this process, and why? Why does this method of analysis identify more comprehensive changes and a more realistic implementation process than traditional approaches?

Another important area of analysis concerns the overall outcomes and what could have strengthened the ability to keep jobs in Buffalo. What could have been done differently? Should unions support activities such as Study Action Teams? If this is a useful process for unions, are there better ways to establish such activities? Some of these questions may be answered by comparing the SAT process to traditional methods.

First, the SAT process helped to integrate the day-to-day knowledge of shop-floor employees, who know specific details of problems, with the broader knowledge of technical specialists. In traditional studies done by management, the ideas and perspectives of the workforce are rarely examined or considered. As a result of the integrated perspective, new ideas and solutions emerge. Independently, the observations of labor and management are significantly different and are rarely brought together.[3]

The second and perhaps most important aspect of the Study Action Team process is that it helps to establish a commitment to implement changes by the workforce and management. Analyses done solely by technical and financial specialists rarely convince plant management and workers to make changes. Without the commitment of key employees, and support from both management and labor, solutions agreed upon by specialists often remain just good suggestions which are never actually implemented.

Another beneficial aspect of the SAT process is that it enables an organization to identify and then find solutions to politically risky problems. Since the union members of SATs cannot be fired for voicing their ideas and concerns, the SAT process allows major problems to be identified which in the past might have been overlooked. Managers are often reluctant to raise problems because they are fearful of admitting to these situations in their departments or in the organization as a whole. A fairly common feeling among managers is the fear that raising such questions could cost them their jobs. Also, the very process of engaging the employees who will be directly affected by a major organizational change creates an environment in which they are more likely to be committed to working in structures which they understand and have helped to develop.

To some extent, the entire SAT process at Trico Products was hindered by the president's initial and ongoing reluctance to establish a formal agreement. Although he accepted in principle the use of the three SATs and provided them with access to technical and financial staff, he never signed an agreement nor agreed to cost-saving targets. The experience at Xerox showed that having clear cost, productivity, and quality targets from the beginning of the process helped to keep the SAT process on track even when several managers left in the middle of the project because they were promoted into the manufacturing plants.[4]

The UAW decided that the practical course of action at Trico was to make the best of the situation rather than further delay getting the teams started or decide to withdraw from the process entirely. They felt they had no other choice than to continue even without having everything in place. In hindsight, another approach might have been tried to obtain a formal agreement from Dick Wolf. Requesting involvement and an agreement from the Board of Directors might have helped create a more accountable process.

The information on cost structures, production information, and new product requirements of customers which local 2100 and region 9 gained through the SAT process had never been made available to them before. This information gave the union a new tool for protecting the interests of workers by examining and then making recommendations for changing production methods. Traditionally, when there were severe economic problems in a particular firm, the UAW became involved in negotiating cost problems solely in terms of what they knew best and had control over—wages, benefits, and employment of workers. Specific productivity improvement changes had rarely been identified as an alternative to cutting wages or laying off workers. Although the members of the shop committee of local 2100 had no previous experience in analyzing and improving manufacturing processes, they quickly became experts.

The results of the Trico project and similar activities at Xerox suggest that the SAT process can give unions an opportunity to explore extensive changes in production, material control, and general costs, as well as customer-supplier relations. Rather than just battling over wages, benefits, and employment, solutions can be identified to reduce overhead and indirect labor and material costs, as well as improve the efficiencies of equipment and manufacturing processes. As David Steinwald, chairman of the shop committee, noted at the end of the SAT process, "it would have been nearly impossible to have saved an additional 300 jobs or obtained the severance package using traditional bargaining methods and lacking access to financial and productivity information."[5] The above conclusions have been seconded by the leadership of local 2100 and the regional director of the UAW, Tom Fricano.

The final agreement between the UAW and Trico was reached largely because of the factual results of the studies conducted by the SATs. These findings identified the importance of keeping specific high-volume operations in Buffalo rather than relocating them to Texas. By agreeing to changes in work responsibility and manufacturing approaches in the toolroom and linkage departments, the union put itself in a strong position for negotiating an extensive severance package and the development of outplacement services.

In retrospect, it would have been extremely helpful to have been able to start the SAT process as soon as there were signs that Trico was in bad shape. If the process could have been established earlier, Dick Wolf and his Board of Directors might have been more receptive to a comprehensive approach for achieving cost reductions and changes, rather than focusing solely on labor costs.

In order to spread the knowledge of the methods and results of the SAT process to the UAW leadership in region 9, a workshop on the risks and benefits of SATs was held at their annual retreat in August 1987. The SAT process used at Trico Products was presented by members of the teams, who examined both the positive benefits and the areas of weakness. Many delegates to the meeting showed a strong interest in learning more about this new approach in case their local membership faced a similar plant closing or major layoff problem in the future.

Government Involvement

The Study Action Team process was an innovative and challenging experiment for the New York State Department of Economic Development. Prior to the Trico project, the strategy of this agency had been to focus on trying to attract new business to relocate to New York and improving access to on-the-shelf technology by existing factories. Although the Department of Economic Development and the governor felt comfortable with the concept of joint labor-management programs, such activities had not been seen as a practical process for solving significant productivity problems of firms.

Pressure from the governor's office was important in getting Dick Wolf to sit down and agree to the SAT process. The state did not accept the conclusion of an earlier consulting report to Trico management which stated that "Trico's middle managers and hourly employees could not change their nonproductive ways."

After seeing the results of the SAT process at Trico, Vincent Tese decided to create the Industrial Effectiveness Program to provide development and implementation funds to companies and unions that establish SAT activities. By providing funding and holding workshops and seminars to promote the Study Action Team approach, New York State is helping to make the SAT process more accessible to other firms and unions; it is encouraging an aggressive examination of cost reductions rather than relying solely on wage reductions and layoffs when companies are faced with extensive needs to reduce costs. Vincent Tese commented at the end of the Trico project that "the Trico experience will make us better prepared to respond in the future...it sets a model that can be used to work with other companies."[6]

Future Issues

Study Action Teams are currently being used not only in New York State and around this country, but also in Poland to help improve efficiency and to create new work structures in some of their plants. The process is also being used to increase the opportunity for workers to contribute to a more democratic form of decisionmaking as Poland changes to a social market economy.

There is an ongoing need to examine how to effectively integrate the ideas and concerns of employees at all levels of plants, and particularly at times of crisis such as Trico Products faced. The involvement of workers in the manufacturing and production decisionmaking areas of companies has not generally been considered important, but it seems likely that unions will need to consider the use of this approach more in the future as traditional methods used to negotiate saving jobs become less effective. In order to use this particular approach in the future, a careful analysis of the risks and benefits are needed, as well as proper training to help establish these activities.

NOTES

*I would like to express my thanks to Mary Mahon and Marie Rudden for their help in editing this article.

1. The Study Action Team (SAT) process is an intensive in-plant method of analyzing problems and implementing necessary changes. Workers and managers work full time on these projects (with some assistance from outside specialists), evaluating production processes and methods, workflow, quality processes, equipment improvements, and changes in the compensation system. The labor-management SAT process was originally started at Xerox in 1982 as a method for restructuring their manufacturing units. Instead of just having engineers and managers analyze production and cost problems, the SAT approach engaged all levels of the organization in the investigation. This method differed from previous approaches by thoroughly evaluating and making changes in all cost areas and not focusing mainly on labor rates, which traditionally are what management focuses on in their productivity analysis. (See Peter Lazes and Tony Costanza, "Xerox Cuts Costs Without Layoffs Through Union-Management Collaboration," *Labor-Management Brief,* July 1984.)

The ultimate goal of the SAT process at Trico Products was to keep as many jobs as possible in Buffalo, as well as cut costs. Ideally, the outcome of their work would be to eliminate the planned move to the Texas-Mexico border.

2. Peter Lazes, "Participative Consulting," *ILR Report,* Fall 1988, pp. 24-27.

3. Max Elden, "Democratization and Participative Research in Developing Local Theory," *Journal of Occupational Behavior* 4 (1) 1983, pp. 21-34.

4. Peter Lazes, Leslie Rumpeltes et al., "Xerox and the ACTWU: Using Labor-Management Teams to Remain Competitive," *National Productivity Review,* Summer 1991, pp. 339-349.

5. Harmon Lecture, Harvard University, April 28, 1988.

6. Thomas J. Lueck, "Saving Jobs in Buffalo: Victory and Loss," *The New York Times,* February 17, 1987, pp. B1-2.

6
Collaborative Restructuring Efforts

Textile and Apparel Labor-Management Innovation Network
Lehigh Valley, Pennsylvania

Robert Coy, *Commonwealth of Pennsylvania*
Saul Rubinstein, *Participative Systems, Inc.*
Michael Shay, *Participative Systems, Inc.*

In 1989, the Pennsylvania Departments of Commerce and Labor and Industry designed the Manufacturing Innovation Network Initiative, or MAIN, to test whether the state could stimulate regional concentrations of related firms to organize consortia. Firms were considered to be related to each other if they served similar markets. These consortia were expected to strengthen the competitive position of the firms by developing new business services, transferring best practices between firms, and forming new production relationships among firms.

Rapidly changing technology and high standards for quality and speed of delivery are forcing firms to cooperate in new and significant ways.[1] The number of strategic partnerships is growing, and the range of issues around which they are organized is increasingly significant. For instance, companies are joining together for research and development, capital investment, concurrent engineering, product development, and to provide technical assistance to suppliers.

Most examples involve cooperation between large companies. However, there are many examples from Europe and Japan, and to a lesser extent the United States, of smaller firms joining together at a regional level to strengthen their competitive position.[2] These firms tend to be clustered in close geographic proximity to each other and are joining forces to achieve a number of goals, including: combining their complementary manufacturing capabilities to produce goods for the final market; establishing service centers that provide shared marketing, engineering, design, and testing services; developing lending consortia that provide investment capital to member firms; and organizing export, training, and educational reform programs.

MAIN, which is managed by the Department of Commerce's Office of Technology Development, is built on two premises. First, some problems are simply too large for individual firms to address alone. Second, collaboration among firms and between firms and unions can create a learning system which can be a powerful force for manufacturing modernization and other innovations.

With respect to the first premise, about 95 percent of Pennsylvania's 17,500 manufacturing establishments employ fewer than 250 workers. Pennsylvania considers firms of this size to be small firms. While small firms are often innovative and flexible, they face certain vulnerabilities. These would include insufficient resources (capital and people) for research and development, training, marketing, and exporting. They often have problems securing investment capital for modernization. Finally, they are unable individually to improve the local business infrastructure that supports them; for example, they are unable to reform the educational system, open up new sources of investment capital, or strengthen the local economic development institutions that provide business services.[3]

The second premise of MAIN is that collaboration between firms, and among firms, associations, and labor organizations where they exist, creates the potential for a learning system that stimulates modernization and innovation. An example from the knitwear industry in Carpi, Italy illustrates this point.[4] About 10 years ago, 600 small knitwear firms in this northern Italian city designed and financed, with government assistance, a service center which enables them to share the costs of marketing research, design, training, and other activities that would be too expensive for individual firms to support. While these services alone are of value to the firms, the interaction between the firms' owners at the service center is of equal importance, for it leads to valuable information exchange and peer pressure to keep pace with the more innovative firms. This stimulates modernization and innovation. The MAIN initiative limited itself to supporting projects targeted at regional concentrations of related firms to maximize the chances that firm representatives would personally interact with each other.

Through MAIN, the state is testing these two premises in four geographically concentrated industries: the apparel industry in the Lehigh Valley, where there are about 250 apparel companies employing 15,000 workers; the plastics industry in Erie, where there are 80 plastics companies employing over 8,000 workers; the tooling and machining industry clustered in Erie, Pittsburgh, Lancaster/York, and the Philadelphia areas; and the foundry industry in Pittsburgh, where there are between 50 and 60 foundries employing 6,000 workers.

The state identified these industry clusters using a request-for-proposal process, not an extensive economic analysis. Trade associations, trade unions and nonprofit economic development organizations were encouraged to submit bids. It was especially hoped that trade associations would respond, assuming that firms would be most likely to identify with them. In addition, we expected that, as a result of this project, trade associations would discover new ways to help their members through the delivery of innovative services.

The state received eight responses from seven trade associations and one economic development organization. Proposals were evaluated by a team of representatives from the Departments of Commerce and Labor and Industry and from academia. The evaluation criteria were as follows: a demonstrated understanding of the industry; the formation of an industry-led steering committee; a realistic project design; the strength of the management team; and the level of private sector financial support.

Based upon the recommendations of the evaluation team, four projects were funded. Three of the four projects were managed by trade associations and one was managed by a nonprofit economic development organization. Two of the projects received $90,000, one $80,000, and one $25,000.

While the proposal guidelines for MAIN were very general so that each industry could design a project tailored to its needs, the evaluation committee placed the greatest emphasis on two criteria. The first was the formation of a strong Steering Committee comprised, at a minimum, of business representatives from the industry and trade union representatives if the industry was unionized. The membership of the Steering Committee could be expanded to include others from the community with a special interest in the industry. For example, some Steering Committees had representation from local economic development organizations, vocational-technical schools, and community colleges. The second requirement was a detailed description of how the Steering Committee would use a strategic audit process to identify the industry structure, key market trends, common problems and opportunities, patterns of innovation, and strategies for improvement.

The importance of the Steering Committee to the success of the MAIN projects must be emphasized. The Steering Committee had three roles; first, to direct all phases of the project and to ensure that it was industry-led and industry-driven; second, to coordinate and integrate services available in the region that can support the industry; and third, to resolve conflicts between stakeholder groups in the industry.

It is also useful to highlight the importance of the strategic audit process. The strategic audit produces information and often surprising results that can lead to what Chuck Sabel of the Massachusetts Institute of Technology has described as "cooperation through studied consensus." This is especially true if the audit relies on personal interviews with industry leaders. Used in this way, the audit becomes a tool to draw more firms and unions into the project, uncover industry leaders, develop new cooperative relationships, and organize the industry for improvement projects.

Key problem areas emerged in all four projects almost immediately after the strategic audits started. Tooling and machining firms identified as their most critical problem a shortage of tool and die makers and, in partnership with high schools, launched a youth apprenticeship program; foundries began to develop a strategy for disposing of foundry sand; plastics companies identified the need for new types of equipment that would be shared by the firms, as well as new training and export programs; and apparel firms focused on developing technology, marketing, new services, work organization, and supervisory training strategies.

Since 1991, the MAIN initiatives have been managed by Pennsylvania's Industrial Resource Centers (IRCs). The IRCs, which were established by Governor Robert P. Casey in 1988, are regionally based, industry-led, nonprofit corporations. Overseen by the Office of Technology Development, the IRCs are the manufacturing equivalent of the agriculture extension service. Staffed by professionals with industrial and economic development experience, they help firms in their regions adopt modern manufacturing technologies and techniques. The IRCs accomplish this goal by working one-on-one with individual companies, and by forming networks of related firms as in the MAIN approach.

This report focuses in detail on one of the MAIN initiatives—the Lehigh Valley Apparel and Textile Innovation Network. This project distinguishes itself from the others by a high degree of union involvement. As such, it is an important example of how a labor-management participation process at the industry level could help spark the restructuring and modernization of a regional industry.

The Lehigh Valley Apparel and Textile Innovation Network

In 1988 there were approximately 125,000 people employed in the apparel and textile industry in the Commonwealth of Pennsylvania, accounting for 13 percent of the total manufacturing employment sector. Over 50,000 of these employees were members of either the Amalgamated Clothing and Textile Workers Union (ACTWU) or the International Ladies Garment Workers Union (ILGWU).

The apparel and textile industry of Pennsylvania has been under severe competitive pressure in recent years. Both production and employment have declined sharply as a result. In 1988, apparel alone accounted for over $21 billion or 15.5 percent of the total U.S. trade deficit. Approximately 60 percent of U.S. expenditure on apparel went to foreign-made garments, and the great bulk of these imports originated in low-wage countries. The failure of this industry to respond to competitive pressures was readily apparent, and Pennsylvania was particularly hard hit. For example, from 1974 to 1985, the industry declined more than 37 percent within the Commonwealth, while nationwide the decline was 16.5 percent.

This innovation effort centers on the Lehigh Valley, including the municipalities of Easton, Bethlehem, and Allentown, and the counties of Northampton and Lehigh. Textiles and apparel represent the largest employment sector in the area.

The industry in the Lehigh Valley has changed from one based on local competition for long runs of limited styles, to one facing short runs, new fabrics, rapid style changes, higher quality standards, and worldwide competition.

Strategy

It was believed that competitive advantage could be returned to this industry by improving production methods and work organization to meet the changing demands of retailers for quick response capability and improved quality. Firms in the Lehigh Valley can take advantage of their proximity to the market by moving from the lower price point niche to the higher end, which is less price-sensitive and more concerned with characteristics such as quality, design, delivery, and rapid response to style changes. Firms able to supply products with these attributes to manufacturers and retailers would be less vulnerable to competition from lower-priced imports.

Relationships

Over the past decade, joint labor-management efforts in planning and problemsolving have produced significant results in individual organizations. Improvements include fuller use of human resources, higher quality products and services, and closer coordination between departments, divisions, and plants. Most of these systems have been developed separately in individual firms. However, based on this experience we believe that many of these lessons could be applied to the problems of smaller firms in a specific industry clustered in a particular geographic region.

It was critical for the firms within the apparel and textile industry to be able to constantly adjust their responses to pressures from domestic and international competitive forces. Flexible and adaptive economies are dependent on a high level of trust among the participants. The industry needed to develop vehicles for increasing the trust level and productive working relationships.

Goals

There were four specific goals in mind as Pennsylvania developed this initiative:

(1) Create a joint effort on the part of labor unions, owners and managers of firms, trade associations, economic development agencies, educational institutions, and state and local government to design and direct an effort toward developing a common understanding of the problems of the apparel and textile industry in the Lehigh Valley, and develop a joint approach toward implementing solutions to these problems.

(2) Demonstrate that economic development efforts in this and other fragmented industries can more effectively be directed to a specific sector concentrated geographically, rather than to individual firms.

(3) Develop vertical and horizontal linkages between firms to deal with inefficiencies, and create new learning opportunities in this fragmented industry.

(4) Establish in the Lehigh Valley an ongoing structure and process dynamic enough to continue to evaluate the needs of the industry and generate solutions.

Steering Committee

The first step of this project focused on the Steering Committee. This group met every month and represented the varied constituencies within the industry, as described above. In order to form a cohesive group, we wanted to establish a common base of understanding of both individual and group needs. The problem of industry fragmentation was mirrored in the Steering Committee, so the process of creating a common vision for the industry had to start with this group. Through a planning process, and by discussing the findings of the strategic audit, a common understanding of the problems of the industry and a common vision of a direction for the industry were developed. Relations between members began to improve, as members shared information on training, technology, marketing and labor force recruitment.

The Steering Committee's membership was as follows:

•the Executive Director of the Atlantic Apparel Contractors' Association and the President of the Valley Apparel and Textile Association

•four owners or senior managers of firms

• four International Union Vice-Presidents (two from the ILGWU, and two from ACTWU)

• the Executive Director of the Bethlehem Industrial Resource Center

• the Superintendent of the Easton Area School District

• the Director of the Computer-Integrated Manufacturing Laboratory at Lehigh University

• the Dean of Community Education, Northampton Community College

• the Principal of Northampton Vocational-Technical School

In organizing the Lehigh Valley Apparel and Textile Innovation Network, we attempted to ensure that:

• all stakeholding organizations were represented in a meaningful way;

• the Network continued to organize itself through working groups, allowing for the broadening and deepening of involvement;

• the activities of all groups resulted in a process of mutual education of each organization's needs, concerns and goals;

• the Network became a forum where the groups could work toward solutions to problems;

• trust relationships developed between the various stakeholders, which would serve as a foundation for additional activities.

Working Groups

The Steering Committee formed working groups made up of its own members and representatives from individual firms, as well as outside resources. Such a mix results in a pool of skills and serves as a method to both broaden and deepen the industry's involvement. The working groups, which are both educational and organizing vehicles, were formed around labor force recruitment and retention, public relations, marketing, and technology.

The results of the Exit Survey, a study of employee turnover, helped the Labor Force Working Group develop an integrated approach to the issues of recruitment and retention by developing an entry-level skills training course through the Commonwealth's Department of Commerce and a local community college; an industry-specific supervisory training program; and a strategy for upgrading the skills of the existing workforce in conjunction with the local vocational-technical high school.

These activities of the Labor Force Working Group had the added benefit of teaching the various stakeholding organizations about each others' concerns and issues. Another activity was the development of internal resources within individual firms to improve communications, problemsolving, quality, and planning. These internal resources are available as trainers in the plants and facilitate group problemsolving.

The Technology Working Group focused on the development of an apparel-specific technology training course at a local area community college. This activity also included the development of a videotape presentation of the new technology available to apparel firms in the hopes of encouraging broader use.

In addition to the above activities, another working group has been developing a program to promote the industry and to improve its image. Such an activity can help local recruitment as well as make New York City manufacturers (the source of most of the work sewn in the Lehigh Valley) aware of innovations taking place within the Lehigh Valley.

Labor's Role in Economic Development

Organized labor can play a unique role in this type of economic development activity. First, labor can project democratic values into decisions regarding the selection of new technologies (such as Unit Production systems, CAD/CAM applications, Programmable Sewing Machines, and Modular Manufacturing) and how these technologies are deployed. If the decisions are made without labor's input, then the cooperation needed to fully take advantage of these investments will be limited. Labor unions must be prepared to serve as the voice mechanism that resolves workers' fears about displacement, or fears of having their skills rendered obsolete. Furthermore, this voice function can encourage substantive input into the selection of the technology and the organizational design that accompanies the technology's deployment.

Second, labor competently trained in business strategy and management is uniquely able to add value, providing substantive input, contributing to the competitive success of the industry. Union officers have been trained by their unions to think critically about management decisionmaking, not simply in terms of economic costs and benefits and rates of return, but also in terms of social costs. Furthermore, both the ACTWU and ILGWU have long histories of providing industrial engineering and technical expertise to employers with whom they have contractual relations.

Labor unions can play a role that assures their traditional concerns for democratic values and principles are projected into the managerial decisionmaking process. Unions can provide a valuable review function by an independent, competent body. In order to fulfill these responsibilities, however, labor needs to obtain the required skills at all levels of its organization.

Strategic Audit

The Steering Committee is responsible for defining and managing an economic development initiative for this industry. A critical tool in this effort is an audit of firm business, marketing, and human resource strategies to identify both the major pressures facing the firms in this industry and their most effective responses—what was working and what wasn't. Meaningful information regarding firms' strategic choices is needed in order to describe how successful firms compete. We expected the following results:

•Identification of overall industry strategies

•Judgments about future direction

•Identification of subgroups within the industry and the strategy of each

•Descriptions of patterns of development and opportunities these present for creating interfirm industry networks.

In conducting this audit we focused on 50 leading firms identified by the unions, employer associations, or other firms as examples of success, innovation, or leadership. Strategy, specific adjustments, and choices made over the last five years were examined, as well as trends the firms expect will shape direction over the next few years. It was important to understand their market niche and any changes they anticipated in price point, quality, delivery, product mix, and batch size. Particular attention was paid to innovative relationships contractors developed with manufacturers and retailers involving new products and services.

The audits involved management and production systems, including the organization of production, and the integration of technology. The research also covered relationships between contractors, subcontracting arrangements, and opportunities for networks to share information, resources, and services. An assessment of training activity was included to determine the skill levels currently pursued by the industry.

Finally, we explored the institutional responses of the ILGWU and ACTWU to the restructuring taking place. The unions' strategies for the future were of interest, as were the responses by the employers' associations, one of which bargains directly with the ILGWU representing its members.

In summary, the strategic audit has become a way for the Steering Committee to:

•describe where this industry is currently positioned and the strategic choices that have already been made;

•identify a strategic vision for the industry; and

•develop a plan to close the gap.

Preliminary Results of Strategic Audit

The apparel industry has changed from one based largely on domestic competition and regional markets, to one based on global markets and international competitors. This has meant a proliferation of products, an increase in season and style changes, and a growth of market niches. Products are more specialized for particular market segments, and quality demands have increased. Further, retailers have sought to minimize their risk and financing costs by dramatically reducing their inventory levels. By reducing inventories, they have also attempted to minimize the need for discounting. They have moved to smaller orders and shorter lead times, hoping to be able to respond to market trends through a reorder strategy dependent upon quick turnaround production. Since contractors typically have no experience in marketing, sales, piece-goods sourcing, design, and relations with retailers, they are ill equipped to deal directly with these market changes. Finally, some low-cost market segments that have continued to provide long runs of standardized products have gravitated to low-wage countries.

There did not appear to be any single strategy followed by the majority of the 50 contractors we visited and interviewed. However, responses by firms to changes in the competitive environment seem to fall into three categories: integrative strategies, partial strategies, and nonresponse.

Integrative Strategies

Our study revealed that 25 to 30 percent of the firms were experiencing significant growth in sales, profits, or employment. These successful firms were union as well as nonunion, some older and well established and others in business for less than 10 years. Our audit of firm business and marketing strategies revealed that these firms have developed innovative ways to deal effectively with the new competition by breaking out of the traditional contractor-manufacturer relationship and structure. The new relationships and strategies have some common characteristics which appear to be transferable to other firms.

The most general characteristic that these firms share is that they have increased the services they provide to manufacturers and retailers. These services include the following:

•product design and design for manufacturability

•pattern-making

•marker-making

•grading

•cutting

•packaging

•shipping

•coordinating production among a group of firms

•ensuring quality control in subcontractors

•sourcing and financing piece-goods

•managing all of the above services among a group of firms (total packaging)

While few contractors provide all of these services, it is important to note that traditionally these functions were controlled by manufacturers. Contractors are offering services they have traditionally never provided. They provide these services for retailers' private labels or for manufacturers who now want to shift responsibility to contractors for such services as design, patterns, grading, and marker-making, thus allowing for more rapid response to market trends through co-locating design and production, and involving multiple firms (contractors) in the design, marketing, and product development end of the business. Contractors in some cases collaborate with manufacturers on "design for manufacturability," so that they can increase the speed of design/ style changes for new seasons. These collaborations are also geared to lower production costs and improve quality. Multiple innovative contractors are able to specialize in a variety of market niches and thereby simultaneously offer a range of products and delivery times that single manufacturers could not develop on their own. Those who provide these services have broken out of the mold of the typical contractor and benefit through increased sales.

Contractors decrease turnaround time and their ability for quick delivery response by increasing their line flexibility for rapid change-overs and broader product mix. In some cases "lead contractors" go beyond their own firms and take responsibility for coordinating large orders among a network of contractors for a given manufacturer. Contractors also go beyond the boundaries of their own shop and take responsibility for quality assurance away from the manufacturer, in some cases sending their inspectors to other subcontractors.

Firms in this category have been able to successfully change their relationship to the market, offering new products and services to manufacturers and retailers, and asserting control in relationships where previously there existed only dependency.

These firms attempted to institute changes in each of the critical dimensions identified (see Figure 1). Further, they appear to have achieved some measure of internal consistency in their systems, integrating across multiple dimensions.

Partial Strategies

These responses were directed toward a particular dimension, i.e., technology, workforce, or other related topics. They tend to be specific programmatic changes in the operations, such as new equipment or training programs. These responses were not directed toward changing the relationship to the market, i.e., manufacturers or retailers. Further, they tended not to be integrated across dimensions. Approximately 40 percent of the firms interviewed fell into this category.

Figure 1

Critical Dimensions of Workforce Restructuring

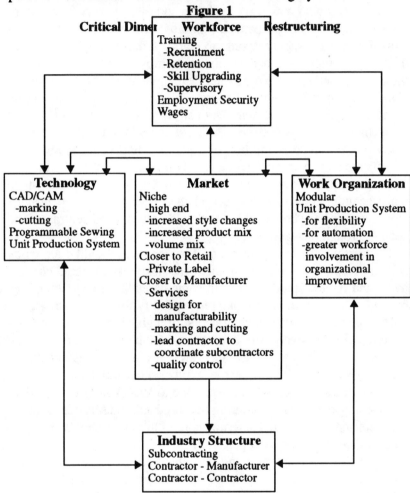

Nonresponse

Firms in this category were simply hoping their competitive situation would improve, and they were not proactive in responding through strategic changes in their operations. Approximately 30 percent of the firms interviewed fell into this category.

Making the Transition

In trying to understand how the innovative plants were able to break out of the traditional relationships between contractors and manufacturers, we detected three general patterns which distinguished them from the balance of the firms in the sample. We have called these patterns *generational, skill-based,* and *new entrants.* The firms characterized as *generational* appear to be making the shift into new services or business strategies as a generation of new owners takes over from the earlier generation. Members of this new generation either ignore the structural boundaries that define the role of a contractor, or simply do not feel the constraints their parents did, and are expanding what contractors typically offer.

The group characterized as making a *skill-based* shift are people who come into the contracting business with nontraditional skill bases such as design, sales, or expertise in computer technology. These people use their skills to drive new competitive strategies, such as product design, CAD/CAM production, or piece-goods sourcing.

The group characterized as *new entrants* is based on a population of new immigrants to the Lehigh Valley from both the Far East and Middle East. These immigrants contract in a nontraditional way, possibly because they had a different tradition in their country of origin, or they didn't see the same constraints. The innovative firms identified have one of these characteristics, having redefined their business by breaking out of traditional patterns.

Labor Force Retention

The apparel and textile industry of the Lehigh Valley in Pennsylvania has faced a severe labor shortage. The industry has experienced great difficulty in its efforts to recruit and retain workers. An assumption by both unions and management has been that the majority of people who left this industry did so primarily because of layoffs, shop closings, or dissatisfaction with compensation levels.

We conducted a survey of 3,213 people who have left this industry in the Lehigh Valley over the past few years in order to better understand what improvements could be made to retain the current workforce. Almost 60 percent of those leaving the industry in the last five years left voluntarily, not as the result of layoffs or shop closings. Further, the primary factors cited were "treatment" issues—supervisors, underutilized abilities, lack of opportunities for advancement, and the pressures of the piece-rate system. These four treatment issues accounted for more than 51 percent of the responses when people indicated what would be their primary reason for departure, while pay was the main factor for only 26 percent of the respondents.

The importance of these treatment factors was reinforced when the new jobs people have taken in other industries were compared with their old apparel jobs. The new jobs were rated consistently higher on factors such as treatment by supervisor, opportunities for promotion, and whether workers felt a sense of accomplishment.

Further, workers in the apparel and textile industry perceived that their old sewing jobs required less skill than their new jobs. This perception might exist, in part, because of the lack of formal training in the apparel industry and the significant amount of training reported by employees in their new jobs.

Improvement of treatment factors may provide the apparel and textile industry the greatest opportunity to retain workers, and the industry itself has significant control over this area.

Conclusions and Implications

These findings have implications for the management systems used by apparel firms in the Lehigh Valley. If this industry is to be successful in retaining the skilled workforce necessary to compete in a global marketplace, it will have to adopt new methods of training, supervision, and compensation. In addition, new systems of production are necessary to meet the changing demands of the market for higher quality products in smaller volumes, with more rapid style changes and quick turnaround production. We believe that the same factors of work organization and skill development that have implications for workforce retention are also critical for marketplace competition. While addressing treatment factors will not solve all of the competitive problems this industry faces, increasing skill levels and allowing for greater use of workers' capabilities can contribute to building and retaining a skilled and motivated workforce, thereby improving quality, productivity, and market responsiveness. This means integrating technology and participation in a way that supports positive human resource practices as well as the changing needs of the market. The Lehigh Valley Apparel and Textile Innovation Network must explore and demonstrate new ways to solve both the competitive problems this industry faces from outside and the very human problems it faces from within.

The effort in the Lehigh Valley is developing some new approaches for solving problems associated with industrial restructuring and increasing competitiveness. One of these innovations is a process of joint labor-management strategic planning at the industry level to identify a future direction for this region, as well as to put in place a more supportive infrastructure. The systems emerging are both social and technical, involving the development of new relationships as well as new systems of production.

The Lehigh Valley Network attempts to help contractors unable to make these changes on their own by providing workshops, conferences, training, direct technical assistance, and access to best-practice examples. The Network helps noncompetitive firms improve by exposing them to new models, and providing the resources and leadership necessary to make the transition.

NOTES

1. "Learning From Japan," *Business Week*, January 27, 1992, p. 52.

2. See, for example, Charles F. Sabel, "Flexible Specialization and the Re-emergence of Regional Economies," in *Reversing Industrial Decline*, ed., Paul Hirsh and Jonathan Witlin (Oxford: Berg Publishers, 1989); Walter H. Plosila, "Developing Networking Relationships: The Experiences of Denmark, Germany, Italy and Sweden" (Rockville, MD: Montgomery County High Technology Council, 1989); and Brian Bosworth, "Getting It Together: Economic Development, Manufacturing Modernization and Collaboration" (Hudson Institute. Forthcoming), pp. 66-75.

3. Philip Shapira, "Modernizing Manufacturing" (Washington, DC: Economic Policy Institute, 1990), pp. 15-18.

4. Walter H. Plosila, p. 35.

7
Labor and Industrial Relations Strategies in the State of Michigan

Michael Schippani•

The 1980s was a period of extensive experimentation in industrial policy in the State of Michigan. The need for a new strategy was obvious to those who were struggling with the rapid changes in the structure and vitality of the economy. The state was hit very hard by the recession in the early 1980s. The global reorganization of the auto industry meant massive job loss, fiscal crises for government, and a declining standard of living for many citizens.

In 1983, first-term Governor James Blanchard and his economic policy staff responded by organizing a policy advisory group to craft a strategy for maintaining and revitalizing the industrial base. The group was led by Douglas Fraser, former president of the International Union, UAW, and Lee Iacocca of the Chrysler Corporation. The deliberations resulted in a three-pronged strategy based on a vision of the future of Michigan as an international center for the development and application of manufacturing technology.

The first part of the plan was to develop an applied technology strategy. The goal was to design public and private programs, and ultimately build institutions, that would be in the business of developing and applying technology to the manufacturing base in Michigan and the nation.

The second part of the state's strategy was to complement the private capital markets with new innovation capital and capital-gap financing. A new institution called the Michigan Strategic Fund was developed to perform a variety of financing functions in an attempt to bridge the gaps perceived to exist in the private financial markets.

The last area of concern was titled "workforce learning and work relations"; that is, education, training, and innovations in labor relations to meet the needs of the changing workforce and to help adapt to the changing labor relations structures and practices in the workplace. This third part of the strategy, investing in "human capital" and reforming the related institutions, proved to be the most difficult part to craft change strategies that could be measured for their effectiveness.

The three-part effort was an aggressive state intervention strategy to create new public investment and program vehicles and to turn around the faltering industrial economy of the early 1980s. These new institutions were expected to deliver a steady stream of services into a revitalized industrial base.

Publicly Supported Institutions for Manufacturing

To implement the overall strategy, state government, with the assistance of private foundations, supported the development of the Industrial Technology Institute, a nonprofit organization staffed by manufacturing engineers and social scientists. The original design for the Institute was to create and develop new technology for manufacturing. The strategy has since been adjusted to include the application of existing and appropriate technology and production processes into the Michigan industrial base by leveraging resources and concentrating on particular geographic areas, industries, and technologies.

The second institution created was the Michigan Modernization Service (MMS), which was designed to serve as the state's major outreach service to the small and medium-sized manufacturers. It is the largest public organization of its kind in the United States with the mission of delivering strategic advice to small and medium-sized firms on technology, training, and marketing issues.

MMS functions through consultations with individual firms and by working on projects with groups of firms. The consultations are carried out by three-person teams with expertise in manufacturing methods and technologies, workforce training, and market analysis and marketing planning. The typical case involves five days of work from each of three members of the team. One of the products is a detailed written report analyzing the firm's performance and a series of recommendations for change.

The individual firm consultations typically cover several areas, including strategic business planning, technology utilization, productivity improvements, general management issues, quality control, workforce training, labor relations (in unionized settings), and market analysis and planning. The service is provided at no cost to the firm.

MMS also works with groups of firms to encourage cooperation among firms and between groups of firms and other players in the economy. This program is carried out through grants to groups of firms, trade associations, or unions. Projects that have been funded include: production networks in the metalworking and furniture industries; research and development strategies for the machine tool industry; and a program for auto parts suppliers, represented by Region 1-A of the United Auto Workers.

MMS has an annual budget of approximately $4 million. The staff consists of a combination of state employees, private contractors, and employees of private, nonprofit organizations such as the Industrial Technology Institute in Ann Arbor.

Focusing on the Smaller-Firm Sector

As a number of researchers have noted, firms with 20 to 500 employees produce over 40 percent of the value added in American manufacturing. MMS and the Industrial Technology Institute made a decision to target the small-firm sector because (1) the smaller firms did not have the resources or the market opportunities that the larger-firm sector had, (2) the original equipment manufacturers (OEMs) were increasing the amount of outsourcing to the supplier sector, and (3) the productivity gaps between the large firms and the small firms was growing (see Figure 1). As a result of the restructuring of the industrial system, wage gaps were growing, unionization rates between the small and large industrial firms were growing apart,[1] and there was a need to focus public attention and, indeed, public investment on the small-firm sector of the industrial economy.

In Michigan, there are about 6,000 small to medium-sized manufacturing firms, employing 500,000 workers, with a total payroll of about $11 billion. In all, they account for close to half of the Michigan manu-

facturing economy. The proportion of the manufacturing base represented by the smaller-firm sector has been steadily increasing. The
percent of manufacturing employment in smaller firms increased from
37 percent in 1979 to 44 percent in 1986.[2]

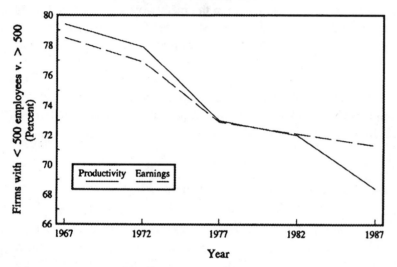

Figure 1
Productivity and Earnings
in Manufacturing Estasblishments
by Number of Employees

SOURCE: Census of Manufacturers
Reprinted with permission from The Industrial Technology Institute.

As the new flexible technologies reduce the importance of economies of scale, and as the large U.S. manufacturers continue to see market share threatened, more and more employment will be in small and
medium-sized shops. Unless more is done to improve productivity and
thereby raise wages, benefits, and conditions, the high industrywide
living standards that exist will be threatened.

A Role for Unions and Workers

Throughout the 1980s we have seen many of the country's leading industrial states treat technology as a central element in the emerging equation of international competitiveness. It is usually only on an *ad hoc* basis, however, and often during a crisis, that those most affected by technological change—the workforce—are brought into the process to play a role in designing change strategies.

The goal of a technology strategy that includes unions and workers would be to mitigate the negative impacts of new technology and begin to empower workers to participate as an equal partner in the process of technological change. To do so would involve the development of programs that include a clear assessment of the effects of technology, an awareness of the possibilities for influencing changes, the exploration of options, and availability of appropriate technical assistance.

The Michigan Modernization Service is a strong actor in the state's technology thrust. Up until very recently, MMS has defined its customer base to include only the management of the companies served by the organization. There has been no formal process to communicate with the workforce or union on any of the issues discussed by the firms' management and MMS consultants.

Beginning in 1988, the state Departments of Commerce and Labor supported the development of a labor-management effort that would provide information and services to strengthen and improve labor-management relations in smaller workplaces where workers are represented by a recognized trade union.

After an intensive period of research and development, the labor-management project developed tools to (1) analyze the union-management relationship in smaller firms within the context of business conditions and the needs of the workforce, (2) recommend appropriate changes, and (3) deliver training on participation strategies.

After field testing the service to over 30 firms and their unions, the state's labor-management project began to transfer the labor relations assessment and training instruments to existing public and nonprofit institutions like MMS. As a result of a strategic planning process, MMS agreed to incorporate a role for the union and the workforce as a part of the consultation process. The case of Philips Drop Forge, outlined below, provided additional evidence to MMS leadership of the importance of involving unions in designing change strategies.

The Case of Philips Drop Forge

The primary business of Philips Drop Forge is the production of steel forgings with conventional drop hammers. Most of the production is for automotive applications. Founded in the early 1900s in downtown Detroit, the company has just under 100 employees who are represented by a local of the International Union, UAW. Due to the change in materials (from forging to castings and powdered metals), newer processes and overseas competition, the firm needed to restructure to remain in business. The owner indicated a need to see a restructuring plan in place and indications of a turnaround before the end of 1990 as a requirement for the continued operation of the business.

A local UAW representative, through the union's regional office, requested that the state consider providing turnaround assistance to Philips Drop Forge. The request was made to the state's Labor-Management Project. A decision was made to offer the assistance of both the Michigan Modernization Service and the Labor-Management Project.

Figure 2 shows a comparative analysis by the state's Labor-Management Project of the separate turnaround recommendations by MMS and the union shop committee at the plant. The reader should look across the boxes to understand the alternative perspectives. For example, while the MMS staff recommended a generic "employee involvement" program as a response to the poor economic conditions of the business, the union leadership insisted that a joint union-management steering committee be organized, trained, and empowered to plan and manage a change agenda for the facility.

The importance of the specific proposals put forward by the union is that (1) they reflect the significance of the collective bargaining agreement, and (2) they emanate from a clear recognition of a worker's organization that has ideas based on experience and that is independent from management with different goals and values.

Figure 2
Philips Drop Forge/UAW

Comparable Issues/Different Perspectives

MMS Action Plan Recommendations	UAW 174 Action Plan Recommendations
a. Introduce employee involvement by communication from owner on poor financial condition of company	a. Empower joint union-management steering committee to manage and plan the change agenda
b. Management and workforce training on problemsolving, SPC, teambuilding, hammerman	b. Address qualifications of supervisors; provide personnel skills training
c. Track incoming material inspection data	c. Smarter steel ordering to reduce scrap Identify sources for better quality steel
d. Conduct hot inspections with cheap fixtures	d. Management must make effort to repair and maintain equipment
e. Group purchasing and better utilization of material	e. Gainsharing plan must be evaluated, fully implemented so that payoff of new initiatives is clear to the workers
f. Preventive maintenance program	
g. Explore viability of gainsharing	

Different Issues

MMS Action Plan Recommendations	UAW 174 Action Plan Recommendations
a. Closer relationship with major customers	a. Company has too many supervisors, white-collar staff
b. Track inventory	b. Collective bargaining agreement will not be opened as a result of this activity
c. Tool control program	c. Entire workforce must be informed and educated about the problems and plans for change
d. Quality team on high-value part	d. UAW research department should analyze finances.
	e. Create health and safety joint training program

Recommendations by MMS for restructuring the manufacturing process at the facility were presented to both top-level management and the entire workforce at an off-site meeting. The proposals were debated and an action plan for the future was agreed upon. Company management, recognizing the need to more formally and completely involve the union in the change process, agreed to support the development of a top-level joint steering committee which would assume responsibility for implementing participation strategies to meet the objectives of the action plan.

Labor as Catalyst to Strengthen an Industrial Sector

Beyond the individual workplace level are a variety of structural issues that planners ignore at their peril. Globalization of manufacturing processes due to capital mobility and the existence of cheap labor havens around the world are seriously affecting the U.S. auto supply industry. Suppliers, faced with higher demands from automakers for quality, just-in-time delivery, lower-cost production, and greater design capabilities have found it increasingly difficult to succeed in a more competitive marketplace. The number of U.S. suppliers has declined as U.S. automakers limit contracts to those suppliers who provide a fuller complement of services and can meet increasing demands. Likewise, most U.S. suppliers have not been successful in winning over Japanese automakers more accustomed to doing business based on long-term relationships.

To respond to this environment, and in the face of inadequate federal policy measures designed to introduce fair trade practices into the system, management and labor must equip themselves to save their businesses and their jobs. However, they must also recognize that each firm acting alone does not have the resources or the expertise to be able to respond effectively at every turn in the road.

Regional Director Bob King of UAW Region 1-A, representing over 100 independent parts suppliers in southwestern Detroit, developed a plan for a labor-management Council of Independent Parts Suppliers. The Michigan Modernization Service provided a planning grant to begin the process. The Council's goals include (1) providing the union and management with new tools to improve company performance and save jobs; (2) strengthening labor-management relations in small supplier shops; (3) developing a program that will help stop job losses and plant closings in the small-shop sector; (4) building a new government/labor/management collaborative process; and (5) targeting appropriate publicly available education, training, and technical services to the union and companies involved in the Council.

The project began with solicitations to 10 firms to establish the Council. Over 20 firms ultimately formed the organizing committee of the Council, with both top management and union leadership from each plant attending meetings.

Over the course of several meetings, participants heard presentations describing the current state of the auto industry and global examples of interfirm strategies. A day-long planning session was held to develop priorities. Groups were organized around (1) interfirm strategies to improve competitiveness; (2) skill development; (3) participation strategies; (4) health, safety, and environmental issues; and (5) employee assistance programs.

As a result of the planning meetings, the membership of the Council crafted a two-part strategy. First, a Market Development and Job Retention program was created to help meet the challenges of external demands. The program included (1) documenting the technology, skills, and production capabilities of member firms; (2) establishing a formal relationship between the Council and the sourcing managers of the large manufacturers; (3) aggregating the production capabilities of member firms and identifying co-production possibilities; and (4) conducting industry-specific research and auto industry information-sharing sessions.

The second part of the strategy involved an Individual Firm Performance and Quality Jobs program. This program was established recognizing the fact that the implementation of any restructuring effort would need to be accomplished at the individual firm level, and that the interrelationship between the nature of industrial relations and the economic performance of the firm was a determining factor. Included in the action plan for the program was (1) implementing UAW Right-To-Know training; (2) developing a cost-sharing program; (3) implementing labor-management training programs; and (4) analyzing the skill demand needs of member firms to determine the content of a training agenda.

The key for this union-led project was to strike a balance between worker needs and business realities, on the one hand, and between education/information and action, on the other. At a recent Council planning meeting, one firm owner stood up to declare "for me this Council represents an opportunity to recognize the union in my plant as a strategic weapon in our effort toward industrial growth and renewal."

The Need for a Strategic Response

Union-initiated industrial restructuring activity raises important strategic questions for trade unions and public policymakers. What institutional resources need to be developed to significantly increase the participation of workers and unions in this environment? How do we shape existing institutions toward the objective of addressing workers' problems in the workplace and strengthening the unions for future struggles in both the workplace and in economic policymaking?

Models of government support for strengthening the role of unions and workers in firm and industry decisionmaking exist in Canada and Western Europe.[3] Many of these competitively successful countries have established high standards of living by investing in modern education, labor market, and industry-specific policies and programs designed by innovative institutional partnerships between government, business, and labor; a partnership where labor plays a more co-equal role than that experienced in the U.S.

The development of a more strategic role for trade unions in the restructuring process is an important part of the process to stop the decline of unionization and to save the U.S. manufacturing base. State government, by commanding or effecting the deployment of technology, training, and financial services could act as a catalyst to counter the short term bias of current federal policies and private sector behavior. A public policy of assistance to workers and unions that complements and underpins all other interventions in the industrial economy can greatly enhance the prospects for maintaining good jobs and improving industry performance.

Epilogue

With an 11,000 vote margin, the newly elected Republican governor, by the stroke of a pen, closed down many of the programs serving Michigan's industrial community in the winter of 1990. Calling them "tinsel on the tree," the new governor shut down programs such as the Michigan Modernization Service. As a result, hundreds of smaller firms and thousands of workers would no longer have the benefit of publicly supported technical assistance in their struggle to maintain jobs and competitiveness.

Along with the loss of MMS went the start-up grant to help the UAW Region 1-A Labor-Management Council of Independent Parts Suppliers. To survive, the leadership organized a membership fundraising effort among the local unions and participating firms. Over 20 firms and the related union locals raised enough membership dues money to maintain the organization and staff, and bought some time to reorganize and identify outside funding sources.

The reorganization plan apparently satisfied federal IRS officials, winning tax-exempt status for the group and building the basis for attracting private foundation funds. The newly named Labor-Management Council for Economic Renewal serves as the education arm of the more action-oriented Labor-Management Suppliers Council.

More recently, the group was the recipient of a grant from the Manufacturing Technology Center (MTC), located at the Industrial Technology Institute. The MTC is one of five centers around the country sponsored by the government-financed National Institute of Standards and Technology. The MTC's Cooperative Capability Project, with the UAW/IPS Labor-Management Council, is assisting member firms and union locals in identifying and building interfirm production activity, or networks, with the goal of capturing business that is disproportionately being outsourced to the nonunion sector by the original equipment manufacturers.

The International Union, UAW, made an industrial policy proposal in 1983 that called for national coordination, democratic decisionmaking, a strong role for government, and the use of social accounting principles in the evaluation of industrial and employment policies and programs. Looking back, it appears that some people were listening.

Michigan in the 1980s was a positive example of the old democratic value that ordinary people and honest employers could depend on government for help in the effort to rebuild industry and create jobs. Michigan in the 1990s is a much different place, as jobs disappear and whole industrial sectors deteriorate. And no one appears to be listening.

NOTES

*At the time of writing, Mr. Schippani worked for the State of Michigan. He is now employed in the research department of the United Automobile Workers union.

1. A July 28, 1990 *Detroit Free Press* article showed that independent automotive suppliers whose workers belong to unions went from 62 percent in 1976 to 22 percent in 1988. Unionization of Big Three assembly plants, however, stayed constant relative to the overall decline in employment.

2. Testimony of John Cleveland, director of MMS, to the Senate Subcommittee on Innovation, Technology and Productivity, December 19, 1989.

3. The most recent example is the Technology Adjustment Research Program funded by the Ontario government. Administered by the Ontario Federation of Labor, the purpose of the program is "to assist the Ontario trade union movement in developing constructive and progressive responses to change in the workplace."

8
Applying Skills-Based Automation Through Participatory Management

The Center for Applied Technology

Frank Emspak
University of Wisconsin–Madison

Origins of the Center for Applied Technology

The Center for Applied Technology was first proposed in January 1987. Governor Dukakis wanted a program that would bring state-of-the-art technology to the traditional industries of Massachusetts as a means of preserving employment. He also wanted to show his concern for issues affecting working people. He asked the Secretary of Labor to cooperate with other state agencies to devise a program. The Secretary worked with agencies such as Massachusetts Centers of Excellence Corporation, the Massachusetts Product Development Corporation, and the Industrial Services Program—all quasi-public corporations, most under the budgetary authority of the Department of Economic Affairs (Commerce). During the spring of 1987, the Centers looked at other state industry-university partnership programs, especially those in Pennsylvania and Michigan. These programs focused on building industry-university partnerships to foster innovation in manufacturing.

The Center for Applied Technology (CAT) was constituted along the lines followed in other states—with one important exception as discussed below. The CAT board reflected the industry-university connection and the technocratic bent of the administration. Thus the members of the board included representatives from three of the most prominent engineering schools in the Commonwealth, business representatives from two high-technology firms, and state agencies dealing with economic development issues. The Center for Applied Technology formally began operations on November 1, 1987.

121

CAT searched for ways to encourage worker participation in the technology design and implementation process. It was this dedication to the notion of worker participation in the design process that distinguished CAT from other agencies in the state or elsewhere who were attempting to assist manufacturers modernize their productive facilities. CAT's work in this area was supported and encouraged by the CAT board.

CAT and Worker Participation

Generally speaking, the labor movement has little influence on the industry-university model of innovation and economic development. CAT wished to alter this traditional model. The objective of worker participation was met through both administrative and program initiatives.

As an example of an administrative action, the Secretary of Labor chaired CAT's advisory board. It was felt that by placing the Center under the titular direction of the Department of Labor, a signal would be sent to the labor movement that CAT was open to labor participation in economic development issues. In addition, meaningful participation of working people in the economic development process also required defining programs in such a way as to encourage participation from all groups using manufacturing technologies.

CAT approached this problem by requiring worker participation in order for university-industry research partnerships to get financial support. CAT did not specify the form that worker participation should take in the research projects, however, it was one of several funding criteria. Financial support by CAT for firm-specific technical assistance also required that a union, if any, or representatives from the workforce be included in any committee that helped define the problems to be solved. In addition, all CAT conferences (there were four) were organized to include both management and labor participation.

While these organizational changes were important in themselves, the actual impact of labor/worker participation on the shape and content of the projects needs to be assessed case by case.

In CAT's view, this formal representation is not enough. CAT was searching for ways that rank-and-file workers could speak in their own right regarding questions of technology design and implementation. CAT was aware of the action research models employed in Scandinavia which might serve as models. However, there are stronger institutions, especially unions, that serve as support for these projects. This country does not have that trade union institutional structure that can lend support to research projects.

Each project was to try to find a way to involve the user-workers in its research. Eventually each research project developed a means of involving the end user. For example, the University of Lowell shop-floor programming project actually hired machinists to evaluate software under review. That phase of their project devised criteria for judging how the software under discussion was designed, referencing the procedures that skilled machinists employed in making a specific part.

Program Development

At the outset of the Center for Applied Technology formation process, the Massachusetts Centers of Excellence (MCEC) had a view of applying state-of-the-art technology to traditional industry via industry-university partnerships. However, it was not clear to CAT that this could be done. While manufacturing in Massachusetts has pockets of modernity, a good deal of manufacturing is also not up to current technical standards. If computers are in use, they are generally in the office and not integrated with the shop-floor manufacturing process.

In September 1987, the author made a presentation to the CAT hiring committee proposing a different model of technology implementation and transfer as an alternative to the state-of-the-art university-industry partnership model. Rather than try to apply state-of-the-art technology, the author suggested that CAT use the resource that is most abundant in the metalworking sector of manufacturing in the Commonwealth—skilled workers. Based on the availability of one resource (skill) and the lack of another (capital), CAT argued that a skill-based strategy which emphasized better use of existing technologies was both immediately applicable and would have the most immediate and lasting impact on industry. Eventually a successful skill-based approach would also put the metalworking industry in a position to use more advanced technologies if they made sense. Thus CAT's idea was to apply appropriate technology, defined as worker-centered and skills-based.

From a design point of view, CAT took traditional engineering criteria for machine or process design—such as speed, repeatability, and accuracy—and added the enhancement of skill as criteria for designing or applying new production methods to a particular shop. In addition CAT was sensitive to ergonomic considerations including noise. After all if workers can't hear because there's too much noise, they probably can't think either.

An industrial system that focuses on skill requires greater emphasis on process and on the worker so, automatically, the worker becomes more central to the picture than the machine. The CAT technical assistance project at the Pneumatic Scale Company in Quincy, Massachusetts met these criteria. Pneumatic was actually two projects—a retraining of the assembly workers, who were among the most skilled craftspeople in the plant and organization of a manufacturing cell to produce spare parts. Deputy CAT director Dr. John Hoops assisted the firm and the union in organizing a training program for the assemblers with Wentworth Institute that allowed the mechanical and electrical assemblers to combine their knowledge with increased familiarity with electronics and hydraulics. Thus the assemblers' skills could keep pace with the changing machinery they produced. The skilled work was kept in the bargaining unit. The jobs of assemblers were kept unified by adding an enhanced technical component.

The work cell was an answer to the chronic problems with spare parts availability and delivery. Placement of the machines was the least difficult task. The organization of production, the role and skill levels of the workers, and the proper provision of work and orders to the work cell became the focus of the union-management discussions, assisted by CAT.

In both examples at Pneumatic, the people were upgraded—not the equipment. Organizational solutions which focused on enhancing skill were the chosen path. Implementation was aided, and indeed made possible, by the active participation in planning and development by the unionized workforce.

From Theory to Practice

CAT's challenge was to take a concept of applied technology based on skill, that is, the worker, and turn it into a legitimate, accepted economic program. The CAT concept had two parts: an engineering notion called skills-based automation, and an implementation pathway based on user (worker) participation. In order to make the concepts real, CAT decided to fund three distinct types of services. First, they funded the Massachusetts Manufacturing Resource Center, a source for information about skills-based automation. Second, CAT funded applied research in the area of manufacturing. Third, CAT staff organized and CAT funded a technical assistance service.

With the organization of three distinct program areas, CAT transformed itself from the conception that the governor had of high-tech and state-of-the-art applications. CAT became an organization that provided down-to-earth advice and assistance to small manufacturers. The name didn't change, but the content did. The nature of the project changed from a grant-giving institution for research with industry, with no labor participation, to a subsidized technology transfer and consultation business with strong labor participation and a supporter of research with a strong bias to labor.

The Massachusetts Manufacturing Resource Center

In June 1988 CAT established the Massachusetts Manufacturing Resource Center (MMRC). CAT's initial vision for the center was drawn from organizations such as the Science Center in Berlin, the Norwegian Computing Center and the Worklife Center. CAT hoped the MMRC would be a place where unions and manufacturers could come together to learn about skill-based manufacturing methods. CAT wanted the Center to publicize the concept and explain the benefits. CAT also wanted the Center to establish a current, and preferably on-line, collection of articles and materials to provide examples of attempts to employ a skill-based method. The MCEC and CAT boards saw the MMRC as a major component of the CAT program and devoted one-third of the program budget to the MMRC.

The project was located at Tufts University and at the University of Lowell. The University of Lowell is one of the Commonwealth's best engineering schools and has a close relationship with industry. It also houses an environmental and health and safety program which enjoys widespread industry and labor support. Tufts has a focus on engineering and technical policy issues. CAT felt that the MMRC could draw on the expertise of both institutions to establish itself as a source of both engineering and policy information.

Program work was divided between the two institutions. The Lowell branch established the MMRC library. It collected articles, case studies, pamphlets, and materials from unions, universities, and companies regarding work organization, skills-based automation, and attempts to implement skills-based systems. The Lowell team also emphasized its contacts with labor, doing some outreach to labor unions and the Massachusetts State AFL-CIO.

The Tufts end of the program began to specialize in the development of a network, as one aspect of making the information available to potential users. Tufts also worked with some manufacturers to assess their views on a skills-based approach with a view to recruiting them to the Board of Directors of the MMRC.

CAT made two assumptions in the original thinking regarding the MMRC. First, they assumed that as the ideas of alternative manufacturing strategies were publicized by the MMRC, business would be willing to use the resources of the Center. Second, they felt that as unions understood the value of a skills-based approach, they would also begin using the Center and vigorously support it. CAT hoped that unions wanting to pursue a skills-based approach would have a resource to draw on for information that would also be "legitimate" in the eyes of management. Therefore the concepts of skills-based manufacturing would get wider exposure, and the requisite political support from management and labor would develop so as to secure continued funding for the MMRC.

For a variety of reasons, the MMRC did not succeed in all of its missions. From the start there were organizational difficulties engendered by the dual location of the MMRC. Problems of coordination and focus were magnified by the location of distinct functions at different institutions. Second, the MMRC did not stabilize as an organization in the first year. A strong board, representing business, labor, and the universities, and which could and would support the MMRC, never really got off the ground. This contributed to the growing lack of financial support. In its original plans, CAT intended to support the MMCR at a high level for three years, by which time it was felt that the organization would have had time to prove its worth. However, under the pressure of continuing and severe state budget cuts, CAT was unable to maintain that high level of support. Although a significant level of support remained, the MMRC had to find other sources of support after only 18 months. Therefore, on one level, the inability of the Commonwealth to make a long-term investment in an alternative manufacturing pathway eventually fatally wounded the MMRC.

The combination of different missions on different campuses combined with limited funding possibilities intensified MMRC's drift away from its original purpose. As mentioned, one part of the Center (Tufts) began to concentrate on electronic networking. In part the theory was to help bring about the type of close cooperation between small metalworking plants that tends to distinguish northern Italy. The system serves to link small concerns for the purpose of marketing and information sharing. Eventually it is intended to be a means with which the smaller firms can get information on-line from the National Institute of Standards and Technology (NIST) regional technology centers, especially the one located at Rensselaer Polytechnic Institute (RPI). However, while the project has done some extremely interesting work, it has also moved away from the skill-based technology aspects. Lack of state funding means that now the network receives most of its funding from the NIST and increasingly is integrated with the NIST center at RPI. As an economic development initiative, especially in regards to technology innovation, the network idea has great potential. It is unclear if, or how, the network will function on behalf of worker participation in the application of technology or proselytizing for skills-based automation.

The University of Lowell branch of the MMRC acquired documentation and information regarding skills-based concepts. From the first it focused more on building relations with the labor movement, which has fewer financial resources to commit to any activity and has rarely committed resources to engineering research/documentation. NIST and other federal agencies are interested primarily in technology transfer or relatively technocratic models of technological innovation. Thus public, i.e., state support, for the Lowell activities is crucial. The Lowell branch was unable to do enough outreach fast enough to establish an independent financial base before the fiscal crunch hit. CAT will be able to support the library and acquisition functions of the Lowell branch, but CAT will not be able to support the other functions at as high a level as wished due to changes in funding.

In short, for an MMRC to succeed, a higher level of institutional, political, and hence funding commitment will be needed. It may be that such an institution is beyond the capacity of one state. It is also clear that an MMRC-type institution needs a champion outside of state government—either in industry or labor— in order to serve as a pole of attraction for political support.

Applied Research

CAT funded six applied research projects. An example of the applied research is the Shop-Floor Programming project that CAT sponsors at the University of Lowell. If the worker is central to the process and not an afterthought, the design of the man-machine interface becomes important. For instance CAD/CAM systems are designed with the engineer in mind. Essentially engineers are writing the programs based on the steps they take when they use computer-aided design. The "thought process" in the CAM software mirrors the CAD thought process.

Do machinists visualize a problem of machining differently from engineers? The Lowell project demonstrated that indeed the answer is yes. Thus, if machinists are to have software that allows them to do parts programming, the internal architecture of the software must be redesigned to match the thought processes of the machinist. In this example, the idea of "user-friendly" takes on a different dimension. It is not a question of making a keyboard "easy" to use, or of providing a menu-driven system with limited selections, but rather a question of redesigning the system itself to more closely approximate the way a skilled machinist envisions a metalworking problem.

The project at Worcester Polytechnic Institute (WPI) approached the problem of worker participation differently. Their objective was to develop a more user-friendly and flexible CAD/CAM system for the production of sheet metal parts. WPI organized a project with a specific metalworking shop and gradually over a period of months worked out a close relationship with the sheet metal workers in the shop. WPI designed a custom training program such that programmers were able to upgrade to more design, and machinists were able to do on-line shop-floor programming of their machines in response to customer demands. Simultaneously, the software was also configured to meet the needs of the machinist users. The CAD/CAM system and course is now available for distribution. A good deal of time was spent by the machinists off the floor at WPI learning the system and providing feedback to the researchers as to how it could be modified.

At the University of Massachusetts, Amherst, the problem was more difficult. Labor relations at the industry partner were poor. The project in its initial phases was also pretty abstract in that it was to define mathematically the tool path for a grinding wheel doing a complex part (a cutting tool). After many discussions with the researcher involved, the company, and the unionized grinders, the grinders were able to participate more fully in the project. The grinders were able to evaluate at the worksite the software produced and visit the University of Massachusetts during working hours to get a better understanding of the entire process.

There are very difficult problems to overcome if we are to involve working people in a meaningful way in a research project. Institutional questions such as paid time off from work are one problem. But cultural problems are another. The university is not the environment that most blue-collar workers are used to. Likewise, most professors are not used to taking the opinions of shop-floor workers seriously. There are also language problems. People speak differently and use different words. There may be a period of education needed, so that all participants in the project can comprehend the significance of the changes in software or tool design that they are advocating. This education period is not simply aimed at blue-collar workers, but also at researchers since they too must learn the significance of proposed design changes on the skills and environment of the worker.

Nonetheless, CAT feels it has taken important first steps in this area and crossed one crucial barrier. The individual professors involved became advocates of the idea. Perhaps, if funding allows, support for work in these areas can be deepened and broadened.

The research projects have led to some industrywide changes, and they do aid some specific firms. However, for a project such as the Lowell project to succeed, significant funding and additional time are needed. As of this writing, the funding outlook is not promising. However, a software development pathway emphasizing worker (blue-collar) skills has significance and can offer a means to bring complicated programming functions into the shop in an economic and practical fashion.

In CAT's view, the research sponsored should be guided by the actual conditions in the field. CAT had to show the industry, by example, that a skills-based, participatory model of technical innovation would work. CAT also realized that demonstration projects that actually performed a service to an industry would help make the program understandable to the legislature, other business, and local unions. Therefore CAT decided to organize "pilot technical assistance projects." In effect, CAT became a small industrial extension service, using a skills-based model of technical innovation. Some of the projects are discussed below.

Technical Assistance Projects

Direct services to the workforce and the manufacturer help validate CAT's other work and also provide models for a worker participation method of technology innovation. So far, CAT has worked in about 15 different factories of varying sizes. Approximately 1,000 people were employed in the various firms. Projects have ranged from laying out a small factory, to designing and implementing a machining cell as part of a larger effort to restructure jobs, skills and the work flow in a sizable factory. As mentioned earlier, the Pneumatic Scale Company project involved not only the design of a cell, but also a general upgrading of skills throughout the affected areas. This, in turn, required a sizable training program. The objective of the project was to ensure the survival of the plant by reducing the time it took to get needed spare parts to the customer. In fact, the time was reduced, mostly due to paperwork types of reorganization, and the company is now prospering. A detailed description of this project would require a chapter in itself.

CAT chose to focus on small and medium-sized firms in the metalworking industry. The choice of firm size was driven by several factors. First, Massachusetts industry is characterized by the smaller firm, so to serve the Commonwealth the smaller firm should be the recipient of aid. Second, most small firms do not have the financial or engineering resources to adequately access the information they need to apply new means of manufacturing to their operations. Third, the number of people employed in smaller firms is a significant sector of the workforce.

CAT chose metalworking for more parochial reasons. Metalworking was and is an important producer of wealth in Massachusetts. Metalworking supports more than its share of service jobs—one service job for each job in metalworking. Metalworkers—especially unionized metalworkers—are also the highest-paid manufacturing workers, so saving jobs in that sector is a priority. But for CAT, one other important reason for choosing metalworking was that the author had worked in the industry for 15 years and thus understood a good deal about manufacturing conditions and skill levels.

The important aspect of all of these technical assistance projects is the participation of the workforce in the projects. By participation, CAT means decisionmaking. In each project, CAT organizes a team of workers to be part of a committee comprised of management and their technical staff (if any), CAT consultant or CAT staff, and the workforce. This committee figures out what needs to be done and how the project should proceed. CAT facilitates that process by providing relevant technical expertise or organizational assistance. The point is to bring the workers' knowledge and expertise into the discussion in a proactive, meaningful way. This does not mean "cooperation" with a preset agenda, but a jointly developed plan for upgrading a particular plant or operation. Generally speaking, the union emerges from this process strengthened organizationally. If nothing else, the union or workers have a much deeper knowledge of the factory and how it works than they did previously. Since one of CAT's design criteria is to enhance skill, most projects also result in an increase in the number of skilled workers and thus usually an increase in wages as well.

However, CAT programs also distinguish themselves in one key area from typical labor-management cooperation programs. CAT tried to organize its technical assistance work so that workers could have a meaningful voice in what technologies would be introduced and how they would be used. In other words, they sought ways to allow working people and management collectively to make the strategic decisions, as opposed to simply asking workers to help implement or make minor modifications. To CAT, the question of design was the starting point, not the problem of implementation.

CAT technical assistance projects also reemphasized a point made in 1950 when firms began experimenting with various productivity and quality programs such as the Scanlon Plan. Then Fortune magazine advised employers that the presence of a union was necessary for these plans to reach their full value. CAT technical assistance projects also showed it to be easier to work in factories where the union was well organized.

In unionized shops, there is an organization of people elected and trusted by workers with whom CAT could speak. They were not afraid to raise questions and could help define the problems with an independence from management not demonstrated in nonunion shops. People could speak with less fear and more openly as they had a contract to protect them. In nonunionized shops, often the people management made available to CAT were those trusted by management. They were not necessarily the most skilled or competent (although they could be), but they owed their position on the committee to management, not to their fellow workers. Thus there tended to be considerable self-censorship and/or willingness to allow traditional authority to define the issues. This process makes it more difficult to isolate and solve problems of production and design. Also, without a contract and grievance procedure, workers, in reality, do not have the ability to speak their mind.

Of course there may be reasons why the existence of a union could present additional difficulties. For example, there may be contractual regulations regarding job placement, training, removal, and pay levels. In addition, the union may decide to choose its representatives on a technology design/change committee. In the unionized plants at which CAT worked—Pneumatic Scale and Mitchell Machine—these so-called problems were not major issues. Regulations regarding job placement allowed CAT to work within a defined and accepted framework. The existence of a union at Pneumatic allowed for an organized approach to training and pay problems. And just as management chose its representatives to the committee on technology/organizational issues based on a combination of knowledge of the area and ability to make decisions, so did the union.

Of course in a union environment the union can always withdraw from a team and thus kill it. However, it is also true that in serious questions of design in a joint worker-management setting, management can withdraw. It has been CAT's experience that management is more likely to resist sharing authority as compared to the union's resistance to gaining it. In other words, management resistance to empowering workers to discuss design issues was the problem. Neither union withdrew or threatened to, even though in varying degrees the firms showed considerable concern with their participation at various points.

CAT has found that technical assistance projects are extremely difficult to organize and manage. Technical innovation is the least of the problems. Getting management to the table and willing to alter their plans at the request of the workers is often the greatest difficulty. Naturally we are dealing with issues of control of the workplace, along with traditional styles of top down authority.

CAT also tries to make sure that the discussions take place in an atmosphere of equality when it comes to making technical decisions about fixtures, machines, etc. This often means that the firm must invest in an education program, or at least encourage team members to work with resources knowledgeable of the area under discussion. Two types of education usually need to occur. There has to be technical education. Workers and management need to be familiar with the technical choices at their disposal. There also has to be education that enables the parties to do joint problemsolving and strategic thinking. In addition, the firm needs to allow time for the education process to take place. Naturally this should occur during the working day, not as an extracurricular activity.

The role of the consultant in these projects is particularly important. The consultant is often fulfilling two functions at once. On the one hand he/she offers technical expertise. On the other hand he/she tries to facilitate meaningful worker participation in decisionmaking. In general, experience has encouraged CAT to provide a different consultant for each role. In some cases, CAT staff does the facilitating, but in larger projects CAT employs people who have expertise in teaching empowerment strategies, organization tactics, how to hold meetings, and so forth. When CAT hires consultants for their technical skills, they also strive to acquaint them with the larger CAT agenda as well.

Over time, CAT has identified a number of people who are now more sensitive to the needs of all of their users.

CAT and Economic Diversification

Part of CAT's job is to service the needs of the small and medium-sized manufacturer. The objective is to maintain the manufacturing base. Massachusetts, however, has an extremely high defense dependency. A good proportion of the work of many of the smaller firms is defense-related—mostly supplying parts to prime contractors. In many cases these firms need to find new customers very soon or they will be out of business.

For years, the discussion of economic diversification has turned on the question of product diversification. It is true there is a need for product diversification, and also for community- and worker-based, multiple-use committees to encourage that diversification. But that is not the whole story.

From CAT's perspective as an organization that works with the manufacturing process, many companies make useful products. But they are making them according to military standards and procedures and are, therefore, not competitive in the commercial market. Thus there is a role for a process-driven strategy of economic diversification. In other words, if CAT can fix up the manufacturing process so that the company can produce for the commercial market, then they have a chance to survive.

To this end, CAT has actively sought to have the various federal defense adjustment bills changed so that there is federal aid to the smaller firms via agencies like CAT to enable them to make the transition from one style of manufacture to another. Naturally, CAT would help firms make this transition using their normal criteria—worker participation and a skills-based production design. So far, the process-driven approach has succeeded in reducing the defense dependency from 60 percent to about 20 percent in a plant that was producing for both commercial and defense markets. In this case, changes in manufacturing technique allowed the firm to lower unit costs and increase quality, thus allowing it to win a substantial commercial contract.

Since its defense business is expected to decline, the ability to manufacture for the commercial sphere will save the firm and the jobs. Obviously a process-driven approach is not the only approach that can be of use, but for firms whose products are similar for the defense industry and for the commercial market, it does offer some assistance. In addition, a process-driven approach to diversification places real value on worker participation, since the changes CAT supports are dependent on the worker. In other words, the workforce is not a spectator to the diversification process but a participant.

CAT as a Political Organization

In certain ways, the CAT project director has a political rather than technical job. In order to move the CAT agenda forward industry, academics, and the labor movement must all support it. Just getting the notion across that technical innovation occurs least expensively and more efficiently when it is based on worker participation and skill is a big agenda item. Obviously, if firms refuse to even try the model, there will be no projects. If CAT cannot convince engineers and others to work with them and for them, they will not get the technical expertise needed. Likewise, AFL-CIO support has been critical for CAT in identifying plants that are in need of assistance and in working with local unions to encourage participation.

Worker participation is also a profoundly political idea. It is derived not only from common sense and experience in industry, but also from a view of how a state-supported agency should function. Most of the people in the state are working people. They pay the taxes. They are the "users." Therefore it seems only fair that economic development must explicitly serve the needs of all the users, not just the managers and technicians. After all, no industry favors the trickle down theory when it comes to their needs; public agencies should not favor trickle down ideas when it comes to the needs of working people either.

CAT has set out consciously to build a constituency of people who recognize the importance of the industrial base in Massachusetts. This is not a glamorous task. Given the extreme budget problems in the state, it takes a high degree of cooperation from the constituent base to maintain the program. So far, CAT has been successful.

Support for manufacturing can take many forms. CAT's contribution to the discussion is trying to get across the notion that a state extension service for manufacturing is not a finance problem; in fact, most of it is manufacturing process. Looked at from a process point of view, workers and their organizations are put in the middle of the innovation process, as opposed to participating later. A process-oriented program would favor in-plant education and apprenticeships. A process-oriented program also focuses assistance on the recipients—the small manufacturer and the workforce—not intermediaries. Process-driven programs do not spend most of their resources at the university or insuring bank loans.

Overall, however, the weight of those who favor support for manufacturing is relatively weak. Even in good times, the Massachusetts programs did not match the scope and intensity of the industrial assistance programs in most other industrialized states, or in many southern states. There is not yet a large enough consensus in the Commonwealth to support a manufacturing extension service in light of the fiscal problems facing the state.

What makes the CAT program unique is its commitment to a worker-centered, skill-based approach. As such, it has more worker involvement than most. It has also been successful in saving or enhancing manufacturing activity in a number of plants. Therefore, even though CAT is not expected to grow substantially over the next few years, it should be able to continue to function.

NOTE

This essay was written for a lecture presented in May 1990. It was edited in August 1991. By that time the Commonwealth of Massachusetts had disbanded the Centers of Excellence, CAT's parent organization. CAT was able to move to another agency, but with no new funds appropriated in the 1991 or 1992 budget.

Frank Emspak was Project Director of the Center for Applied Technology from November 1, 1987 until April 1, 1991.

9
Can the End of the Social Democratic Trade Unions be the Beginning of a New Kind of Social Democratic Politics?

Charles F. Sabel
Massachusetts Institute of Technology

The title of this essay is a provocation directed at the smaller and smaller group of people in the advanced capitalist democracies who are viscerally disturbed by the trade unions' self-evident disorientation and loss of influence on macroeconomic decisions and the reorganization of firms. We know who we are. Despite our differences, we believe that persons who cannot exercise their autonomy in choosing their work and how to do it are diminished in an essential aspect of their personhood; and we believe that autonomy in these things can rarely be achieved by individuals acting in isolation. Because our ideas about how good society can be are bound up with these beliefs, we are always looking for signs that the strongest trade unions—those in the social democracies of Northern Europe—are successfully adjusting to the new conditions of international competition, and that their renewal can serve as a model and guide to the reconstruction of more embattled labor movements.

The first half of the provocation, hinted at in the title and spelled out in the body of the essay, is that this hope is unwarranted. I will not belabor the end of the industrial proletariat and its consequences for traditional forms of trade unionism.[1] I argue instead that social democratic unions suppose in their organizational foundations a certain concept of corporations, of relations among them, of careers within them, and of the boundary between them, "private" life, and the public sector. As actual conditions diverge more and more from this concept, the social democratic unions have more and more trouble addressing the difficulties that employees face in their workday lives, and less and less ability to make effective use of their powers to regulate production. The first part of the essay gives a compressed analysis of the way the corporations' successful adjustment to the crisis changes their organization in the relevant dimensions. The second part argues that social democratic unions will very likely, but not necessarily, encourage these transformations, yet are just as likely to be victims of these successes.

The other half of the provocation in the title and the essay is the idea that to the extent social democratic unions do adjust to the new environment, they perform activities associated more with political entities such as parties and social movements than with trade unions, although neither political parties nor social movements today define themselves as performing these particular tasks. The argument is a bit devious here, so it is only fair to tip my hand. Thus, the third part of the essay looks at effects of corporate reorganization on career patterns and the conception of work as a distinct sphere of activity; the fourth part innocently deduces the features of a labor movement which can take account of these effects. The concluding section asks much less innocently whether an organization with those features is a trade union in any reasonable understanding of that term at all. It contends that it is not a trade union but rather a new form of political activity. The reader is left wondering whether, if true, this finding is a good or a bad thing. So we end the excursion all in the same boat.

The Reorganization of the Firm

There is widespread agreement that firms respond to the current economic environment in one of two very general ways. The first is by cutting the production costs of standard goods. This can be done through automation of traditional production lines, subcontracting to low-wage producers, or some combination of both. Firms pursuing this strategy are always at the mercy of new low-cost entrants. Hence, they are permanently tempted to cut costs by reducing pay, worsening working conditions, introducing machines that can be operated by cheaper or less labor, or shifting production to low-wage areas. This is or soon becomes a *sweating strategy,* whether pursued by large firms or small. It is hard watching, among other things, the current massive layoffs of middle managers in U.S. firms that did for a time pursue this strategy, to see how anyone given a choice could prefer it in the long run to the alternative.

The second response is a *strategy of permanent innovation*. The aim is to respond to and stimulate demand for products or services that correspond to consumers' wants more exactly than mass-produced goods. All products are regarded in this strategy as if they were capital goods, and valued according to the relation between their price and their ability to satisfy particular wants (the more favorable the price/performance ratio the better), rather than according to their absolute price (the cheaper the better).[2]

This second strategy depends on the reintegration of conception and execution in production. Marketing, design, and manufacturing must proceed concurrently, with those responsible for building the product helping to define what it will be in the first place and *vice versa*. Only in this way is it possible to cut development times in the measure required to get products to market when they are still in demand, and to reduce development costs to amounts that can be recovered through sale of short runs of affordably priced goods.

The reintegration of conception and execution has among its many other consequences three closely related effects which are of immediate significance for the organization of trade unions. The first is to raise the general level of skill required in production. Skill is the ability to perform complex tasks guided only by indicative instructions. The more superiors at all levels in the firm are pressed by constraints of time and money to instruct their subordinates to "use their judgment," "do their best," or simply "solve the problem," the more the subordinates are called on to exercise their skills. It is impossible to apply instructions where there are none, and the further a firm progresses down the track of permanent innovation, the less likely it is that the production of any particular product will be codified in rules. Notice I am not claiming that all employees in firms following this strategy are always acquiring and using all the skills for which they might potentially have a use. The claim is simply that whereas in the sweating strategy model the tendency is toward de-skilling, the tendency here is towards skill acquisition.[3]

The second consequence is to change the relation between firms, particularly large firms, and their subcontractors from one of domination to one of collaboration.[4] Just as the reintegration of conception and execution within firms leads to increased cooperation among different departments and across grades of hierarchy, so too it requires increased cooperation among the firms jointly producing a single final product. Subcontractors were, in effect, treated like semiskilled workers in the mass-production system: they executed a set of detailed blueprints provided by the customer, and secured orders by entering the lowest bid for a particular job. In a system of permanent innovation, where even the largest firms cannot master (because they cannot reliably anticipate) all the key technologies necessary to define and build rapidly changing products, subcontractors increasingly collaborate in the specification of the design and manufacturing setup. Asked to build a particular component or subassembly, for example, a subcontractor may propose modifications that reduce its cost of manufacture or improve its performance; asked to contribute expertise in the formulation of a plastic compound for an automobile company, for another example, a chemical firm may install and oversee the operation in the customer's plant of the machinery which shapes the new compound. This is not to claim that there are not disparities of power in relations between large firms and subcontractors in this system. Again the contrast is with the organization of mass production, particularly as it is denatured through sweating. In mass production, subcontractors were permanently, but not necessarily increasingly, subservient to their large customers. In sweating, a bad situation gets worse. In a system of permanent innovation, the tendency is for it to get better, though plainly not for all subcontractors all at once.

The third consequence is the regionalization of production, by which I mean the geographic clustering of firms providing similar or complementary products or services to the same or related markets.[5] This third effect follows in large measure from the first two. Thus, the shorter the product life cycles, the riskier it is to hold inventories at any stage of the production process—hence the need for just-in-time logistics, in which parts are produced and delivered as needed. Often (but by no means always) this means establishing production facilities in close proximity to the customer; and once established, these facilities attract other customers of the same sort. The shorter the product life cycle, moreover, the more likely it is that indispensable knowledge about production will become local knowledge—embedded in the half-articulated practices of persons who are in daily contact and who alone are in a position to grasp the implications of what they say and do. The more knowledge is commonly known to be of this type, the more firms will want to locate in the locale where it circulates. Finally, the more specialized firms or operating units of firms become, the more they are likely to depend for some of the services they need on the public or cooperative institutions of their locale. Training, quality control testing, and industrial medicine geared to the needs of a particular branch or sector are all examples of services that firms may want to have provided collectively; and, once again, the provision of such services by municipal authorities or a cooperative of firms or some combination of both attracts other firms in the same line of business. Thus, just as the integration of conception and execution blurs the hierarchical boundaries within firms and the frontiers among them, so too it blurs the distinction between the public and private sectors.

This does not suggest that there has been or will be a night-to-day transformation. Because firms will want to cluster some of their key activities does not mean that all will be clustered. It may often be more advantageous to purchase subassemblies or even services from an established supplier than to invest in creating a local supplier. But the expectation is that the established subcontractor owes its success in part to its location in a prospering regional economy specialized in its business. Thus regionalization of production can go hand-in-hand with internationalization in the sense that firms reinforce their own core locales by linking them to similarly organized production systems elsewhere.

To sidestep several debates that are, I think, out of place here, consider two general qualifications regarding the model of the flexible, high-wage economy as a whole. First, the permanent-innovation economy is not necessarily an economy of small firms, although it is, compared to the world of mass production, an economy of small production units or establishments. The model supposes that economies of scale—the bigger the plant, the cheaper the product—are less and less important. Otherwise the specialized product would be prohibitively more expensive than the standard ware. Hence the size of establishments should be (and according to much evidence is) constant or falling, always with respect to the size distribution of plants in particular industries in the period of mass production.[6] But firms can also grow through exploiting economies of scope: the more diverse the current production, the lower the incremental cost of a new product. By providing financial, marketing, or research and development services to establishments in different but related lines of work, a corporation can expand by enabling its constituent parts to specialize and diversify. There is, however, no reason to think that these services must be provided by a corporation with a controlling interest in the operating units, as opposed to a bank, a trading company, or a federation of the (independently owned) operating units themselves. Even if it is a corporation which does the coordinating, furthermore, the control it exercises will be radically different from the centralized, bureaucratic control typically exercised by the headquarters of an American corporation in the past. Economies of scale are achieved through specialization of resources: ever more dedicated or specialized machines, ever more narrowly (semi) skilled workers, and ever more centralized structures. Economies of scope are achieved by "generalizing" resources or turning them to more and more diverse uses. This means more and more flexible equipment, more skilled and autonomous workers, and more supple organizations. As a glance at the management literature will reveal, managers themselves are extremely worried that the decentralized organizations they are building will fly fissiparously apart.[7] People in the labor movement are obviously and rightly concerned with the distribution of power in firms. But these days the size of a corporation is a less and less informative indicator of how authority is distributed within it.

The second qualification has been anticipated by the repeated observation that the shift to a flexible economy is not an all-or-nothing proposition. The permanently innovative, flexibly specialized, high-wage, high-skill economy is a limiting case. Some markets or parts of markets remain stable; some technologies, however plastic by historical standards, are more refractory than others. It is risky to try to shift from mass production to permanent innovation in a single leap, partly because it is unclear what the new model corporation really is (the point made just above), partly because building it, whatever it is, requires resources such as skilled labor which cannot be conjured into existence where they do not exist, and partly because firms cannot be sure that the unstable environment to which they are adjusting will not unexpectedly stabilize in a way that is more hospitable to a variant of mass-production techniques. For all these reasons, firms hedge their bets on rationalization, preferring hybrid strategies that combine elements of mass and flexible production in a fashion that allows the firms to move in the direction of whichever pole is more attractive. In an unstable world, all irreversible decisions are dangerous traps, including the decision to abandon the ability to respond efficiently to stability. The consequence of these hedging strategies is that almost every firm and every group of firms deviates from the limiting case of permanent innovation. But for present purposes, that is less consequential than the fact that they deviate as well from the traditional models of firm organization upon which the modern labor movement in both Western Europe and North America is premised. Corporate reorganization has a long way to go before the typical firm resembles the ideal type sketched here. But it has already demonstrated its competitive virtues with such clarity that it is necessary to rethink how the labor movement can encourage such benefit from these changes.

Some of the Things We Don't Know About How the Labor Movement Can Encourage and Benefit from Corporate Reorganization

Inconclusive as the model of the fully flexible corporation is, it is still more substantial than our knowledge of how such firms are or can be created in a particular economy, or of how labor can help create them and benefit from its efforts. There is little in the current debate on the future of the labor movement to challenge this assertion directly; but there is a great deal which presumes knowledge of these matters that I do not think is in hand. The purpose of this section, therefore, is to look critically at the two major and related arguments that connect the idea of labor's participation in economic restructuring to the reorganization of the labor movement. Being clear(er) about what we don't know strikes me at the least as a good way to avoid a comforting, semiconscious reliance on familiar models and tropes in rethinking the tasks and structure of the labor movement. At the most, a clear view of the inappropriateness of new variants of old models to current conditions focuses attention more precisely on what is truly novel in the current situation. For what it is worth, I have at one time or another argued both of the positions I criticize, and I am therefore at least as discomfited as anyone else by the criticism.

The first explanation of why some national economies, and collaterally some national labor movements, move more quickly and successfully in the direction of permanent innovation is simply that even as they industrialized, some economies never went very far down the path of mass production.[8] Smaller, more differentiated markets and craft traditions of production reinforced each other so that, despite appearances to the contrary, the key elements of a flexible economy—skilled labor, flexible equipment, and the managerial know-how to constantly recombine them—were constantly reproduced. Conversely, these same traditions put barriers in the way of a forced-draft extension of mass-production models. When the new conditions of competition put a premium on flexibility, the West German, Austrian, Italian, Japanese, and Swedish economies did what came naturally: because the strategy of permanent innovation had many affinities with past practice whereas the sweating model looked like a radical break with tradition, they "chose" the former as the safer proposition. Where, as in the United States and Great Britain, less of the craft tradition had survived, the balance of potential costs and benefits was reversed, and the firms moved the other way, at least initially. The lesson for labor in this view is simply to revive and adjust to current conditions in craft traditions of organization wherever they have not survived and adjusted automatically.

As a description of what makes for competitive success and failure, this type of account is unbeatable. But as an explanation, it is circular to the point of vacuity. Suppose we call all the rules and routines that regulate the distribution of authority in production economic institutions. Then this view explains the existence in a particular economy of institutions favoring flexibility as the result of the historical presence in that society of institutions encouraging flexibility (or at least encouraging the creation of institutions that encourage flexibility). If you think you can explain the sedative effects of opiates by noting their formative powers, you will find this kind of account satisfying; otherwise not.

To see the practical limits of this kind of tautologous formulation, it is only necessary to look a little more closely at the suggestion to revive craft principles in the organization of labor. Surely the craft idea of defining union jurisdiction according to the materials worked in each task—pipes to the pipe-fitters, bricks to the bricklayers—is an invitation to permanent jurisdictional disputes in an age when the constant introduction of new materials makes it hazardous to guess what will be made of what. But the craft tradition of hiring halls, labor exchanges, and chambers of labor, where unions take substantial responsibility for training and allocating skilled labor, can arguably be seen as an intimation or (exceptionally, as in the case of Sweden) even a precursor of the kind of labor market institutions appropriate to a flexible economy. If firms increasingly subcontract design and production of key subassemblies, why can't labor become a systems supplier of skilled labor? If the tendency is toward more collaborative relations between workers and managers within firms and between firms and their subcontractors, why is collaboration between the firm and the union as organizer of the local labor market less probable?

The point here is that to elaborate the case against "craft" jurisdiction over jobs and for "craft" organization of the labor market is to specify which of the structuring principles of the craft economy might efficiently structure the emergent flexible system and why. To do *that*, however, is to begin to replace the flexibility-begets-flexibility argument with a model or proto-model of a flexible economy that shows just how specific institutions prove to be adapted to the current environment.

This is just what the second argument promises to do. I will call this the model of resurgent social democracy, because many of the institutional features it identifies as favoring the transition to a flexible economy and reinforcing the labor movement through that transition are characteristic of the Northern European social democracies, particularly those in countries such as Germany, Austria, and Sweden. Indeed, the model is appealing in no small measure because it suggests that institutions indigenous not just to the West but to the left in the West could unexpectedly prove a politically palatable alternative to wholesale initiation of Japanese practices, which otherwise seems the humiliating price required to maintain economic competitiveness.

Like the more general institutional view, the model of resurgent social democracy identifies costs and benefits which move firms' choices away from sweating in the direction of the permanent-innovation strategy.[9] The emphasis is on the costs imposed and benefits provided by the system of industrial relations broadly understood. The most important cost regards layoffs: a combination of legal and political constraints obliges firms to negotiate expensive severance arrangements whenever they seek to reduce the workforce. This makes management think twice and twice again before rationalizing, relocating, and subcontracting production work as prescribed in the sweating model. Labor, the familiar argument goes, is increasingly viewed as a fixed cost; and firms must consider carefully how to make efficient use of an asset of which they cannot dispose.

Here is where four key benefits of social democratic industrial relations come in. First, there is a system of plant-level dispute resolution based on considerations of equity and substance rather than precedent and procedure. Outcomes, in theory, are supposed to secure the firm's competitiveness while respecting the interests of employees, not to determine which employees are entitled to what given the language of the collective bargaining agreement and the common law of the plant. It would be easy to overstate the difference: workers in the social democratic systems have plenty of legal and customary rights, and bargaining in, say, the Anglo-American system is influenced by complex and encompassing ideas of equity.

But in the Anglo-American system, at least as it existed in the early 1980s, the definition of rights was tied to the definition of jobs and seniority in ways that made reorganization at work a constant threat to established patterns of entitlement.[10] To accept changes in the definition and scope of one's job was to accept greater vulnerability to managerial discretion. In the social democratic system, standards are established to govern treatment of whole classes of employees—those above a certain age, the skilled, those with families, those requiring training—and so long as there are good prospects of satisfying these standards by any combination of, say, job transfers, compensatory training, and indemnifications, individuals do not have rights to particular places in the production system. Hence reorganization is not held hostage to adjudication of such rights.

The remaining features of the social democratic system as portrayed in this argument regulate relations between labor and capital outside the plant. The first and in many ways most important is simply labor's right to participate in the definition of administration of training programs.[11] As demand for skill increases, labor's place in the institutional order becomes more central, the argument goes, because labor already occupies a central place in the training system; and this is true regardless of whether unions come to manage local labor markets on the hiring hall model or in some other, unspecified way.

The second and third supra-plant features of the social democratic system are industrywide collective bargaining and the elaboration of framework labor regulations. Industrywide collective bargaining obviously establishes minimum wages and working conditions and guarantees that flexibility at the plant and company level does not lead to company unionism in which workers and managers in each production unit try to advance their own (collective) interest, regardless of its consequence for others in a similar situation. It also allows for experimentation, industry-by-industry, with new ways of collectively establishing a fair distribution of the burdens of reorganization and adjusting the standards of equity applied at plant level to the new forms of work organization resulting from rationalization. Framework legislation, finally, coordinates public provision of training and social insurance with needs of firms and industries; it also protects and extends labor's right to gain, through some form of participation in managerial decisionmaking, the kind of information and veto powers necessary to make substantive regulation of industrial reorganization workable. Without the knowledge to judge what can reasonably be expected of a firm in a particular situation, and without the power to effectively obstruct solutions that violate its sense of equity, labor would have to seek protection through imposition of a much finer mesh of plant-level rules.

The net effect of the social democratic model is to make a choice of the sweating strategy of prohibiting expenses and the strategy of permanent innovation affordable and remunerative, if not painless. Moreover, the more rapidly the new strategy spreads, the better for the unions. The demand for skill draws unions more and more into the process of reorganization itself, reinforcing their position with respect to the firms at the same time it refurbishes their appeal to their members. Indeed, if the process goes far enough, the unions will eventually come to exercise *de facto* rights of determination that they have not been able to obtain directly through legislation. Hence the resurgence of social democracy, and particularly social democratic industrial relations, which seemed threatened by the breakdown in the new world economy of tripartite or neocorporatist systems of wage bargaining that helped these countries reduce both inflation and unemployment in the 1970s and early 1980s. The lesson for economies that do not already have social democratic industrial relations systems as depicted in this model is clearly to build them, starting with the creation of training systems in which labor plays a central part.

This view certainly has more bite than the generic institutional explanation. The problem with it is not, I think, that it is vacuous but that, taken at face value, it is wrong. First, a strong labor movement in the sense of resurgent social democracy is neither a necessary nor a sufficient condition to encourage restructuring along the lines of the permanent-innovation strategy. Moreover, there is good evidence that trade unions and the labor movement more generally are unexpectedly being weakened by the very changes that they are directly and indirectly encouraging, including the changes that favor use of more highly skilled labor.

Developments in countries as diverse as Switzerland, Japan, and France show that a social democratic labor movement is not a necessary condition for flexible adjustments. All these countries have adopted flexible adjustment strategies, although the shift in this direction is more recent and less comprehensive in France. Swiss national unions are nonentities by almost any imaginable standard; there is debate about whether Japanese unions are company unions in the sense defined a moment ago or rather in the perjorative U.S. sense of yellow-dog organizations which betray their members to do the bidding of their masters in management. But there is no doubt that they are company unions in one sense or another. In France, less than 9 percent of the workforce is organized in unions. The question publicly posed for debate in that country is whether there can be unions without members.[12]

It is, to be sure, possible to explain how firms in each of the countries were moved, at least partly because of the particularities of their relation to labor, to decide in favor of the flexible strategy. Japanese firms have practices of granting long-term job security to their core workforce dating back to the 1920s. French unions have by law the right to participate in the decisionmaking of a great number of public entities with responsibility for monitoring and shaping the labor market. Swiss firms have long traditions of flexible production, and correspondingly developed complex formal and informal systems of dispute resolution consistent with that strategy.[13] But the more complex and particular each of these explanations becomes, the closer it gets to the generic institutional argument in which flexibility begets flexibility. If you nodded in approval as that argument was dismissed a moment ago, you cannot use it as a makeweight to save the resurgent democratic model. The strength of that model is its parsimony; and elaborating it in response to counterexamples only weakens its foundation.

The same difficulties arise in the defense of the claim that the social democratic model of industrial relations is a sufficient condition for extension of the flexible economy. The argument suggests that the stronger the unions in the social democratic sense, the more likely that firms will perceive the costs of the sweating strategy as prohibitively high and the costs of flexible reorganization as attractively low.[14] But all change, even change ultimately for the better for almost everyone, imposes short-term costs. Suppose the unions become so strong that they can successfully not only oppose a switch to sweating, but also pursue a variant of the high-skill strategy in which the costs of transition are fairly shared. The result, as illustrated in the bankruptcy of the Austrian state-owned steel and metalworking firms that are the traditional fortress of the country's trade unions, is first stalemate, then catastrophe.[15] However much one is inclined to favor the expansion of union influence, this is, at best, too much of a good thing.

Here too, of course, it is possible to patch the argument by specifying that it holds only within a particular range: when labor has sufficient power to block sweating but not enough to be tempted to believe it is invulnerable to changes in the environment, and is able to defend the status quo indefinitely. But insofar as the specification looks forward to the outcomes it aims to include and exclude, it again arouses suspicion of circularity. Just as troubling, the notion that more trade union power is not necessarily better undercuts the (to me) politically attractive suggestion that the model of resurgent social democracy offers an alternative to democratization of the workplace through legislation. Surely employers will tend to suspect that there is a point at which an increase in union influence on decisionmaking begins to impede flexibility rather than encourage it. If advocates of the model of resurgent social democracy concede that such a point exists without being able to locate it precisely, managers will voice those suspicions sooner rather than later.

Labor, indeed, may not merely reap fewer benefits from restructuring than the model suggests. It may find its organizational integrity undermined by the very process of economic reorganization it encourages and from which members benefit as individuals. Whether this happens or not depends on the influence of reorganization on background conditions that the model, in its appealingly parsimonious forms, ignores.

Take as an example the organizational consequences for German unions of increasing demand for skill and the resulting extension of training programs.[16] Traditionally, youths went to work full time upon completion of their apprenticeships and were assimilated into the overlapping worlds of the shop floor and the union in the years that followed. Many would subsequently continue their educations by attending classes. But even when they left the shop floor to become technicians or engineers, often with highly responsible jobs, they remained attached to the values which had formed them, and tolerant of if not loyal to the unions. In any case they defined themselves as distinct from university-trained managers, for whom the idea of a career was associated with the idea of progression up a formal hierarchy rather than with growing technical prowess.

Today this pattern and the distinctions on which it is based are disintegrating. Young people spend a shorter and shorter time on the shop floor between completing their apprenticeships and continuing their educations. For the most ambitious and talented, more and more of the time spent on the shop floor at any stage in their careers is spent in special project groups where teams of engineers, managers, technicians, and skilled workers perfect new products or install new production systems. The union is simply not a constitutive element of the training system on the shop floor as these new cohorts of skilled workers experience it. They are, to all appearances, not antiunion, but quite indifferent to its existence. Because the most active trade unionists and the bulk of union officials have, in Germany as elsewhere, been recruited from among the skilled workers, this indifference threatens the organization's ability to renew itself, and is clearly perceived by union leaders as doing so.

A second German example concerns the effects of subcontracting and the blurring of the boundaries among corporations more generally. As subcontractors take more and more responsibility for design and production work once done in-house, the plant or firm-level institutions that defend employee interests are less and less able to even monitor, let alone control, developments. The problems are aggravated when, as is frequently the case, the work is subcontracted to firms in industries other than the client's, and hence organized by different unions: unionized seamstresses upholstering seats in an automobile firm are members of the metalworkers union in Germany, but members of the textile and garment workers union if employed by a seat-making firm supplying the auto plant just-in-time from an adjacent facility. The engineers and skilled workers designing the microprocessor used in an advanced fuel-injection system are likely to be working for an electronics firm that is not organized by any union at all. Given that the social democratic model of substantive dispute resolution presumes the possibility of making a comprehensive assessment of the costs and benefits of various possible compromises, the fragmentation of control over the process of restructuring endangers the capacity to formulate and assess just the kinds of comprehensive bargains upon which the success of the substantive system depends.

A third example concerns the effects of changes in the boundaries and operation of the public sector. The reorganization of the economy on flexible lines changes the division of labor between the public and private sectors. The earlier discussion of the regionalization of production and the increased public provision of services to industry indicated one aspect of this change. Another regards the growing barrier against the entry of the unskilled into the flexible economy. So long as much of the skill needed for work could be learned on the job, the state could provide unemployment insurance and other forms of social assistance independent of systematic job training and placement. The state assured citizens of a subsistence income, and the economy eventually provided jobs which allowed those who wanted to work their way into economic and social security the chance to do so. The more necessary it is to possess substantial generic skills to get *any* job, however, the more important it becomes to integrate the provision of social services and training into a package customized according to the needs of particular clients or client groups.

But this recombination and customization of services often requires a profound reorganization of social welfare bureaucracies, including decentralization of authority to the local level and devolution of the responsibility for providing many services to community or other non-profit groups with the kind of local knowledge on which the effectiveness of the program depends. These pressures for reorganizing the bureaucracy and opening it to the outside world are further increased by the ambition—often inspired by the experience and model of the large firms and their reconstitution—to break monopolies in the provision of services ranging from medical care to garbage collection both as a spur to efficiency and as a protection against administrative arrogance.[17]

The cumulative effect is that the fluidity of production relations, as indicated particularly by an increase in subcontracting, is becoming as typical of the public sector as it is of private industry. And as in private industry, the consequence for unions is an increase in jurisdictional disputes whose occurrence is a sign of an increasingly poor fit between the organizational boundaries of the labor movement and the boundaries of the relevant units of economic and social welfare activity. Sweden is the most clamorous example of disruption which can result when public- and private-sector unions fight each other over the right to represent employees or classes of work which have passed in one form or another from public to private control. In Sweden, as elsewhere, these conflicts resonate with and thus amplify the jurisdictional disputes provoked by reorganization within the private sector.[18]

The aim in criticizing the model of resurgent social democracy is no more to suggest that labor's role in organizing the training system of shaping corporate decisions is irrelevant to its future than criticism of the generic institutional model is meant to demonstrate that economic adjustment is not influenced by institutional patterns.

Historical barriers to the extension of mass production and historical dispositions for flexible economic organization, including especially those associated with the social democratic system of industrial relations, help stack the deck against pursuit of the sweating strategy and for a program of permanent innovation. The difficulty with both the general and the particular institutional arguments is that in identifying important continuities between the emergent flexible economy and its antecedents, the former is assimilated into the latter in a way that obscures vital differences between them: differences, indeed, which affect the role in the new economy of just those institutions such as training that appeared to warrant the assimilation of new to old in the first place.

In the next two sections, I reverse the procedure. Rather than searching for even a crude blueprint for the future in the past, I look only for those old building materials that can be used to erect the new system. Instead of treating the flexible economy as a distinctive elaboration of certain historical traditions in new circumstances, I try to outline a plan of construction by reflection on the novelty of the current situation as it has emerged in the preceding discussion.

The Localization of the Labor Market

Firms, we saw, are opening themselves to one another (through the transformation and extension of subcontracting relations) and to the society in which they are more and more embedded (through increasing reliance on public or at least collective provision of training and other services as well as new forms of social insurance). This double opening is leading, I argued earlier, to the regionalization of production: at the limit the fundamental unit of production is not the firm, but an ensemble of firms and public or community institutions in a particular locale.

Regionalization has two closely related effects on the organization of labor markets and hence on the boundary conditions that any labor movement operating in such markets would need to respect. First, the blurring of boundaries among firms that follows from the reintegration of conception and execution means that even as the demand for skill increases, individual jobs become less and less secure. When even the largest firms expect to turn to system suppliers to provide crucial expertise, but cannot predict when and for what sort of know-how they will do so, who at what level of the firm can be sure of his or her job? Where is the stable core of the economy? When high-flying employees can expect to be rotated from autonomous division to autonomous division or project group to project group to develop a sense of loyalty to the corporation as a whole, but the corporation cannot define itself as a unified entity except by pointing to the common experience of the high flyers, what sort of loyalty will the latter develop? Under these circumstances, to pursue a career does not mean to progress rung by rung up the bureaucratic ladder as envisaged in the concept of the closed labor markets central to the social democratic system of industrial relations: many rungs are gone and the very structure on which the ladder rests may disappear. Nor does it mean, as in craft labor markets, to master a well-defined body of knowledge by moving from firm to firm in a predictable pattern: the definition of what knowledge is relevant is constantly changing. Rather it means to assess constantly which of all the current or potentially acquired skills ought to be developed in the light of changing market conditions and one's unfolding self-conception.

Second, the blurring of the boundary between the firm and society is paralleled for the individual in the blurring of the boundary between work and other crucial spheres of experience. The devolution of authority within organizations and the growing need for skill and teamwork require employees even in large corporations to exercise on the job the kind of autonomy and responsibility for the use of resources that in capitalist democracies have typically been regarded as the prerogative of groups such as homeowners or the self-employed: those whose control over some form of capital entitled them to a corresponding kind of economic sovereignty. "Private" or even "family" values such as self-reliance in complex situations are highly valued, perhaps even indispensable at work. Conversely, however, the less secure jobs become and the less meaningful the traditional ideas of a career, the more employees must rely on extra-firm associations established through the family, professional groups, churches, political parties, hobby groups, or social movements to learn what kinds of jobs are imperiled, what kinds expanding, and where to acquire the skills necessary to compete for them. By definition, an information network that followed the contours of the firm would be of no help in these regards precisely because the information of value concerns possibilities beyond the corporate boundaries—the disintegration of which creates the insecurity in the first place. The more the social and the economic become fused through regionalization, the more the home invades the workplace and *vice versa*. Changes in gender relations, related but not reducible to changes in the organization of work, further mute the distinction between the two by formalizing the division of labor in the household (if only by making it a matter for family discussion), and making family needs as the job prospects of each partner in the more and more numerous two-earner households a constraint on job choices.[19]

Social democratic unions are coming to grief because they are not adjusting to these effects of reorganization, although they are in many ways the best positioned of all contemporary labor movements to make such adjustments. The unions (perhaps with the exception of those in Sweden) are losing their formative influence on the skilled workers because they are extraneous to the complex systems of post-apprenticeship training that define new kinds of careers and loyalties. Because their basic units of organization are the plant, the firm, and the branch, unions cannot regulate the increasing movement of work and workers across these boundaries. Because they presume a stable division of labor between the public and private sectors, and treat the public sector as if it were a firm in the traditional sense, unions are bewildered by efforts to redistribute responsibility between the state and civil society, efforts which often entail reorganization of the state itself.

Towards a New Model Union

To do better these unions will, in a sense, have to follow the lead of the firms: push responsibility for decisionmaking down to the local, operative level, and open the local unions and plant-level institutions in each area to one another and to the whole range of economically relevant local actors from municipal authorities to environmental and social movements, and even political parties with whom they may have little or only hostile contact.[20] By inserting themselves into the regional economy at the points where the firms connect with one another and where they as a group join the local society, the unions can make themselves indispensable to management as systems suppliers of skilled labor and indispensable to their members as guides and advisors in their passages from job to job and home to work and back. Continuing education for the skilled, extensive training for the semiskilled, extensive job counseling that bundles general social services and training of both sorts in packages individuals and families can use are the first, indispensable steps to this end. If the social democratic unions can learn to do that much locally, it will be almost child's play to redefine the advisory and tutelary role of the national union.

Unions in the United States seem to have an incomparable harder row to hoe.[21] Social democratic unions are victimized by the success of a broad movement towards flexible reorganization that they encourage. In the United States, the respective costs and benefits of the two adjustment strategies are often indeterminate, and firms frequently oscillate between them. But whichever course firms choose, and perhaps most directly by their wavering, they do the unions harm.[22] If the unions oppose cost-cutting strategies they are defending their members' privileges; if they condone them, they are protecting their organizations at the members' expense. If they block attempts to increase flexibility, they are dinosaurs, unable to understand the motivations of the modern workforce and the exigencies of competition in world markets; but if they cooperate with strategies aimed at increasing productive flexibility, they make themselves and their members hostage to management's half-hearted and vacillating dedication to this course of action. Even the fear of a reversion to cost-cutting strategies— provoked perhaps by high-level corporate struggles far beyond the influence of plant-level or division management—is enough to reveal that labor's gradual abandonment of its traditional forms of self-defense make it vulnerable to incalculable risks. U.S. unions would, I suspect, love to have the problems of their social democratic counterparts; and that is perhaps one of the reasons they tend to discount the gravity of those difficulties if they take notice of them at all.

But it is easy to overlook the vulnerabilities of the strong and the strength of the vulnerability. The social democratic unions' position in the largest plants, the continuing allegiance of the middle-aged workforce, and the unions' political influence make it easy for them to downplay the dangers of delayed adjustment, hard for the national center to see why it should cede power to the local periphery, and harder still for any one powerful union to see why it should abandon its jurisdictional claims to the benefits of a rival. Conversely, the confusing fluidity of the American corporations and the debility of American labor mean that local unions may enjoy more freedom than their more closely regulated social democratic counterparts to establish themselves as an indispensable component of an emergent regional economy should the occasion present itself for them to do so.

Such possibilities are, I think, much less remote than a simple survey of the disorganized and dispirited state of national—or, as their Canadian affiliations entitle them to say—international unions in the United States would suggest. At the plant level, many unions have become engaged during the last decade in various forms of worker participation or employee involvement. In the many successful but scattered programs of this type, blue- and white-collar workers take an active role in assessing the competitiveness of the plant and determining ways to improve it.[23] To do this they and the unions who represent them must have access to virtually all the information that management considers in making its decisions. The result in the best cases is a system of substantive dispute resolution and *de facto* labor-management codetermination which approximates the social democratic systems. But whereas the latter presumes rigid plant boundaries, many of the emergent plant-level systems in the United States grow out of cooperative efforts by managers and employees to establish which products the operating unit can, after the requisite reorganization, profitably make, and which must be abandoned to other makers. Thus cooperation in this setting is from the first directed toward limiting the risks of an organizational vulnerability which, given the impossibility of fixing firm boundaries with any reliability, is broadly seen as a constituent fact of corporate life. For the moment, these open-ended success stories remain isolated: plants in the same corporation or region can have wildly different experiences in this regard, depending on the accidents of personality and timing; and national unions are either ignorant of local successes or too threatened by the popularity of the leaders they create to even debate their significance. But if one of the building blocks of a new labor movement is a local union rooted in the firm's decisionmaking yet not barricaded behind its formal boundaries, construction materials of this kind are being produced in the United States.

Similar considerations apply to training programs and the creation of subcontracting networks, although unions have been reticent to participate in either of these foundational elements of the new regional economies. Here too local initiatives are indispensable. The pattern in training is for a group of firms, varying in size according to the nature of the local economy, to join with a community college or vocational training center to create a new kind of apprenticeship which blends traditional forms of vocational education with the relevant components of an undergraduate-level technical curriculum.[24] New degree programs transform traditional machinery and other trades into paraprofessions. Often the project is initially funded with the help of state or federal monies. In this case too the fluidity of the situation is a potential advantage. If apprenticeship were recreated in the United States now, and if the unions participated in its formation, it could be done in a way that gives labor a central place in a system of life-long training—a system that does not draw the line between initiation into a trade and continuing education that vexes much of the social democratic labor movement. But for the moment, U.S. unions are so absorbed with their day-to-day problems and the defense of the interests of their current members that they are less likely to embrace these efforts to regenerate skill than to ignore or even to oppose them in favor of programs to *re*train older, displaced workers.

The growing efforts to create subcontracting networks of diverse kinds also involve consortia of large and small firms, public—typically state—agencies, and educational institutions. Sometimes the initiative comes from large corporations, sometimes from trade associations, sometimes from *ad hoc* groups of small firms, sometimes from the public sector. Again the results are mixed. There are plenty of reliable successes strewn among the tales of disaster. But win or lose, the effects seldom succeed in overcoming the unions' preoccupation with other matters or fear that they lack the competence to participate knowledgeably in decisions for which they may later be held accountable. Yet again it is clear that if the unions could vanquish their reticence, they could be rebuilding themselves by building a structure indispensable to the local economy—and difficult to construct with the organizational tools of social democracy.

If your imagination stretches easily to comprehend these separate possibilities, then it will take only a slight additional effort to comprehend the possibility of a strategy that makes realization of each easier by connecting it to the others. Take the common case of a local union fighting for the innovation strategy in alliance with one faction of plant management against the rear-guard, cost-cutting methods of a second. Suppose next that the union and its allies participate in a training consortium that, among other things, undertakes to remedy the spot skill shortages that clouded the prospects of the permanent-innovation strategy and provided a convenient argument to oppose it. Suppose further that the union and its allies in management simultaneously participated in a consortium of large and small firms dedicated to improving subcontracting relations, and thus removing yet another potential obstacle to the flexible alternative. Suppose, finally, that a state government provides funds and advice to help the local union pursue all these tasks at once, and—welcome to America—you will have imagined just the program which the State of Michigan and a local of the United Automobile Workers in the auto parts sector pursued until the governor who supported the plan was unexpectedly defeated for reasons unrelated to his economic initiatives.[25] Had this plan succeeded, or if any of the many, less formal ones that survive it prospers, one result would be to create local constituencies (other firms, educational institutions, public officials) who will take the union's side in its struggle against the cost-cutting strategy. If successes multiply, a second result would force unions to reverse the firms' strategy of using labor's concessions at one plant as justification for demands for give-backs at another. Instead, unions favoring the permanent-innovation strategy could begin whip-sawing recalcitrant management, using the examples of managers elsewhere who participated to their benefit in cooperative strategies as a means of convincing their recalcitrant local interlocutors to do the same.

Does It Matter Whether
There Are New Model Unions?
Whether There Are Unions At All?

To us, the us addressed at the beginning of this essay, the answer to both these questions is self-evidently yes. People who are not much interested in labor these days are so sure that unions have no future that they seldom can be troubled to read essays alleging they might; those who believe unions do have a future or should are so desperate for some conformation of their hopes that they take the mere fact that essays appear on the topic as a sign that labor is more vigorous than it appears. But this essay about the future of the unions had indirectly raised the question whether we—and I am still talking about us— should care about the fate of the new model union, and indeed whether that organization is reasonably regarded as a union at all.

The answer to the first question is clearly connected to the unions' role in economic adjustment. If (almost) everyone should reasonably prefer the innovation strategy to the sweating strategy in the long run, and strong unions in the social democratic or new model sense encourage diffusion of the innovation strategy, then (almost) everyone should support either social democratic or new model unions.

But in the light of the foregoing discussion it is hard to extract much of a defense of new model unions from this kind of shaky syllogism. First, the argument supposes that unions play a critical role in determining the choice between strategies as though most of what managers did was decided by what unions did or how industrial relations are organized. Those things count—a lot. But we saw, first, that a social democratic industrial relations system is neither a necessary nor a sufficient condition for the choice of the innovation strategy, and, second, that social democratic unions do not automatically become new model unions. On the contrary, they are more likely to be victims of the reorganization they encourage.

The upshot is that the preceding discussion provides reasons for supporting several types of unionism if you care strongly about the outcome of economic adjustment, but no reasons for supporting unions more than, say, programs to encourage training or build subcontracting networks. Presumably more of all these things is better than less, and doing them concurrently or at least in a coordinated way is better than doing them disjointedly. But the model of resurgent social democracy is too ramshackle a theory of economic adjustment to suggest how scarce resources should be allocated even among this limited group of tasks.

The one strong conclusion which discussion of the model of resurgent social democracy *does* allow is, paradoxically, that whatever robust labor organizations emerge from and take root in the process of economic reorganization will not be trade unions in any traditional sense. Trade unions in the sense of social democracy or of American industrial unionism are concerned with the interests of employees at work, where work typically means a long-term association with a par-

ticular occupation in a single firm. But if the foregoing analysis of the
effects of reorganization is correct, the new model labor organizations
will have to be concerned with addressing problems that cross the
boundaries among firms and between work and other vital life activities. A labor organization that tries to distinguish its members' interests
at work from their general interests in well-being could not, in this
view, effectively represent their interests at all.[26]

But why call an organization that represents some aspects of members' general interests in well-being a trade union, or even a labor organization? I can think of little reason especially if that organization
operates in association with social service agencies, schools, churches,
and political parties. I say little reason rather than none at all because I
imagine this organization might play a distinctive role in wage determination. But the more wages are set through individual negotiations
between employees and firms on the one hand and more and more
encompassing minimum wage or minimum social income legislation
on the other, the less distinguishing a mark this will be.[27]

No, the more natural but troubling way to think about organizations
that represent their members' general interests in well-being is to
regard them as engaged in politics. The characterization is natural
because to defend its members' general interests in well-being an organization must articulate and advance a vision of life, including ideals
of justice, views about the proper distribution of control over economic
activity, and so on. If an organization that does these things is not a
political organization, what other kind of reorganization might it be?
But because the same kinds of everyday definitions that make it reasonable to say that the new model union is not a union but a political
organization obstruct efforts to say what kind of political organization
it might be. Plainly unions are not parties in any traditional sense,
because parties, we just saw, traditionally leave concerns about work to
unions. More precisely, concern with work exhausts itself in concern
for "the economy," which typically means macroeconomic decisionmaking, except insofar as such decisionmaking is in the hands of virtually self-governing institutions (as is often the case with, for example,
central banks). Nor are these new model political organizations easily
assimilated to social movements. Either these movements are concerned with the situation of particular groups, in which case they aim
to regulate workplace conditions only insofar as those conditions

threaten their constituents' interests: for example, feminist groups fight sexism on the job and seniors' associations fight ageism. Or the social movements are concerned with what they regard as public interests such as a healthy environment or safe consumer products. In that case they aim to regulate production insofar as it is necessary to eliminate threats to these public interests: for example, by legislating reductions in pollution or creating incentives to or improving the safety of products by making firms strictly liable for harm caused by their wares. Thus social movements are not trying to regulate the relation between the economy and other spheres of life in general.[28] On the contrary, it would be more accurate to say that the proliferation of these movements is a response to the failure of the existing division of labor between parties and unions to define a form of regulation adapted to current circumstances; and that this response presumably makes the task of finding a general solution harder by creating more and more precise divisions among groups and interests that will eventually need to be reconciled both on and off the job through complex compromises.

New model political organizations cannot, therefore, be social movements. If they are doing their jobs, they will be reducing the need for social movements, or rather the need for social movements to do some of the things they currently do in the way they do them. Certainly this will require collaboration between the new model entities and the social movements; but this does not suggest that one will absorb or come to approximate the other, any more than cooperation with political parties suggests analogous outcomes.

Hence the disturbing provisioned conclusion: there is nothing in the logic of the current reorganization that warrants the assumption that we will have trade unions in the future. And if we have them they will be filling a political function that we can specify only in the sketchiest outline. But then it may well be that reflection on the void that would exist if these almost indefinable political entities did not take the place of trade unions is the beginning of another and more robust kind of argument for creating them.

NOTES

This essay builds on a program of research and writing on corporate reorganization and its implications for trade unionism that I am conducting with Horst Kern of the University of Göttingen. See our "Trade Unions and Decentralized Production: A Sketch of Strategic Problems in the West German Labor Movement." *Politics and Society* 19, no. 4 (1991), 373-402, for a detailed discussion of the German case. Neither Kern, nor my colleague Michael J. Piore, with whom I also continually discuss the issues raised here, are responsible for my excesses.

1. For arguments along this line, see Colin Crouch, "The Future Prospects for Trade Unions in Western Europe." *Political Quarterly* 1 (1986): 5-8; Walter Müller-Jentsch, "Industrial Relations Theory and Trade Union Strategy." *International Journal of Comparative Law and Industrial Relations* 4, 3 (1988): 177-190; and Jelle Visser, "In Search of Inclusive Unionism?" *Bulletin of Comparative Labor Relations* 18 (Special Issue 1990): 39-67.

2. For more details, see Michael J. Piore and Charles F. Sabel. *The Second Industrial Divide: Possibilities for Prosperity.* New York: Basic Books, 1984.

3. Horst Kern and Michael Schumann. *Das Ende der Arbeitsteilung?: Rationalisierung in der industriellen Produktion: Bestandsaufnahme, Trendbestimmung.* Munich: Beck, 1984, started this debate. The view does not go unchallenged. See Richard Hyman, "Flexible Specialization: Miracle or Myth?" In *New Technology and Industrial Relations,* eds. Richard Hyman and Wolfgang Streeck. Oxford: Basil Blackwell, 1988; and the discussion in Stephen Wood, "The Transformation of Work?" In *The Transformation of Work?,* London: Unwin Hyman, 1989.

4. See, for instance, Walter W. Powell, "Hybrid Organizational Arrangements: New Form or Transitional Developments." *California Management Review* (Fall 1987).

5. For more details, see Charles F. Sabel, "Flexible Specialization and the Re-emergence of Regional Economies." In *Reversing Industrial Decline? Industrial Structure and Policy in Britain and Her Competitors,* eds. Paul Hirst and Jonathan Zeitlin. Oxford: Berg, 1989, pp. 17-70.

6. Rainer Bartel, "Organisationsgrößenvor- und nachteile: Eine strukturierte Auswertung theoretischer und empirischer Literatur." *Jahrbuch für Sozialwissenschaft: Zeitschrift für Wirtschaftswissenschaften* 41, 2 (1990): 135-159 provides a good review of the literature on the size of production units.

7. See, for instance, the discussions in Christopher A. Bartlett and Sumantra Ghoshal. *Managing Across Borders: The Transnational Solution.* Boston: Harvard Business School Press, 1989; and Rosabeth Moss Kanter. *When Giants Learn to Dance.* New York: Simon and Schuster, 1989.

8. This argument can be found in different places and under many different guises. A representative sample: Charles F. Sabel. *Work and Politics: The Division of Labor in Industry.* Cambridge: Cambridge University Press, 1982, pp. 220-31; Piore and Sabel. *The Second Industrial Divide,* pp. 115-62; James P. Womack, et al. *The Machine That Changed the World: The Story of Lean Production.* New York: Rawson Associates, 1990; and Peter Katzenstein, "Industry in a Changing Germany." In *Industry and Politics in West Germany: Toward the Third Republic,* ed. Peter Katzenstein. Ithaca, NY: Cornell University Press, 1989, pp. 13 ff.

9. The criticism about to be directed at this argument applies to much of my earlier work as well. See, for example: Anton Benya and Charles F. Sabel, eds. *Gewerkschaftsstrategie in den achtziger Jahren: Die Hauptreferate auf dem 10, ÖGB-Bundeskongress.* Vienna: Verlag der Österreichischen Gewerkschaftsbundes, 1983; Wolfgang Streeck, "On the Institutional Conditions of Diversified Quality Production." In *Beyond Keynesianism: The Socio-Economics of Production and Employment,* eds. Matzner Egon and Wolfgang Streeck. London: Edward Elgar, 1991; Lowell Turner. *Democracy at Work? Labor and the Politics of New Work Organization.* Ithaca, NY: Cornell University Press, 1991; and Kathleen A. Thelen. *Continuity in Crisis: Labor*

Politics and Industrial Adjustment in West Germany 1950-1987. Ithaca, NY: Cornell University Press, 1991.

10. See, for example, Katharine Van Wezel Stone. "The Post-War Paradigm in American Labor Law." *The Yale Law Journal* 90, 7 (1981): 1509-1580, and Katharine Van Wezel Stone. "Labor Relations on the Airlines: The Railway Labor Act in the Era of Deregulation." *Stanford Law Review* 42 (1990): 1485-1547.

11. See Wolfgang Streeck, et al. *The Role of the Social Partners in Vocational Training and Further Training in the Federal Republic of Germany.* Berlin: CEDEFOP, 1987.

12. Pierre Rosanvallon. *La Question Syndicale.* Paris: Calmann Lévy, 1988, addresses this question.

13. On Japan, see Ronald Dore. *Flexible Rigidities: Industrial Policy and Structural Adjustment in the Japanese Economy, 1970-80.* Stanford: Stanford University Press, 1986; Ronald Dore, Jean Bounine-Cabalé, and Jean Tapiola. *Japan at Work: Markets, Management and Flexibility.* Paris: OECD, 1989; and Masahiko Aoki. *Information, Incentives, and Bargaining in the Japanese Economy.* Cambridge: Cambridge University Press, 1988. On France, see Jean-Daniel Reynaud. *Les Syndicats en France.* Paris: Seuil, 1975; François Sellier. *Strategie de la Lutte Sociale: 1936-1960.* Paris: Les Editions Ouvrières, 1961; and Rosanvallon. *La Question Syndicale.* For Switzerland, see Beatrice Veyssarat. "Industrial Flexibility in Switzerland: The Social and Institutional Aspects of Degeneration and Revivals." In *Worlds of Possibility: Flexibility and Mass Production in Western Industrialization,* eds. Charles F. Sabel and Jonathan Zeitlin. New York: Cambridge University Press, forthcoming; and Mario Vuilleumier. *Horlogers de l'Anarchisme. Emergence d'un Mouvement: La Federation Jurassienne.* Lausanne: Payot, 1988.

14. See, among others, Lowell Turner. *Democracy in Overalls.*

15. See Franz Summer. *Das VOEST Debakel.* Vienna: Orac, 1987, for more details.

16. For more on this, see Horst Kern and Charles F. Sabel. "Trade Unions and Decentralized Production:A Sketch of Strategic Problems in the West German Labor Movement." *Politics and Society* 19, 4 (1991).

17. See for Germany, Helmut Wollmann. "Stadtpolitik-Erosion oder Erneuerung des Sozialstaats-von unten?" *Leviathan* special number 7 (1986); and for Sweden, Benny Hjern. "The Swedish Social Welfare Municipality." In *International Review of Comparative Public Policy,* eds. Nicholas Mercuro and Douglas E. Ashford. Greenwich, CT: JAI Press, 1990.

18. Horst Kern and Charles F. Sabel, "Trade Unions and Decentralized Production." See Nils Elvander. *Den Svenska Modellen: Loneforhandlingar och Inkomstpolitik 1982-1986.* Stockholm: Allmanna Forlaget/Publica, 1988; Kristina Ahlen. "Swedish Collective Bargaining Under Pressure." *British Journal of Industrial Relations* 27, 3 (1989) for more on Sweden.

19. See, for example, Jurgen Hoffmann et al. *Jenseits der Beschlußlage: Gewerkschaft als Zukunftwerkstatt.* Cologne: Bund, 1990, 45-57.

20. Michael J. Piore. "Administrative Failure: An Hypothesis About the Decline of the U.S. Union Movement." Department of Economics, MIT, September 1989 presents an example of such new union practices. Ironically, the "radical" French unions have, in an attempt to stop the dramatic membership decline, initiated a series of nonworkplace-related services, which moves them close to the type of open, multifunctional organization abstractly referred to in the text. See Michel Noblecourt. *Les Syndicats en Questions.* Paris: Les Editions Ouvrières, 1990.

21. For general discussions of the fate of American unions, see Richard B. Freeman and James L. Medoff. *What Do Unions Do?* New York: Basic Books, 1984; Seymour M. Lipset, ed. *Unions in Transition.* San Francisco: Institute for Contemporary Studies, 1986; Charles Heckscher. *The New Unionism.* New York: Basic Books, 1988; Michael Goldfield. *The Decline of Organized Labor in the U.S.* Chicago: University of Chicago Press, 1987; and Joel Rogers. "Divide and Con-

quer: Further 'Reflections on the Distinctive Character of American Labor Laws'." *Wisconsin Law Review* (January-February 1990): 1-147.

22. See Thomas A. Kochan, Harry C. Katz, and Robert B. McKersie. *The Transformation of American Industrial Relations*. New York: Basic Books, 1986.

23. Team concepts do not go unquestioned. For representative views, see Harry C. Katz. *Shifting Gears: Changing Labor Relations in the U.S. Automobile Industry*. Cambridge: MIT Press, 1985; and Mike Parker and Jane Slaughter. *Choosing Sides: Unions and the Team Concept*. Boston: South End Press, 1988.

24. For a case study, see "BRADD Program Aids Southern Kentucky Manufacturers." *Advanced Manufacturing* 4, 2 (1991): 1-2.

25. See chapter 7 in this volume.

26. See Jurgen Hoffmann et al. *Jenseits der Beschlußlage: Gewerkschaft als Zukunftwerkstatt.* Cologne: Bund, 1990, pp. 34-95 for a debate along these lines.

27. See Bob Hancké. "The Crisis of National Unions: Belgian Labor in Decline." *Politics and Society* 19, 4 (1991).

28. The seminal statement here is Jean L. Cohen. "Strategy or Identity: New Theoretical Paradigms and Contemporary Social Movements." *Social Research* 52, 4 (1985).

10
Training and the
New Industrial Relations

A Strategic Role for Unions

Wolfgang Streeck
University of Wisconsin–Madison

In the past decade, training seems to have emerged as a core subject of what to many promises to become a new type of industrial relations: more cooperative and consensual, less adversarial and conflictual, with fewer costly power struggles. More and more employers have come to accept that a modern economy's competitiveness depends on the skills of its labor force. Many union leaders, in turn, no longer object to the idea that secure employment at high wages requires above all economic competitiveness. To deal with what are perceived as critical skill shortages, employers in many countries and industries urge governments and unions to join them in concerted training offensives. Governments, for their part, have moved training to the center of labor market policies. As skill formation turns into a central issue of economic policy and labor relations, previously opposed group interests and the general interest finally seem to converge; distributional conflict promises to give way to productive cooperation; and eventually what appears to be outdated political antagonism may be displaced by peaceful competition for the best ideas on how jointly to organize and implement the upskilling of a country's, industry's, or company's labor force.

Still, few unions have yet thought through the implications of the resurgence of training as an industrial relations issue for their own strategy and status. Beyond general acknowledgments of the importance of skill formation, there is considerable skepticism and suspicion, especially about the intentions of employers. Among many unionists, memories of the destruction of the craft tradition under mass production in the name of economic necessity and rationality are still vivid. More recently, unions in many places have observed an industrial restructuring process that was above all aimed at "doing more with less"—less labor, that is. The training efforts that accompanied this were too often intimately linked with downsizing, speed-up, unemployment, and intensification of work to offer strategic promise from a union perspective. Moreover, the frequent and conspicuous emphasis on "social" and "attitudinal" skills, especially in firms and sectors that have gone through the trauma of downsizing, is bound to raise suspicions that employers' real objective in training is the restoration of unquestioned managerial prerogative. And are there not enough cases where "retraining" or "further training" are no more than a cover for outright de-skilling? Or where alleged skill needs in fact serve to justify the reintroduction of discretionary wage differentials?

In the burgeoning "new industrial relations" rhetoric (for a more moderate version, see Heckscher 1988), all of this alleged to have changed recently. Employers are said to "need" high skills—as well as "good industrial relations" in a participatory work organization because of fundamental changes in their competitive environment. As markets and technology allegedly force employers into high-wage and high-skill production—turning them into "good employers" as a matter of economic self-interest—the implication seems to be that there is no longer a need for unions to *impose* benevolent labor practices through mobilization and application of collective political power. Now it is suggested, and not just by traditional unions foes, that unions can and should instead concentrate their efforts on the implementation of such changes as economic restructuring, modernization, and flexibility, thereby finally taking on *productive* rather than merely *distributive* functions and moving from *conflict* to *cooperation* as their main new source of influence and organizational status.

Union reluctance to embrace tripartite cooperation on training as a central new industrial relations subject ultimately derives from its unclear implications for the role of unions and the structure of industrial relations in general. In the following, I wish to argue that popular images of a harmonious "new industrial relations" based on common interests in high skills are dangerously simplistic—mixing truths and delusions, profound insights and business school rhetoric, in an almost perfect melange. The principal flaw here is a misconstrued relationship between productive cooperation and distributive conflict, or between cooperative policy and adversarial politics, suggesting that the benevolent market pressures that give rise to "flexible specialization" signal the obsolescence of struggles over and for power. This is not just a misreading of the evidence which, as will be illustrated in more detail, supports the old insight that conflict and cooperation not only do not *preclude,* but often in fact *presuppose,* each other. In addition, by implying that unions that care about productive concerns can be no more than agents of management-determined economic necessities, it also deters unions from constructive and creative rethinking of present, primarily distributional policies. The point I would like to make here is that one can fully agree with the proposition that unions should embrace skill formation as the centerpiece of a new, cooperative, and productivistic strategy, and at the same time insist on unions' need for a strong, independent power base giving them, just as in the past, a capacity to impose rules and obligations on employers that they would not voluntarily obey or accept. I will argue that the latter no less than the former is in fact an indispensable condition for a successful joint union-management strategy of industrial upskilling, even from the perspective of governments and employers. To do this, I begin with a brief general discussion of the relationship between unionism and the sphere of production.

Unions and the Supply Side

Mainstream unions in the postwar period have almost universally conceived of themselves as agents of distributive and redistributive politics, not of production. As such, they were reluctant to discuss their activities in terms of their impact on, or their contribution to, efficiency and productivity—and indeed usually such discussions were forced upon them by employers, conservative governments, and hostile academics. Nevertheless, the ideological self-stylization of unions as exclusively devoted to distributive concerns,[1] enabling them to decline direct responsibility for the well-being of national economies and individual enterprises, was not only historically new but also factually incorrect. This was because, through their very concentration on distribution, unions in the Keynesian-Fordist world of postwar Social

Democracy contributed to economic performance both by more or less explicitly accepting managerial prerogative at the workplace, and by helping stabilize aggregate demand and increase the economy's propensity to spend at the macro level. In fact, unions' very power in distributive politics was conditional on the productive functions that their emphasis on distribution performed for the economy as a whole; and it was only because of these that unionism could come to be regarded by governments and employers as serving not only particularistic but also general interests.[2]

Today the Keynesian configuration is history (Skidelski 1979). For many reasons, the critical problems of the economy have migrated from the macro to the micro level, from the demand to the supply side, from the amount of output to its structure—and from distribution to production. In the process modern unionism has been thrown into disarray. Having comfortably located themselves in the distributive politics of macroeconomic demand management, unions are now faced with an apparently irreversible breakdown of the felicitous convergence of particularistic interest representation and the promotion of the general interest that had in the Keynesian period sustained both their institutional position and the economy.

Why do unions typically have such a hard time asserting themselves in the changed political economy of the 1980s and 1990s? The supply side has been called the "kingdom of the bourgeoisie" (Przeworski and Wallerstein 1982, p. 59). At first glance, production requires above all cooperation and compliance, not conflict and resistance. Likewise, structural change and industrial adjustment have to be responsive to market conditions; if they are driven or constrained by distributional politics, the result is all-too-often disastrous. Moreover, unlike the demand side which is governed by politicians, the supply side and the microeconomics of individual enterprises are run by managers; while politicians are subject to a similar set of incentives and strategic imperatives as union leaders, and therefore are often sympathetic with them, managers are not. Also, the micro level is a world, not only of diverse conditions in different sectors and workplaces, but also of competitive market pressures. Unions that get entangled in these may lose their capacity to impose general rules on the economy as a whole, find their internal politics and their organizations fragmented by divergent member interests, and run the risk of being torn apart by identification of their members with the competitive needs and interests of their employers.

Not that there was, even in an orthodox view, no place at all for unions in an economy driven from its supply side. Today unions are again and again invited to "cooperate" with management in restructuring, in rebuilding competitiveness, improving quality, increasing productivity, and other efforts. But typically such cooperation is not meant to entail much more than union leaders explaining to their membership why it is necessary to comply with whatever management determines is required—for example, more training and retraining. The rewards held out for such cooperation are improved economic performance, with an uncertain share of the benefits accruing to union members, and perhaps management absention from trying to break unions and run the workplace unilaterally. Indeed not a small number of union officials all over the western world today pursue cooperative policies for exactly these reasons, and for no others. Correspondingly, unions in stronger industries or with a more secure organizational base often prefer not to get involved in a kind of cooperation that seems to offer them essentially no other role than that of subordinate agents of management-determined economic, or "strategic," necessities.

Drawing on training as my example, I argue that just as in the past on the demand side, there are today on the supply side numerous opportunities for unions to combine independent, powerful representation of member interests with a pursuit of general social and economic interests. Exploring such opportunities indeed requires cooperative policies and strategies. But the type of cooperation needed here is far from passive acceptance of managerial decisions or self-limitation of unions to the implementation of them. Quite to the contrary, forceful intervention in, and regulation of, managerial behavior are required, with unions potentially and eventually appropriating, through collective political action, a significant share of the responsibility for productive performance. This is so, and indeed cooperation is *necessary* in the sense that it is competitively superior to managerial unilateralism, because the supply side of a modern industrial economy is a kingdom of the bourgeoisie only on the surface. In reality, it is rather a *magic kingdom* full of paradoxes and contradictions, the most important of which is that the king cannot properly govern, either in his own interest or in that of his subjects, unless he is himself governed by these—a king who needs to be constrained by a powerful citizenry in order to be able to accomplish what he would like to accomplish; a king, as a prisoner of his passions, faces dilemmas that he can solve only if he is compelled to do so by others.

Skills and Effective Supply

Union involvement in skill formation may well be the successor in the post-Keynesian political economy to what wage formation was for unions under Keynesianism, being as important and performing the same functions for them. Understanding the politics and institutional dynamics of training constitutes a major step towards a *theory of effective supply* to succeed older theories of effective demand, and may help unions adjust their position in the political economy to new conditions and realities. In training as well as, before, in demand stabilization, the possibility for unions to perform a useful function for both their members and the society at large derives from the fact that their opponents—capitalists or management—are confronted with vexing dilemmas between their collective long-term and their individual short-term interests. In the Keynesian world, this was the dilemma between the need for high and stable purchasing power and the desire to cut costs. The solution was cooperation between employers, forced upon them by unions through the exercise of collective power in industrial conflict, and often also by governments through legal intervention. More specifically, unions imposed on employers a more or less uniform and rigid wage pattern, thereby taking wages out of competition and insuring investors against the downward spirals in purchasing power that may result from competitive cost-cutting. In this way, collective action of workers created the stable and growing product markets that enterprises in the era of mass production needed to invest and grow.

In a market economy, training poses similar problems for employers on the supply side to that of aggregate demand stabilization on the demand side, and it offers similar opportunities to unions to build a base of independent power. What wage bargaining was for distributional unionism, training may become for unions working on and through the production side of the economy and making their peace with it: an opportunity for *conflictual cooperation*, or cooperation through conflict; for redistribution in the general interest; and for deep involvement of unions in the management of an advanced industrial economy and society. In short, this is because:

1. In certain growing but highly competitive product markets, a rich supply of skills, and especially of broad, experientially based general work skills, constitutes perhaps the most important source of competitive advantage for firms.

2. The skills that are most needed in such markets are of a kind that can be generated only with the active involvement of employers. This is because such skills are most likely to be generated through work-based learning in close proximity to the work process, and clearly *not* in schools.

3. While the acquisition of today's critical skills requires the utilization of workplaces for nonwork purposes, most employers, *if left to their own devices*, will not do enough for skill formation, in part because of individually unsolvable problems of calculating expected returns on investment, and in part because in an open labor market skills are, in an important sense, collective, or public, goods (Becker 1975).

4. Unions, if properly supported by public policy, have the capacity to make employers train, and may well develop the motivation to do so.

I have elaborated these points elsewhere (Streeck 1989). For the present purpose, I would like to confine myself to a few selective observations.

The Relationship Between Modern Technology, Work Organization, and Skills

Modern technology is less than instructive with respect to the skills needed to operate it (Brödner 1990; OECD 1988). The reason is that microelectronic circuitry can support radically different patterns of work organization. Vastly increased capacities to process and transmit information allow for centralization of control and differentiation of tasks far beyond what has been possible only a decade ago. At the same time, they also enable organizations to delegate decisions to flexible subunits with integrated, overlapping functions, so as to respond better to more complex and specific demands from their environment. Different patterns of work organization give rise to different skill needs. A centralized and functionally differentiated organization requires a small number of highly skilled employees located in staff-like departments remote from the actual production process, and a large number of unskilled or semiskilled operators with narrowly specialized tasks waiting to be eliminated by automation. By comparison, a decentralized and functionally integrated work organization will have short hierarchies and will require a relatively even distribution of skills.

Beliefs about a trend towards upgrading work in modern production systems, about urgent needs for improvements in initial and further training, about a "skill gap" in the workforce, or about skills as a crucial resource for international competitiveness are all premised on the assumption that in the future, most productive work will be done in less centralized and less functionally differentiated organizations. To the extent that firms will be compelled to exploit the potential of microelectronic information technology for decentralizing and reintegrating work tasks, it is argued that they will have to rely on a large supply among their workforce of a *combination of cognitive-technical, attitudinal, and social skills* that together form the basis for what may be called "decentralized competence"—where competence means both the organizational autonomy and the individual ability of workers to make correct and responsible decisions embedded in and related to the context of the organization at large.

The Relationship Between Product Markets, Product Strategies, and Productive Flexibility

While the skill needs of employers using new technology depend on how employers choose to organize work, that choice, in turn, is related to the product market in which a firm operates. Decentralized competence seems to be particularly conducive to, or outright required for, small-batch production or customized production of goods or services designed to fit the specific needs of individual clients. This is because decentralized competence provides organizations with a high degree of internal flexibility in general and a capacity for fast retooling in particular, i.e., for switching from one product, or batch of products, to another.

Producing a diverse and changing range of products at a high quality level requires not only a strong engineering capacity that allows for a high rate of product innovation. It also demands close interaction between the organization and its customers, as well as between different organizational functions such as marketing and product engineering, or product engineering and production. For this to be possible, employees in different parts of the organization must be able to understand each other's job, and sometimes to substitute for one another. That is, their qualifications must overlap (Gustavsen 1986). Moreover, rapid product change is facilitated by work groups integrating, like small firms, a wide range of tasks and thereby becoming more independent from concurrent decisions or supporting activities of differentiated, functionally specialized units. This calls for duplication of skills across organizational subunits. Productive flexibility thus necessitates redundant (i.e., overlapping or duplicated) organizational capacities that can be economically sustained only if other overheads, like quality control, supply management, or worker supervision, are cut—which again demands integration of previously separate, specialized tasks in front-line production work.

Overall, it appears that today's product markets place a premium on customization (Piore and Sabel 1984), and that firms that are flexible enough to engage in small-batch or customized production can command higher profit margins, are less vulnerable in their market position, and are likely to enjoy more long-term stability. Ultimately, this is based on the experience that in the highly competitive 1970s and 1980s firms, or national economies, that were capable of offering more diversified and customized products fared better than more traditional producers of standardized mass products. There is some disagreement as to why this should have been the case, to what extent product markets have really changed, and how large the new markets for what has been called "diversified quality production" (Streeck 1991) actually are. What seems clear, however, is that the economic attraction for employers of small-batch or customized production is often conditional on the prevailing wage level in a given country or region—firms that can bring down their wages far enough may have the alternative to survive as mass producers. The problem is that in a more and more global economy, mass markets tend to be increasingly taken over by producers from newly industrializing countries where wages are so low that firms in old industrial countries may, for all kinds of reasons, find it impossible to compete.[3]

In addition, it seems that the distinction between mass and customized markets is more fluid than is often believed. Given the productive flexibilities made possible by information technology, especially in combination with a work organization that emphasizes decentralized competence, small-batch producers and customizers are often able to transform mass markets into markets for more customized products, as mass producers in the course of industrialization transformed craft markets into mass markets. This is because high productive flexibility makes it possible to narrow the cost differential between customized, or semicustomized, and mass production to a point where the (still) higher price of nonstandardized goods or services is compensated by their better match of the customer's individual needs. To the extent that advances in customized and semicustomized production methods make this possible, mass markets shrink and differentiated quality markets grow.

In sum, as product markets fragment, the market a firm serves becomes increasingly subject to "strategic choice." Simultaneously, as technologies become more undefined and malleable, the products that are produced with them, and the organization of work that surrounds them, are less determined than in the past by a technology's intrinsic properties; they, too, have to be strategically chosen. Given existing technologies and demand structures, a firm can in principle aspire to be either a quality-competitive producer of customized goods with a flexible, fluid, and decentralized work organization, employing highly skilled workers at a high wage, or an efficient price-competitive producer of standardized goods with a centralized and formalized organizational structure, unskilled labor, low wages, and high-wage dispersion (see Carnevale 1991; CSAW 1990).

The Institutional Sources of Skill Use and Skill Development

The long controversy on the direction of skill development under capitalism can now by and large be considered settled. Whether or not employers prefer de-skilled over skilled labor cannot, in Bravermanian fashion, be decided deductively and once and for all. The question can sensibly be answered only when placed in the context of wage-setting mechanisms, the regulation of employment contracts, patterns of work organization, styles of technology use, and firms' strategic product market decisions (Sorge and Warner 1988). Today managerial choices between downskilling and upskilling are clearly not driven by technology as such; microelectronic circuitry can be used for cutting costs by eliminating skills and human intervention, as well as for increasing product quality and variety by enriching the productive capacities of well-trained workers. Downskilling presupposes, among other things, downward flexibility and wide dispersion of wages, enabling employers to adjust wages to relatively declining labor productivity, as well as high numerical flexibility of employment, permitting rapid adjustment of labor input to market fluctuations and making it unnecessary to provide for workers' internal redeployability through training. By comparison, rigid and high wages, an egalitarian wage structure, limited access of firms to external labor markets, and limitations on the deployment of new technology for "rationalization"—by making it impossible for firms to be profitable in mass markets for standardized, price-competitive products and forcing them to try and serve differentiated, quality-competitive markets—tend to forbid downskilling and instead induce firms to raise the skill level of their workforce.

The Importance and the Difficult Economics
of Work-Based Learning

Consensus is growing that today's advanced work skills are best acquired at or near the workplace (for the United States, see OTA 1990). Workplace-based training, where it is up to its new task, is quite different from traditional on-the-job training. Its task is to impart, for the mass of the workforce subject to easy, flexible hiring and firing, cheap, narrow, workplace-specific skills supplementing the general skills produced in public educational institutions. The growing need to use the workplace for training purposes is related to the fact that with fast-changing and highly flexible technology, and with fast product turnover, work routines can never become so established that execution can be neatly separated from conception. Work in such environments amounts to continuous experimentation with, and permanent "debugging" of, new processes and machine setups. On the part of operators, this requires, in addition to high cognitive skills (literacy and numeracy), an intuitive feel for the work that can only be gained from experience, as well as a range of motivational, attitudinal, and social skills that cannot be adequately developed outside "real work" production situations with their pressures and constraints. This is one reason why countries like Japan and Germany, where most industrial skill formation takes place in work settings, are so advantaged by their human capital endowment. Put in more general terms, the skills required for advanced industrial competitiveness are most likely to be available where it is possible to transform the workplace into a place of learning in addition to a place of work (i.e., to place a large share of the training burden on firms and managements and make them accept the utilization of the enterprise not just for production but also for skill formation).

Mainstream labor economics proceeds from the seminal insight that in an open labor market, returns on investment in general skills cannot be internalized by individual firms since such skills are transferable from one employer to another. This is why such skills will not be produced unless the costs are borne by the worker as an individual or as a taxpayer (i.e., in the latter case, by the general public). Keeping expenditure on and responsibilities for general and specific skills apart is greatly simplified if general skills are taught outside the workplace in specialized training organizations—schools—while specific skills are generated at the workplace. To the extent that the workplace is used to produce general skills, which is not likely to be typical, workers must be willing to accept a pay cut equivalent to the cost of the general training they receive, or the government must reimburse employers for their expenses. The first solution presupposes that general training can indeed be paid for out of a share of a worker's wage during the training period; both assume that the costs and returns of training at the workplace can be reliably established.

All these assumptions have come under heavy pressure. As has been pointed out, there is for a variety of reasons a fundamental school failure with respect to the formation of general work skills. As a result, to the extent that an economy depends for its competitiveness on high skills, a growing share of its general training effort has to be carried out at its workplaces. Typically, the costs of such training are high and can be recovered by individual employers only over a long period far exceeding the time of training, and with some reasonable commitment by workers not to move to another employer. The benefits of workplace training for employers inevitably become vulnerable to being pirated by competitors. Unlike previous types of market failure, this problem cannot be remedied by unilateral public provision, since that fails to produce the desired type of skills.

Moreover, the exact costs of workplace training defy conventional accounting and can therefore not easily be reimbursed. Workplace learning is optimally effective in a group-based or team-centered work organization that is more open and "porous" than what traditional industrial engineering prescribes. While this may in one sense increase costs, or at least make costs less easy to detect, it may at the same time engender quality improvements and productivity increases. To this extent, workplace training may pay for itself. In any case, an offer by the public sector to pay employers for general training at the workplace is likely to encourage all kinds of "creative accounting." Also, employers may feel induced to rely on more traditional, classroom-style training, the costs of which are easier to establish. The inevitable conclusion is that adequate utilization of the workplace as a learning site requires that employers pay a significant share of the costs of general training.

The difficult economics of workplace training require public intervention of a kind that makes unilateral provision look simple by comparison. The assumption by employers of responsibility for training in workplace-unspecific skills, as appears optimal for competitive performance, demands effective imposition of *social obligations to train*, as a substitute for insufficient individual market incentives and as a way of taking training costs out of competition. In open labor markets, employers competing with each other will always be under a temptation to "cheat" by not investing in general training and hiring skilled workers from their competitors. What is more, the mere prospect that others may behave in this way is likely to deter employers from training even if the result will be a general skill shortage. Societies that have at their disposal institutional or cultural mechanisms by which to oblige firms to cooperate in training are likely to enjoy competitive advantages as they will be able to protect their firms from the dysfunctional consequences of market-rational behavior for the production of skills as collective goods. The governance of workplace training, like that of workplace relations and the employment contract in general, is best assigned to legally supported and facilitated joint regulation between management and labor at the point of production. The same reasons that speak for collective bargaining as an alternative to both managerial unilateralism and direct government intervention in the workplace also speak for an orderly sharing of responsibility for governing the workplace as a place of learning.

Union Policies on Training: From Consumption to Investment

Unions in advanced industrial countries differ widely in their attitudes towards training. The spectrum extends from outright hostility among radical unions of unskilled workers (as in parts of the Communist French CGT), to indifferent lip service to the idea of shared, public responsibility for skill upgrading; and to long-standing support for, and involvement in, initial and continuous training (e.g., in Denmark or Germany). However, even where unions have accepted training as a current concern, there usually is still a long way to embracing it as a core subject of union strategy.

This is not only because there is a temptation for unions that support training to do so in the traditional framework of distributive politics, conceiving of training as a basically consumptive nonwage benefit. More important, training tends to be regarded by many unionists as an investment employers make out of economic self-interest, as required by technology and product market conditions. To this, the principal *modus operandi* of unionism—the creation of entitlements for workers—does not seem to apply. As long as it is assumed that "employers know what they are doing" (i.e., that product market signals are sufficiently instructive for employers to "do what is needed" on training), there is simply no reason for unions as unions to expend scarce bargaining power on making employers train. For this to make sense, union confidence in employers' ability to act with economic rationality must be less than complete. An active union policy on training, in other words, presupposes that the limited capacities of the self-proclaimed king of the supply side to act in his own interest are thoroughly appreciated.[4]

A positive union policy on training may also take off from the insight that advanced skills require investment not just by employers but also by workers, and that such investment is indeed more likely if supported by negotiated entitlements—albeit, of course, to invest rather than consume. More generally, the opening for unions becoming agents of a more-than-distributive training policy lies in the *incompleteness*, as it were, of the human resource investment functions of both employers and workers—being due to a lack of resources on the part of the latter, and the inherent limits of rational return-on-investment calculations for the provision of work-based training in high, broad, experiential skills on the part of the former. Here as elsewhere, gaps in the instructive capacity of product markets and technology have to be filled, and conflicts between individual and collective rationality overcome, by institutional rules and social norms enabling rational economic actors to act in their rational economic interest.

Union Intervention in Training

Independent union intervention in cooperative training and human resource policies must combine the imposition of institutional *constraints* on managements that foreclose low-skill, low-wage paths of industrial adjustment, with the creation of institutional *opportunities* for managements to pursue successfully a high-skill and high-wage policy. Constraints and opportunities must be built simultaneously; while the former without the latter suffocates economic performance, the latter without the former results in a dual economy with widely divergent conditions and performance levels, and very likely an under-utilization of productive opportunities due to unchecked temptations for employers to defect from more demanding high-skill and high-wage production patterns.

How specifically unions can deploy their political and organizational capacities to build the constraints and opportunities required to make employers train, and what those constraints and opportunities could be in a given economic and political setting, depends on the situation and, of course, the creativity of the actors involved.[5] What can generally be said is that cooperation on training is not only compatible with conflict, but indeed may require a conflictual capability of unions for its success. Examples where rigorous pursuit of, in part quite traditional, union objectives—if necessary against employer resistance—complements and makes effective a cooperative strategy on training are:[6]

1. Defense of high wages and a relatively flat wage structure, so as to foreclose the option of low-wage, low-skill employment. High and downwardly rigid wages force employers to raise the productivity of their workers to match the given price of their labor, rather than depress wages to the level of workers' given marginal productivities. The more flexible the wage, the lower the interest of employers in training. The higher the wage spread, the more selective employers' training investment will be.[7] Given the inherent indeterminacy of skill needs and the benefits of a rich skill environment for advanced competitiveness, highly selective and targeted human resource investment is, almost by definition, likely to be economically suboptimal.

2. Insistence on obligatory, standardized workplace training curricula that firms have to follow if they want to train for a particular skill or occupation. These curricula must be broadly defined, so as to prevent overspecialization and provide the ground for future, further training. Standardized curricula also serve the important function of enabling workers to quit and carry their skills with them. This ability constitutes a major source of union and worker power that can be defended only if training regimes are centralized.[8] Moreover, by barring employers from generating skills that are too workplace-specific, generally binding curricula provide the constraint as well as the opportunity to produce exactly the kind of broad, polyvalent skills that they need most.

3. Use of the union workplace organization, or whatever structure of worker representation may exist at the workplace, to ensure that training follows the standardized curriculum and neither becomes too workplace-specific nor is absorbed in productive work. Without an effective, on-the-ground enforcement mechanism, unions and workers cannot live with a high differential between training and skilled wages. Effective union supervision of workplace training, ensuring that it remains just that, is an important safeguard against the temptation for

management to extract more productive work from trainees, thereby neglecting their firm's own longer-term interests.

4. Defense, or extension, of legal and other provisions that protect employment continuity and stability. Employers who can satisfy their skill needs and change the skill composition of their workforce by firing old and hiring new workers will have less incentive to train than employers who face fewer employment rigidities. An economy where employers have the option of turning to the external labor market for skills, instead of training or retraining their existing workforce, will tend to suffer from a general skill deficit. This is so not least since the expectation on the part of employers that their competitors will seek external rather than internal adjustment constitutes a strong disincentive to train, even in periods of obvious skill shortages and even for firms that feel severely constrained by these.

5. Imposition of a flat wage regime with the few wage grades and job classifications, which rewards knowledge rather than activities performed. Wage structures of this kind allow for easy redeployment of workers, which affords firms a degree of internal flexibility that makes the constraints of external employment rigidity bearable. Even more important, with the right kind of pay system workers will not only be willing to acquire skills but will also accept internal mobility—in part because it helps them learn.[9]

6. Active pursuit, as an objective in its own right, of an anti-Taylorist policy of work organization, aimed at imposing on employers negotiated obligations to move towards broad job descriptions, a low division of labor, long work cycles, and reintegration of tasks. In addition to improving working conditions, such a policy contributes to making low-skilled labor unusable by eliminating the type of jobs for which it was in the past typically hired. Coupled with external employment rigidities and internal employment flexibility, de-Taylorization of work organization thus constrains as well as induces employers to invest in training.[10]

7. Negotiation of training and retraining plans with employers, setting a mutually agreed human resource policy for enterprises, regions, or industries. Such agreements would have to create enforceable entitlements for workers to be trained and retrained at the workplace on a current basis, not just in emergencies, and under general as well as workplace-unspecific curricula. Given that firms lack instructive eco-

nomic criteria as to what kind of skills and how many they need; and given the advantages quality-competitive firms, industries, and regions derive from a rich supply of excess skills, there will be ample space to accommodate egalitarian demands for underendowed groups in the workforce to be included in training. In fact, it will be through negotiated entitlements to learn at work that unions will contribute most to the broad and unspecific skill formation that firms in demanding markets need but find so hard to generate on their own.

A Strategic Perspective?

Unions today have a unique chance to return in a productive way to their craft heritage (Piore 1986). Craft unions were producers of skills as well as sellers. Up to the present day, there are industries in the United States where high standards of training at the workplace, and indeed the very provision of such training, depend on strong craft union presence and disappear with the decline of unionization.

But it is also true that in their distributional battles with Bravermanian employers, craft unions often redefined skill in terms of exclusive rights of their members to narrowly demarcated jobs.[11] In that process, unions' contribution to the production of skills began to take second place to the defense of craft prerogatives. Where craft unionism, or important elements of it, survived, it all-too-often deteriorated, under the pressure of employers' de-skilling strategies, into a reactive defense of status and privilege. In such cases training lost its productivist meanings: at the worst, it became reserved for small groups of carefully selected apprentices, with restricted access serving to maintain a high differential between skilled and unskilled wages, and turned into an increasingly well-paid, waiting period for accession to the labor aristocracy, without much of a meaningful curriculum.[12] This, in turn, made it easier for employers to attack unions as special interest groups impeding both industrial progress and fair access to good jobs. De-unionization and the destruction of apprenticeship can thus be presented by employers as efficient as well as equitable.

In a perverse alliance, then, industrial employers bent on de-skilling and craft unions narrowly representing only their members, often enough played into each other's hands. The dismal results were unhappily reinforced when industrial unionism appeared and found in de-skilling the promise of a homogeneous workforce easy to organize in inclusive unions around distributional concerns and without entanglement in the sphere of production. This configuration prepared the ground for the postwar compromise between capital and labor, in which the latter agreed to leave production to management and accomplish its egalitarian objectives through distributive collective bargaining and social policy. With the ascent of Fordism, training was no longer much of a concern.

There is nothing in the present return of skills onto the industrial relations agenda that would compel unions to give up the egalitarian values they inherited from industrial unionism. In fact, in a world in which redundant skills may be necessary for competitive economic success, the two traditions of unionism may now be able to converge in a policy of negotiated general upskilling, conducted and enforced in *cooperative conflict* with employers and in *creative partnership* with governments, and indeed much facilitated by the internal organizational dynamics of industrial unionism. Who will be king on the supply side is far from being a foregone conclusion.

NOTES

*I am grateful to Joel Rogers for constructive comment. The usual disclaimers apply.

1. In reality, of course, the matter was more complicated. In all western countries in the post-war period, there were sporadic demands by unions for involvement in managerial decisions. Mainstream unionists typically had a hard time deciding if these were a right-wing sellout to capital, or a Communist attack on the market economy and, with it, free collective bargaining. The mainstream *Nur-Gewerkschafter,* to use Marx's term, hated both. To keep his distance from the inscrutable ambivalence and the puzzling political contradictions of productivism, right or left, he would insist that the union's proper concern was fundamentally different from management's; that the two were confounded only at the union's and, perhaps, the economy's and democracy's peril; and that while management was in charge of efficiency, or economic issues, the union was to look after equity, or the social questions. Coexisting with this strand of unionism were other, older strategic orientations that sometimes looked "cooperative," or "yellow," and sometimes "radical," or "red." Their difference from mainstream centrism was that they sought an active role for unions in the efficient organization of production. In some countries, these in fact became the mainstream: the "left" version in Sweden, the "right" version in Japan, and a peculiar blend of the two in Germany (*viz.* that chameleon-like institution, codetermination). The matter is made even more confusing by the fact that rhetoric and behavior did not always coincide, so that one found, for example, distribution-minded centrists supporting wage moderation in the name of economic growth.

2. For the workplace, Freeman and Medoff (1984) have produced econometric evidence that unions, even in the United States and in contradiction of received wisdom, increase productivity. For more recent confirmation, see Mishel and Voos (1991).

3. Firms in high-wage areas that do not want, or are unable, to develop productive flexibility may also, of course, relocate to low-wage countries.

4. Again, this does not appear to be a clear-cut left-right issue. Confidence in the superior economic wisdom of owners and managers can be found both among "cooperative" unionists for whom cooperation consists of rallying their members behind management-defined economic inevitabilities, and among "arms-length," "adversarial" opponents of cooperation who want to confine unions exclusively to extracting distributive concessions. The latter position implies that the economic basis for such concessions can be safely produced and reproduced without union "involvement," i.e., by management acting on its own.

5. A different but related question that I will *not* address here is how unions with weak or declining organizational capacities, for example in the United States, can use involvement in skill formation to build or protect such capacities. Much depends in this respect on whether employers, and perhaps the state, perceive existing skill deficits as so critical, and their own means to deal with them as so limited, that they are willing to pay a political price to whoever may be able and willing to help them out. This would imply that if unions could come up with an effective contribution to skill formation that only they can make (or that they can make better than others), they could in principle "sell" that contribution in the same way and for the same kind of returns as they have in the past sold their more traditional "product"—peace at the workplace. As Joel Rogers reminds me, unions thrive if their policies satisfy three conditions: they must be advantageous to their members and possible members; they must give employers something that they want, but cannot get on their own; and they must make a visible contribution to the "common good." Promotion of effective skill formation, especially at the workplace, may very well do all of the above.

6. As will easily be recognized, my list draws in large measure on the German experience (Hilton 1991; Lane 1989; Streeck et al. 1987). However, this is only because I happen to know that experience better than others. To the extent that there may be lessons from the German case for other countries, these would consist of a number of *general principles* rather than concrete institutional cookbook recipes. I believe that most of those principles have to do with the insufficiency of a market mode of skill formation; the crucial importance of using the workplace as a place of learning; the dangers of off-loading training to the state; the need, resulting from this, for mechanisms generating social obligations for employers to train, thereby transcending the limits of a liberal-voluntaristic training regime; and the potentially extremely productive role unions can play in generating such obligations. On the basis of what I think I have learned from the German case, I would be inclined to predict that where such principles are neglected, skill formation and advanced industrial competitiveness will lag behind German (and Japanese) standards.

7. A low wage spread at a high overall wage level induces employers to distribute their human resource investment more evenly. This presupposes relatively low training wages, especially for young people—which may or may not be difficult to concede for unions. The narrower the gap between training wages and skilled wages, the larger the productive component of a trainee's activities at the workplace, as distinguished from its investive, training component.

8. While this might appear alien in an American context, it is not so at all. Not long ago apprenticeships were a major mechanism of skill formation in the United States. Their rapid decline in the recent past derives from the combined effects of de-industrialization, declining real wages, and de-unionization, not from a basic incompatibility of externally regulated and standardized workplace-based training with the American culture.

9. While a low wage spread above a high wage floor creates an incentive for employers to train, it may constitute a disincentive for workers to learn. The latter seems to have been one of

the unanticipated consequences of Swedish "solidary wage policy." Unions taking an active role in skill formation will have to search for a "saddle point" where wage differentials are low enough for employers to be willing to provide training to the workforce at large, and high enough for workers to justify the effort of undergoing training. (To make remaining wage differentials effective with respect to training, they should to the greatest possible extent be based on knowledge.) One would expect that the ideal level of wage differentiation should be found somewhere between the extremely high American and the extremely low Swedish wage spread.

10. To advance more comprehensive job demarcations as well as facilitate the move towards an ability-based payment system, unions could negotiate higher wages for workers who have undergone training, regardless of whether or not their additional qualifications are actually used. This will be a strong incentive for managements to reorganize work in such a way that the new skills can in fact be utilized—which will in turn make it easier for unions to push for a less fragmented work organization. Being forced to use newly generated qualifications by reorganizing work so as to accommodate them, managements will be educated about the possibilities and advantages of high-wage and high-skill production, and in this way unions may provide further training to management in their own long-term interests.

11. That is, where they were given the chance to do so, especially in the Anglo-Saxon countries. For a variety of reasons, the development was quite different in Germany and Scandinavia. Still, the differences are gradual and not categoric, and at least historically the dynamic described here was present everywhere.

12. This was the case particularly in Britain where apprenticeship typically deteriorated into "time served," at declining pay differentials between skilled workers and apprentices. As a result it almost completely disappeared.

Chapter 10 References

Becker, Gary, 1975. *Human Capital: A Theoretical and Empirical Analysis, with Special Reference to Education.* New York: Columbia University Press.

Brödner, P., 1990. "Technocentric-Anthropocentric Approaches: Towards Skill-Based Manufacturing," in M. Warner, W. Wobbe and P. Brödner, eds., *New Technology and Manufacturing Management,* New York: John Wiley and Sons.

Carnevale, Anthony P., 1991. *America and the New Economy.* San Francisco: Jossey-Bass.

CSAW (Commission on the Skills of the American Workforce), 1990. *America's Choice: High Skills or Low Wages!* Rochester, NY: National Center on Education and the Economy.

Freeman, Richard B., and James L. Medoff, 1984. *What Do Unions Do?* New York: Basic Books.

Gustavsen, B., 1986. "Evolving Patterns of Enterprise Organization: The Move Towards Greater Flexibility," *International Labour Review* 125:367-82.

Heckscher, Charles C., 1988. *The New Unionism: Employee Involvement in the Changing Corporation.* New York: Basic Books.

Hilton, Margaret, 1991. "Shared Training: Learning from Germany," *Monthly Labor Review* 114:33-37.

Lane, C., 1989. *Management and Labor in Europe.* London: Edward Elgar.

Mishel, Lawrence, and Paula B. Voos, eds., 1991. *Unions and Economic Competitiveness.* New York: M.E. Sharpe.

OECD (Organization for Economic Co-Operation and Development), 1988. *New Technologies in the 1990s: A Socio-Economic Strategy.* Paris: OECD, esp. Ch. 3, "Flexibility in the Workplace," pp. 67-93.

OTA (U.S. Congress, Office of Technology Assessment), 1990. *Worker Training: Competing in the International Economy,* OTA-ITE-457. Washington, DC: U.S. Government Printing Office, Chapter 3, "Human Resources for Competitiveness," pp. 73-97.

Piore, Michael, 1986. "The Decline of Mass Production and the Challenge to Union Survival," *Industrial Relations Journal* 17:207-13.

Piore, Michael, and Charles F. Sabel, 1984. *The Second Industrial Divide: Possibilities for Prosperity.* New York: Basic Books.

Przeworski, A., and M. Wallerstein, 1982. "Democratic Capitalism at the Crossroads," *Democracy* (July):52-68.

Skidelsky, R., 1979. "The Decline of Keynesian Politics," in C. Crouch, ed., *State and Economy in Contemporary Capitalism.* London: Croom Helm.
Sorge, Arndt, and Malcolm Warner, 1988. *Comparative Factory Organization.* UK: Gower, 1996.
Streeck. Wolfgang, 1989. "Skills and the Limits of Neo-Liberalism: The Enterprise of the Future as a Place of Learning." *Work, Employment and Society* 3:90-104.
Streeck, Wolfgang, 1991. "On the Institutional Conditions of Diversified Quality Production," in E. Matzner and W. Streeck, eds., *Beyond Keynesianism: The Socio-Economics of Production and Employment.* London: Edward Elgar.
Streeck, Wolfgang, J. Hilbert, K.H. vanKevelaer, F. Maier, H. Weber, 1987. *The Role of the Social Partners in Vocational Training and Further Training in the Federal Republic of Germany.* Berlin: European Centre for the Development of Vocational Training (CEDEFOP).

Appendix I
International Competition and the Organization of Production
Economic Realities and the Emerging Patterns of Industrial Relations

Seminar Advisory Board 1989-90

Ron Blackwell
Amalgamated Clothing & Textile Workers Union

Peter Lazes
Cornell University Program for Employment and Workplace Systems

Oscar Marchesio
Studio Giano

James Parrott
International Ladies Garment Workers Union

Charles Sabel
Massachusetts Institute of Technology

Michael Schippani
Michigan Modernization Services Program

Wolfgang Streeck
University of Wisconsin

Seminar Presentations 1989-90

Charles Sabel
Massachusetts Institute of Technology
Economic Restructuring - Theoretical Issues

Michael Barzelay
Harvard University
Economic Restructuring in Andalucia, Spain

Sune Sunesson
Lunds University, Malmo, Sweden
Alternative Forms of Development - The Scandinavian Model

Peter Lazes
Cornell University
Western New York Auto Industry Project

Wolfgang Streeck
University of Wisconsin
West German Codetermination

Bruce Herman
Center for Labor-Management Policy Studies, Columbia University
Restructuring the Emilia-Romagna Economy

Saul Rubinstein
Participative Systems Inc.

Michael Shay
Participative Systems Inc.

Robert Coy
Department of Commerce and Industry, State of Pennsylvania
Pennsylvania's Collaborative Restructuring Efforts

Michael Schippani
Director, Michigan Labor-Management Partnership Project
Economic Revitalization in Michigan

Lee Smith
Executive Director, New York State Industrial Cooperation Council
New York State Efforts to Promote ESOPs, Worker Participation and Cooperative Restructuring

Frank Emspak
Director, Massachusetts Center for Applied Technology
Massachusetts Centers for Excellence

192

Appendix II
International Competition and the
Organization of Production
Economic Realities and the Emerging Patterns
of Industrial Relations

Conference Participants
October 5-6, 1990

Victor Gotbaum (Center for Labor-Management Policy Studies)
Seamus O'Cleireacain (Center for Labor-Management Policy Studies)
Sumner Rosen (Center for Labor-Management Policy Studies)
Michael Wei (Center for Labor-Management Policy Studies)
Stephen Sleigh (Center for Labor-Management Policy Studies)
Bruce Herman (Center for Labor-Management Policy Studies)
Stavros Gavroglou (Center for Labor-Management Policy Studies)
Michael Kapsa (Center for Labor-Management Policy Studies)
Doris Suarez (Center for Labor-Management Policy Studies)
Ron Blackwell (Amalgamated Clothing & Textile Workers Union)
Peter Lazes (Cornell University)
Oscar Marchisio (Studio Giano, Milan, Italy)
James Parrott (International Ladies Garment Workers Union)
Charles Sabel (Harvard University)
Michael Schippani (Michigan Modernization Services Program)
Wolfgang Streeck (University of Wisconsin)
Bernard Brown (City University of New York Graduate School)
Robert Coy (Department of Commerce and Industry,
    State of Pennsylvania)
Frank Emspak (Massachusetts Center for Applied Technology)
Saul Rubinstein (Participative Systems, Inc.)
Michael Shay (Participative Systems, Inc.)
Edward Sadlowski (United Steel Workers of America)
Joe Romano (United Steel Workers of America)
David Bensman (Rutgers University)
Kathy Cannings (Harvard University)
Bennett Harrison (Carnegie-Mellon University)
Maryellen Kelley (Carnegie-Mellon University)
Susan Houseman (Upjohn Institute for Employment Research)
William Lazonick (Columbia University)
Ann Markuson (Rutgers University)
Jack Metzgar (Midwest Center for Labor Research)
John Steward (McKinsey & Company)

Bibliography

Abernathy, William J., Kim B. Clark, and Alan M. Kantrow. *Industrial Renaissance: Producing a Competitive Future for America.* New York: Basic Books, 1983.

Accornero, Aris. *Gli anni' 50 in fabbrica.* Bari: De Donato, 1973.

Adams, W., J. Brock, and Y. Ramstad. "Industrial Policy and Trade Unions/ Comment," *Journal of Economic Issues* 19, 2 (June 1985) pp. 497-511.

Ahlen, Kristina. "Swedish Collective Bargaining Under Pressure," *British Journal of Industrial Relations,* 27, 3 (1989).

Albrecht, Karl. At America's Service. Homewood, IL: Dow-Jones Irwin, 1988.

Amin, Ash. "Flexible Specialization: Miracle or Myth?" In *New Technology and Industrial Relations,* R. Hyman and W. Streeck, eds. Oxford: Basil Blackwell, 1988.

Angelina, Maurizio. "Rapporti fra organizzazioni artiginane ed enti locali nell'esperienza della CNA di Bologna." In *La politica industriale delle regione,* Andrea Tosi, ed. Milan: CLUP, 1983. "Antitrust and Capitol Hill: Industrial Policy, Foreign Competition, and the 'Siege' Syndrome," *Antitrust Law and Economics Review* 17, 2 (1985) pp. 73-96.

Antonelli, Gilberto. *Innovazioni tecnologiche e struttura produttiva: la posizione dell'Italia.* Bologna: Il Mulino, 1984.

Aoki, Masahiko. *Information, Incentives, and Bargaining in the Japanese Economy.* Cambridge: Cambridge University Press, 1989.

Armington, Catherine and Marjori Odle. "Small Business—How Many Jobs?" *Brookings Review* (Winter 1982) pp. 14-17.

Audretsch, David. "R&D Rivalry, Industrial Policy, and U.S.-Japanese Trade," *Review of Economics and Statistics* 70, 3 (August 1988) pp. 438-447.

Auerbach, Stuart. "U.S. Firms Lag Japanese in Spending," *Washington Post,* June 29 1990.

Bade, F.D. "Large Corporations and Regional Development," *Regional Studies* 17, 5 (1983).

Bagnasco, Arnoldo. *Tre Italie.* Bologna: Il Mulino, 1977.

_____. *La costruzione sociale del marcato.* Bologna: Il Mulino, 1988.

Bahl, Roy. "Industrial Policy and the States: How Will They Pay?" *Journal of the American Planning Association* 52, 3 (Summer 1986) pp. 31-318.

Baldissera, Alberto. "Alle origini della politica della disuguaglianza nell'Italia degli anni ' 80: la marcia dei quarantamila," *Quaderni di Sociologia* 31 (1984).

194

Balloni, Valeriano, ed. *Esperienze di ristrutturazione industriale.* Bologna: Il Mulino, 1985.

Barbagli, Marizio, Vittorio Capecchi, and Antonio Cobalti. *La mobilita sociale in Emilia-Romagna.* Bologna: Il Mulino, 1988.

Bartel, Rainer. "Organisationsgrofenvor - und Nachteile: Eine Strukturierte Auswertung Theoretischer und Empirischer Literatur," *Jahrbuch fur Sozialwissenschaft: Zeitschrift fur Wirtschaftswissenschaften* 41, 2 (1990) pp. 135-159.

Bartlett, Christopher A., and Sumantra Ghoshal. *Managing Across Borders: The Transnational Solution.* Boston: Harvard Business School Press, 1989.

Barzelay, Michael. "Andalusian Socialism: Political Ideology and Economic Policy in an Autonomous Community in Spain." Paper presented at the American Political Science Association meetings, Washington, DC, August 1986.

Barzelay, Michael, and Linda Kaboolian. "Structural Metaphors and Public Management Education," *Journal of Policy Management and Analysis* (Fall 1990).

Bassi, S., R. Bennati, CdF. Biotec, O. Marchisio, M. Melotti, S. Pinazzi, and M. Ruffino. "Strumenti di lavoro: i casi." In *Frammenti di innovazione*, O. Marchisio, ed. Milan: Franco Angeli, 1988.

Bearse, Peter J., et al. "A Comparative Analysis of State Programs to Promote New Technology Based Enterprise," *New England Journal of Business and Economics* 5, 2 (1979).

Beauregard, Robert., ed. *Economic Restructuring and Political Responses,* Vol. 34 of *Urban Affairs Annual Review.* London: Sage, 1989.

Becattini, Giacomo. "The Development of Light Industry in Tuscany: An Interpretation," *Economic Notes* 3 (1978).

_____. "Sectors and/or Districts: Some Remarks on the Conceptual Foundations of Industrial Economics." In *Small Firms and Industrial Districts in Italy,* Edward Goodman and Julia Bamford with Peter Saynor, eds. London: Routledge, 1989.

Becattini, Giacomo, ed. *Mercato e forze locali: il distretto industriale.* Bologna: Il Mulino, 1987.

Becker, Gary. *Human Capital: A Theoretical and Empirical Analysis with Special Reference to Education.* New York: Columbia University Press, 1975.

Behn, Robert, "Management By Groping Along," *Journal of Policy Analysis and Management* (Fall 1988) p. 646.

Bennis, Warren, and Burt Nanus. *Leaders: Strategies for Taking Charge.* New York: Harper & Row, 1985. Benson, J. Kenneth. "The Interorganizational

195

Network as a Political Economy," *Administrative Science Quarterly* 20, pp. 229-249.

Benya, Anton, and Charles Sabel. *Gewerkschaftsstrategie in den Achtziger Jahren: Die Hauptreferate auf dem 10.OGB- Bundeskongress.* Vienna: Verlag der Osterreichischen Gewerkschaftsbundes, 1983.

Biagi, Marco. *Cooperative e rapporti di lavoro.* Milan: Franco Angeli, 1983.

Bianchi, Patrizio. "Servizi reali e politica industriale a livello locale," *State e Mercato* 16 (1986) pp. 123-146.

Birch, David. "The Job Generation Process." Final Report to Economic Development—Program On Neighborhood and Regional Change, Massachusetts Institute of Technology, 1979.

_____. *Job Creation In America.* New York: Free Press, 1987.

Birch, David, and S. McCracken. "The Small Business Share of Job Creation—Lessons Learned from the Use of a Longitudinal File." Unites States Small Business Administration, 1982.

Blakely, Edward. "Innovation as National Industrial Policy," *International Journal Of Technology Management* 2, 5-6 (1987) pp. 731-742.

Bluestone, Barry, and Bennett Harrison. *The Deindustrialization of America.* New York: Basic Books, 1982.

Boltho, Andrea. *Japan: An Economic Survey 1953-1973.* London: Oxford University Press, 1975.

Bonacich, Edna. "U.S. Capitalism and Korean Immigrant Small Business." Department of Sociology, University of California, 1978.

Bonacich, Edna, et al. "Koreans in Small Business," *Society* 14 (1977) pp. 54-59.

Bonacich, Edna, and J. Modell. *The Economic Basis Of Ethnic Solidarity: Small Business in the Japanese-American Community.* Berkeley: University of California Press, 1980.

Bonazzi, Giuseppe. "La lotta dei 35 giorni alla Fiat: un'analisi sociologica," *Politica ed Economia* 11 (1984).

Boonelamp, Clemens. "Industrial Policies of Industrial Countries," *Finance and Development* 26, 1 (March 1989) pp. 14-17.

Bosworth, Brian. *Getting It Together: Economic Development, Manufacturing, Modernization and Collaboration.* Indianapolis, IN: Hudson Institute, forthcoming.

"BRADD Program Aids Southern Kentucky Manufacturers," *Advanced Manufacturing* 4, 2 (1991) pp. 1-2.

Brinkman, Richard. "The Genesis of a New Policy: Equity and Efficiency," *Journal of Economic Issues* 20, 2 (June 1986) pp. 335-344.

Briskin, Lawrence. "An American Industrial Policy: Recalculating the Zero Sum," *Industrial Management* 30, 3 (May/June 1988) pp. 7- 13.

196

Brodner, P. "Technocentric-Anthropocentric Approaches: Towards Skill-Based Manufacturing." In *New Technology and Manufacturing Management*, M. Warner, W. Wobbe, and P. Brodner, eds. New York: Wiley, 1990.

Brown, Bernard. *Socialism of a Different Kind: The Reshaping of the French Left*. Westport, CT: Greenwood Press, 1982.

_____. "Worker Participation in France." In *Managing Modern Capitalism*, M. Hancock and J. Logue, eds. Westport, CT: Praeger-Greenwoood, forthcoming.

Brown, Charles, and James Medoff. "The Employer Size Wage Effect." Working Paper No. 2870, National Bureau of Economic Research, 1989.

Brown, Charles, James Hamilton, and James Medoff. *Employers Large and Small*. Cambridge, MA: Harvard University Press, 1990.

Brown, William. "Industrial Policy and Corporate Power," *Journal of Economic Issues* 19, 2 (June 1985) pp. 487-496.

Bruderl, Josef, and Peter Preisendorfer. "Betriebsgrosse als Determinante Beruflicher Gratifikationen," *Wirtschaft und Gesellschaft*, 4 (1986).

Brusco, Sebastiano. "The Emilian Model: Productive Decentralization and Social Integration," *Cambridge Journal of Economics* 6, 2 (1982).

_____. "Flessibilita e solidita del sistema: l'esperienza Emiliana." In *Industrializzazione senza frattura*, F. Fua and C. Zacchia, eds. Bologna: Il Mulino, 1983.

_____. "Small Firms and Industrial Districts: The Experience of Italy." In *New Firms and Regional Development in Europe*, D. Keeble and E. Wever, eds. London: Croon Helm, 1986.

_____. *Piccole imprese e distretti industriali: una raccolta di saggi*. Turin: Rosenberg and Sellier, 1989.

Brusco, Sebastiano, and Charles Sabel. "Artisan Products and Economic Growth." In *The Dynamics of Labour Market Segmentation*, F. Wilkinson, ed. New York: Academic Press, 1981.

Burt, Ronald S. "Models Of Network Structure," *Annual Review of Sociology* 6, (1980) pp. 79-141.

Butera, Federico. *L'orologigio e l'organismo*. Milan: Franco Angeli, 1985.

Carland, James, et al. "Differentiating Entrepreneurs from Small Business Owners: A Conceptualization," *Academy Of Management Review* 9 (1984) pp. 354-359.

Carmignini, Fabrizio. "Il sindacato di classe nella lotta dei 35 giorni alla FIAT," *Politica ed Economica* 11 (1984).

Carnevale, Anthony. *America and the New Economy*. San Francisco: Jossey-Bass, 1991.

Castells, Manuel. *Technology, Space and Society*, Vol. 28 in *Urban Affairs Annual Review*. London: Sage, 1980.

Cella, Gian Primo, and Tiziano Treu. *Relazioni industriali: manuale per l'analisi della esperienza italiana*. Bologna: Il Mulino, 1982.
_____. *Relazioni industriali: manuale per l'analisi della esperienza italiana*. Bologna: Il Mulino, 1982.

Churchill, N, and V. Lewis. "The Five Stages of Small Business Growth," *Harvard Business Review* 16 (1983) pp. 30-50.

Coffey, William, and Mario Polese. "Local Development: Conceptual Bases and Policy Implications," *Regional Studies* (April 1985).

Cohen, Elie. "Le'moment lois Auroux' ou la desublimation de l'economie," *Sociologie du Travail* 28, 3 (1986), pp. 277-79.

Collida, Ada Becchi, and Serafino Negrelli. *La transizione nell'industria nell'industria e nelle relazioni industriali: l'auto e il caso Fiat*. Milan: Franco Angeli, 1977.

Conrad, Alfred. *Enterprise Organization*. Miroda, NY: The Foundation Press, 1977.

Contini, Bruno, and Riccardo Revelli. "The Process of Job Destruction and Job Creation in the Italian Economy," *Labour* 1, 3 (1987).

Contini, Stefania, Raffaele Lungarella, and Franco Piro. *L'economica emiliana nel dopoquerra*. Bologna: Marsilio, 1979.

Coombs, Rod, Paolo Saviotti, and Vivien Walsh. *Economics and Technological Change*. Totawa, NJ: Rowman & Littlefield, 1987.

Cooper, Arnold. "The Palo Alto Experience," *Industrial Research*, 12 (1970) pp. 58-61.

Crouch, Colin. "The Future Prospects for Trade Unions in Western Europe," *Political Quarterly* 1 (1986) pp. 5-8.

Cummings, Scott. *Self-Help in Urban America: Patterns of Minority Business Enterprise*. Port Washington, NY: Konnikat, 1980.

Cunningham, J, and M. Kotler. *Building Neighborhood Organizations*. Notre Dame, IN: University Of Notre Dame Press, 1983.

Commission on the Skills of the American Workforce. *America's Choice: High Skills or Low Wages!* New York: National Center on Education and the Economy, 1990.

Cyert, Richard, and David Mowery, eds. *Technology and Employment*. Washington, DC: National Academy Press, 1987.

D'Angelillo, Massimo. *Servizi reali: politiche industriali e servizi alle imprese in Italia e in Europa*. Bologna: I Quaderni di Quarantacinque, 1987.

Darity, William. "The Managerial Class and Industrial Policy," *Industrial Relations* 25, 2 (Spring 1986) pp. 212-227.

Dekker, Wisse. "Prospects for Collaboration and a Common Industrial Policy in Europe for the High-Technology Industries," *International Journal of Technology Management* 1, 3/4 (1986) pp. 297-307.

198

Dewar, Margaret. "Development Analysis Confronts Politics: Industrial Policy on Minnesota's Iron Range," *Journal of the American Planning Association* 52, 3 (Summer 1986) pp. 290-298.

Dluhy, Milan, and Kan Chen, eds. "Steering the Path Between Ambiguity and Overload: Planning as a Strategic Social Process." In *Interdisciplinary Planning: A Perspective for the Future*. New York: Center for Urban Policy Research, 1986, pp. 117-121).

Doeringer, Peter, et al. *Invisible Factors in Local Economic Development*. New York: Oxford University Press, 1987.

Domhoff, G. "Social Clubs, Policy Planning Groups, and Corporations: A Network Study of Ruling-Class Cohesiveness," *Insurgent Sociologist* 5 (1975) pp. 173-184.

Dore, Ronald. Flexible Rigidities: *Industrial Policy and Structural Adjustments in the Japanese Economy*. Stanford, CA: Stanford University Press, 1986.

Dore, Ronald, Jean Bounine-Cabale, and Jean Tapiola. *Japan at Work: Markets, Management and Flexibility*. Paris: OECD, 1989.

Dorfman, Nancy. "Route 128: The Development of a Regional High Technology Economy," *Research Policy* 12 (1983) pp. 299-316.

Dunne, Timothy. "Plant Failure and Employment Growth in the U.S. Manufacturing Sector." Mimeo. Pennsylvania State University, December 1987.

Dunne, Timothy, et al. "Patterns of Firm Entry and Exit in U.S. Manufacturing Industries," *Rand Journal of Economics* 19, 4 (Winter 1988) pp. 495-516.

Eaton, Jonathan, and Gene M. Grossman. "Optimal Trade and Industrial Policy Under Oligopoly," *Quality Journal of Economics* 101, 2 (May 1986) pp. 383-406.

Eaton, Thomas, and R. Conant. *Cutting Loose: Making the Transition from Employee to Entrepreneur*. Chicago: Probus Publishing, 1985.

Edelman, Murray. *Constructing the Political Spectacle*. Chicago: University of Chicago Press, 1988.

Ehringer, Ann. "Wellsprings of a New Industrial Policy," *New Management* 5, 1, (Summer 1987) pp. 52-53.

Eisinger, Peter. *The Rise of the Entrepreneurial State*. Madison: University of Wisconsin Press, 1988.

Elden, Max. "Democratization and Participative Research in Developing Local Theory," *Journal of Occupational Behavior* 4, 1 (1983) pp. 21-34.

Elvander, Nils. *Den Svenska Modellen: Loneforhandlingar och Inkomstpolitik 1982-1986*. Stockholm: Allmanna Forlaget/Publica, 1988.

"European Industrial Policy," *Journal Of World Trade Law* 20, 3 (May/June 1986) pp. 349-353.

Evans, David. "Tests of Alternative Theories of Firm Growth," *Journal of Political Economy* 95, 4 (1987) pp. 657-674.

Fardin, G., M. Casoli, and L. Cerato. *Come cambia la fabbrica: Nuovi sistemi produttivi e professionalita.* Turin: Fondazione Giovanni Agnelli, 1986.

Fink, Donald. "Industrialization Policy Focuses on Aircraft Sector," *Aviation Week & Space Technology* 132, 16 (April 1990) pp. 36- 39.

Flam, Harry, and Elhanan Helpman. "Industrial Policy Under Monopolistic Competition," *Journal of International Economics* 22, 1/2 (February 1987) pp. 79-102.

Freeman, Richard B., and James L. Medoff. *What Do Unions Do?* New York: Basic Books, 1984.

Friedman, David. *The Misunderstood Miracle: Industrial Development and Political Change in Japan.* Ithaca, NY: Cornell University Press, 1988.

Friedmann, John. *Planning in the Public Domain.* Princeton, NJ: Princeton University Press, 1987.

Gabel, H. Landise, and Anthony Hall. "United Kingdom: Industrial Policy Toward the Automobile Industry," *Journal of Management Case Studies* 1, 2 (Summer 1985) pp. 102-107.

Gabler, Ted, and David Osborne. *Reinventing Government: How the Entrepreneurial Spirit is Transforming the Public Sector.* Reading, MA: Addison-Wesley, 1992.

Gallagher, C., and H. Stewart. "Jobs and the Business Life Cycle in the U.K." Research Report No. 2, University Of Newcastle Upon Tyne, Department of Industrial Management, 1984.

Gallie, Duncan. "Les Lois Auroux: The Reform of French Industrial Relations?" In *Economic Policy and Policy Making Under the Mitterrand Presidency, 1981-1984,* H. Machin and V. Wright, eds. London: Frances Pinter, 1985.

Garibaldi, Francisco. "Problemi di politica rivendicativa: la natura dei rapporti cooperativi tra i lavoratori rispetto alla struttura dell' impresa. Esperienze e problemi di progettazione organizzativa nei metalmeccanici bolognesi." In *Frammenti di innovazione,* Oscar Marchisio, ed. Milan: Franco Angeli, 1988.

_____. "The Crisis of the Demanding Model and the Search for an Alternative in the Experience of the Metal Workers Union in Emilia-Romagna." Paper presented at Bielefeld University, March 30, 1989.

Gartner, William. "A Conceptual Framework for Describing the Phenomenon of New Venture Creation," *Academy Of Management Review* 10 (1985), pp. 696-706.

Garvini, Robert, Franco Calistri, and Ornella Cilora. *A quatra Italia: il lavoro e la politica industriale nei distretti e nelle areee integrate in Italia.* Rome: Edlesse, 1988.

Genovese, Frank. "An Examination of Proposals for a U.S. Industrial Policy," *American Journal of Economics and Sociology* 47, 4 (October 1988) pp. 441-453.

Gibbons, R., and L. Katz. "Layoffs and Lemons." Department of Economics, Massachusetts Institute of Technology, 1989.

Giugni, G. *Il sindacato fra contratti e riforme, 1969-1973.* Bari: De Donato, 1973.

Glaessel-Brown, Eleanor. "Immigration Policy and Colombian Textile Workers in New England: A Case Study in Political Demography." Doctoral dissertation, Massachusetts Institute of Technology, 1984.

Gold, Bela. "Some International Differences in Approaches to Industrial Policy," *Contemporary Policy Issues* 4, 1 (January 1986) pp. 12-22.

Golden, M. "Austerity and Its Opposition: Italian Working Class Politics in the 1970's." Doctoral dissertation, Cornell University, 1983.

_____. *Labor Divided: Austerity and Working Class Politics in Contemporary Italy.* Ithaca, NY: Cornell University Press, 1988.

Goldfield, Michael. *The Decline of Organized Labor in the U.S.* Chicago: University of Chicago Press, 1987.

Goldsmith, Edward. *The Great U-Turn: De-Industrializing Society* Devon, UK: Green Books, 1988.

Goldstein, Harvey A., and Edward M. Bergman. "Institutional Arrangements for State and Local Industrial Policy," *Journal of the American Planning Association* 52, 3 (Summer 1986) pp. 265-276.

Goodman, Edward, Jullia Bamford, and Peter Saynor. *Small Firms and Industrial Districts in Italy.* London: Routledge, 1989.

Granovetter, Mark. "The Strength of Weak Ties," *American Journal of Sociology* 78, 6 (1973) pp. 1360-1380.

Greene, Richard. "Tracking Job Growth in Private Industry," *Monthly Labor Review* 59 (September 1982) pp. 3-9.

Gualtieri, Giuseppina, ed. *Acquisizioni, fusioni, concorrenza.* Bologna: NOMISMA, 1988.

Gustavsen, B. "Evolving Patterns of Enterprise Organisation: The Move Towards Greater Flexibility," *International Labour Review* 125, 4 (1986) pp. 367-382.

Hackman, J. Richard, and Richard E. Walton. "Leading Groups in Organizations." In *Designing Effective Work Groups,* Paul Goodman, ed. San Francisco: Jossey-Bass, 1986.

Hall, Bronwyn. "The Relationship Between Firm Size and Firm Growth in the U.S. Manufacturing Sector." Working Paper No. 1965, National Bureau of Economic Research, 1986.

Hall, Graham. *European Industrial Policy.* New York: St. Martin's Press, 1986.

Hancke, Bob. "The Crisis of National Unions: Belgian Labor in Decline," *Politics and Society* 19, 4 (1991).

Harris, Candee. "U.S. Establishment and Enterprise Microdata: A Data Base Description." The Brookings Institution, 1982.

_____. "The Handbook of Small Business Data: A Sourcebook and Guide for Researchers and Policy-Makers." The Brookings Institution, 1983.

Harrison, Bennett. "Concentration Without Centralization: The Changing Morphology of the Small Firm Industrial Districts of the Third Italy." Paper presented to the International Symposium on Local Employment, National Institute of Employment and Vocational Research, Tokyo, Japan, September 1989.

Harrison, Bennett, and Barry Bluestone. *The Great U-Turn: Corporate Restructuring and the Polarizing of America.* New York: Basic Books, 1988.

Hatch, C. Richard. "Learning From Italy's Industrial Renaissance," *Entrepreneurial Economy* 6, 1 (July/August 1987).

Hayden, Gregory, Douglas Kruse, and Steve Williams. "Industrial Policy at the State Level in the United States," *Journal of Economic Issues* 19, 2 (June 1985) pp. 383-396.

Hayward, Jack. *The State and the Market Economy, Industrial Patriotism and Economic Intervention in France.* New York: New York University Press, 1986.

Heckscher, Charles. *The New Unionism: Employee Involvement in the Changing Corporation.* New York: Basic Books, 1988.

Heifetz, Ronald A., and Riley M. Sinder. "Political Leadership: Managing the Public's Problem Solving." In *The Power of Public Ideas,* R. Reich, ed. Cambridge, MA: Ballinger, 1988.

Heskett, James. *Managing in the Service Economy.* Boston: Harvard Business School Press, 1986.

Heymann, Phillip. *The Politics of Public Management.* New Haven, CT: Yale University Press, 1987.

Hicks, Larry. "Intel's Chief Urges U.S. Industrial Policy," *Sacramento Bee,* May 3, 1990.

Hilton, Margaret. "Shared Training: Learning from Germany," *Monthly Labor Review* 114, 3 (March 1991) pp. 33-37.

Hirschman, Albert. "Introduction: Political Economics and Possibilism." In *Bias For Hope.* New Haven, CT: Yale University Press, 1971.

Hjern, Benny. "The Swedish Social Welfare Municipality." In *International Review of Comparative Public Policy,* Nicholas Mercuro and Douglas E. Ashford, eds. Greenwich, CT: JAI Press, 1990.

Hoerr, John. "Will Industrial Policy Be Dr. Cuomo's Rx for the Economy?" *Business Week,* April 11, 1988, pp. 78-80.

Hoffmann, Jurgen, et al. *Jenseits der Beschluflage: Gewerkschaft als Zukunftwerkstatt.* Cologne: Bund, 1990.

Holmes, J. "The Organization and Locational Structure of Production Subcontracting." In *Production, Work, Territory: The Geographical Anatomy of Industrial Capitalism.* A.J. Scott and M. Storper, eds. Boston: Allen and Unwin, 1983.

Horwitch, Mel. *Post-Modern Management: Its Emergence and Meaning for Strategy.* New York: The Free Press, 1988.

Hyman, Richard. "Flexible Specialization: Miracle or Myth?," *New Technology and Industrial Relations.* R. Hyman and W. Streeck, eds. Oxford: Basil Blackwell, 1988.

Hyman, Richard, and Wolfgang Streeck, eds. *New Technology and Industrial Relations.* Oxford: Basil Blackwell, 1988.

I bilanci delle impreesse cooperative 1988. Bologna: Lega Emilia-Romagna, 1989.

Il Polo Scientifico e Tecnologico Bolognese. Bologna: ERVET, 1987.

Jacquier, Jean-Paul. *Les cow-boys ne meurent jamais, l'aventure syndicale continue.* Paris: Syros, 1986.

Johnson, Chalmers. "The Institutional Foundations of Japanese Industrial Policy," *California Management Review* 27, 4 (Summer 1985) pp. 59-69.

Johnson, Russell, and Paul Lawrence. "Beyond Vertical Integration—The Rise of the Value-Adding Partnership," *Harvard Business Review* (July-August) 1988.

Jovanovic, Boyan. "Selection and Evolution of Industry," *Econometrica* 50 (1982) pp. 556-569.

Jovanovic, Boyan, and Rafael Rob. "Demand-Driven Innovation and Spatial Competition Over Time," *Review of Economic Studies* 54, (1987) pp. 63-72.

Julliard, Jacques. *Autonomie ouvrie re: etudes sur le syndicalisme d'action directe.* Paris: Gallimard, 1988.

Kanter, Rosabeth Moss. *The Change Masters: Innovation for Productivity in the American Corporation.* New York: Simon and Schuster, 1983.

_____. *When Giants Learn to Dance.* New York: Simon and Schuster, 1989.

Katz, Harry C. *Shifting Gears: Changing Labor Relations in the US Automobile Industry.* Cambridge, MA: Massachusetts Institute of Technology Press, 1985.

Katzenstein, Peter. "Industry in a Changing Germany." In *Industry and Politics in West Germany: Toward the Third Republic,* P. Katzenstein, ed. Ithaca, NY: Cornell University Press, 1989.

Kern, Horst, and Charles Sabel. "Trade Unions and Decentralized Production: A Sketch of Strategic Problems in the West Labor Movement," *Politics and Society* 19, 4 (1991).

Kern, Horst, and Michael Schumann. *Das Ende der Arbeitsteilung? Rationalisierung in der industriellen Produktion: Bestandsaufnahme, Trendbestimmung.* Munich: Beck, 1984.

Kerr, C., J. Dunlop, F. Harbison, and C. Meyers. *Industrialism and Industrial Man: The Problems of Labor and Management in Economic Growth.* Cambridge, MA: Harvard University Press, 1960.

Kimberly, John. "Issues in the Creation of Organizations: Initiation, Innovation and Institutionalization," *Academy of Management Journal* 22 (1979), pp. 437-457.

Kingdon, J. *Agendas, Alternatives, and Public Policies.* Boston: Little Brown, 1984.

Kjellberg, S.O. "Free Trade as Industrial Policy," *CMA Magazine* 60, 4 (July/August 1986) p. 50.

Kochan, Thomas, Harry C. Katz, and Robert McKersie. *The Transformation of American Industrial Relations.* New York: Basic Books, 1986.

Komiya, Megumi. "The Japanese Computer Industry: An Industrial Policy Analysis," *Information Society* 6, 1,2 (1989) pp. 1-20.

Kotabe, M. "The Roles of Japanese Industrial Policy for Export Success: A Theoretical Perspective," *Columbia Journal of World Business* 20, 3 (Fall 1985) pp. 59-64.

Kubota, H. "A Statistical Survey of the Situation of Small and Medium Subcontracting Firms in the Federal Republic of Germany," *Journal of Industry and Management* 16 (1983).

Lama, Luciano. *Il potere del sindacato.* Rome: Riuniti, 1978.

Lane, C. *Management and Labor in Europe.* London: Edward Elgar, 1989.

Lane, Marc. *Legal Handbook For Small Business.* New York: Amacom, 1977).

Lange, Peter, George Ross, and Maurizio Vannicelli. *Union Change and Crisis: French and Italian Union Strategy and the Political Economy, 1945-1980.* London: Allen & Unwin, 1982.

La Rosa, M. *Il modello giapponese.* Milan: Franco Angeli, 1988.

Lassini, Angelo. *Gli interventi regionali per i servizi alle imprese.* Milan: Franco Angeli, 1985.

Lawrence, Paul, and D. Dyer. *Renewing American Industry.* New York: The Free Press, 1983.

Lawrence, Robert. "Is Trade Deindustrializing America?" *Brookings Papers on Economic Activity* 1 (1983).

Lax, David A., and James K. Sebenius. *The Manager as Negotiator: Bargaining for Cooperation and Competitive Gain.* New York: The Free Press, 1986.

Lazes, Peter. "Participative Consulting," *ILR Report* (Fall 1988) pp. 24-27.

Lazes, Peter, and Tony Costanza. "Xerox Cuts Costs Without Layoffs Through Union-Management Collaboration," *Labor Management Brief* (July 1984).

Lazes, Peter, Leslie Rambouillets, et al. "Xerox and the ACTOR: Using Labor-Management Teams to Remain Competitive," *National Productivity Review* (Summer 1991) pp. 339-349.

Lehman, James, and Thomas D. Willett. "National Security and Industrial Policy: The Need for a Public Choice Perspective," *Contemporary Policy Issues* 4, 1 (January 1986) pp. 36-47.

Leonard, Jonathan. "On the Size Distribution of Employment and Establishment." Working Paper No. 1951, National Bureau of Economic Research, 1986.

Lindblom, Charles. *The Policy-Making Process.* Englewood Cliffs, NJ: Prentice-Hall, 1980.

Lindblom, Charles, and David K. Cohen. *Usable Knowledge: Social Science and Social Problem-Solving.* New Haven, CT: Yale University Press, 1979.

Lipset, Seymour M., ed. *Unions in Transition.* San Francisco: Institute for Contemporary Studies, 1986.

Locke, Richard. "The Resurgence of the Local Union: Industrial Restructuring and Industrial Relations in Italy," *Politics and Society* 18, 3 (1990) pp. 347-379.

Locke, Richard, and Serafino Negrelli. "Il caso FIAT Auto." In *Strategie di riaggiustamento industriale,* M. Regini and C. Sabel, eds. Bologna: Il Mulino, 1989.

Loveman, Gary. "Changes in the Organisation of Production and the Skill Composition Of Employment." Department of Economics, Massachusetts Institute of Technology, 1989.

Lowe-Beer, John. *Protest and Participation: The New Working Class in Italy.* Cambridge: Cambridge University Press, 1978.

Lucas, Robert. "On the Size Distribution of Business Firms," *Bell Journal of Economics* 9 (Autumn 1978) pp. 508-523.

Luciano, L. (intervista di Fabrizio D'Agostino), *Il potere del sindacato.* Rome: Riuniti, 1978.

Lueck, Thomas J. "Saving Jobs in Buffalo: Victory and Loss," New York Times, February 17, 1987, pp. B1-2.

MacDonald, James. "Entry and Exit on the Competitive Fringes," *Southern Economic Journal* 52 (January 1986) pp. 640-652.

Maguire, Lambert. *Understanding Social Networks.* Beverly Hills, CA: Sage Publications, 1983.

Maire, Edmond. *Nouvelles frontieres pour le syndicalisme.* Paris: Syros, 1987.

Majumdar, B. "Industrial Policy in Action: The Case of the Electronics Industry in Japan," *Columbia Journal Of World Business* 23, 3 (Fall 1988) pp. 25-34.

Marchisio, Oscar. "La progettazione organizzativa fra negoiazione ed identita: i casi della regione Emilia-Romagna." In *Il modello giapponese,* Michele La Rosa, ed. Milan: Franco Angeli, 1988.

Marcus, Alfred, and Allen M. Kaufman. "Why is it Difficult to Implement Industrial Policies: Lessons from the Synfuels Experience," *California Management Review* 28, 4 (Summer 1986) pp. 98-114.

Marshall, A. *Industry and Trade.* London: MacMillan, 1919.

Matsushita, M. "The Legal Framework of Japanese Industrial Policy," *Brigham Young University Law Review* 2 (1987) pp. 541-570.

Merini, Alberto, and Emilio Rebecchi. *L'altra faccia della luna.* Bologna: CLUEB, 1986.

Miller, R, and M. Cote. "Growing the Next Silicon Valley," *Harvard Business Review* (July-August 1985) pp. 114-123.

Mishel, Lawrence, and Paula Voos, eds. *Unions and Economic Competitiveness.* Armonk, NY: M.E. Sharpe, 1992.

Moore, Gwen. "The Structure of a National Elite Network," *American Sociological Review* 44 (1979) pp. 673-692.

Moore, Mark H. "What Sort of Ideas Become Public Ideas?" In *The Power of Public Ideas,* Robert B. Reich, ed. Cambridge: Harvard University Press, 1990.

Moss, Bernard H. "After the Auroux Laws: Employers, Industrial Relations and the Right in France," *West European Politics* 11, 1 (January 1988) pp. 68-80.

Mothe-Gautray (ch4, note 7)

Müller-Jentsch, Walter. "Industrial Relations Theory and Trade Union Strategy," *International Journal of Comparative Law and Industrial Relations* 3 (1988) pp. 177-190.

Murray, F. "Production Decentralisation and the Decline of the Mass Worker," *Capital and Class* 19 (1983).

Nanetti, Raffaella. *Growth and Terrritorial Policies: The Italian Model of Social Capitalism.* New York: Pinter, 1988.

Neu, Werner, Karl-Heinz Neumann, and Thomas Schnoring. "Trade Patterns, Industry Structure and Industrial Policy in Telecommunications," *Telecommunications Policy* 11, 1, (March 1987) pp. 31-44.

Neumann, Manfred. "Industrial Organization and Public Policy," *International Journal of Industrial Organization* 6, 2 (June 1988) pp. 155-166.

_____. "Industrial Policy and Competition Policy," *European Economic Review* 34, 2-3 (May 1990) pp. 562-567.

Nilsson, K. Robert. "The EUR Accords and the Historic Compromise: Italian Labor and Eurocommunism," *Polity* (Fall 1981).

Noblecourt, Michael. *Les Syndicats en Questions.* Paris: Les Editions Ouvrieres, 1990.

Norhia, N. "Institutional Innovations in High Technology Based Entrepreneurial Communities: The 128 Venture Group as a Case Study." Sloan School Of Management, April 1986.

Norton, R. D. "Industrial Policy and American Renewal," *Journal of Economic Literature* 24, 1 (March 1986) pp. 1-40.

Norton, R. D., and J. Rees. "The Product Cycle and the Spatial Decentralization of American Manufacturing," *Regional Studies* 13 (1979) pp. 141-151.

Office of Technology Assessment (OTA). *Worker Training: Competing in the New International Economy.* Washington, DC: Government Printing Office, 1990.

Okimoto, Daniel. *Between MIT and the Market: Japanese Industrial Policy for High Technology.* Stanford, CA: Stanford University Press, 1989.

Organization for Economic Cooperation and Development (OECD). *Agencies for Industrial Adaptation and Development.* Paris: 1978.

_____. "Employment in Small and Large Firms: Where Have the Jobs Come From?" *Employment Outlook* (1985).

_____. *New Technologies in the 1990's: A Socio-Economic Strategy.* Paris: 1988. (Esp. Ch.3, "Flexibility in the Workplace")

Osborne, David. *Laboratories of Democracy.* Boston: Harvard Business School Press, 1988.

Osterman, Paul. *Employment Futures: Reorganization, Dislocation, and Public Policy.* New York: Oxford University Press, 1988.

Paleczek, O. "Interfirm Cooperation: An Instrument to Improve Small Business Competition." Paper presented to the 16th European Small Business Seminar, Sweden, 1986.

Parker, Mike, and Jane Slaughter. *Choosing Sides: Unions and the Team Concept.* Boston: South End Press, 1988.

Pearce, Joan, and John Sutton. *Protection and Industrial Policy in Europe.* London: Royal Institute For International Affairs, 1986.

Pennacchi, Laura, ed. *L'industria italiana: transformazioni strutturali e possibilita di governo politico.* Milan: Franco Angeli, 1981.

Perrow, Charles. *Complex Organizations: A Critical Essay.* New York: Random House, 1986.

Perrucci, Robert, and B. Lewis. "Continuity and Change of Interorganizational Network and Community Elite Structure." Paper presented at the 80th Annual American Sociological Association, 1985.

Peters, Thomas J., and Robert H. Waterman. *In Search of Excellence: Lessons from America's Best-Run Companies.* New York: Harper & Row, 1982.

Peterson, Richard, and D. Berger. "Entrepreneurship in Organizations: Evidence from the Popular Music Industry," *Administrative Science Quarterly* 16 (1971) pp. 97-107.

Pinchot, Gifford. *Intrapreneuring.* New York: Harper & Row, 1985.

Piore, Michael. "The Decline of Mass Production and the Challenge to Union Survival," *Industrial Relations Journal* 17 (1986) pp. 207-13.

_____. "Administrative Failure: An Hypothesis about the Decline of the U.S. Union Movement." Department of Economics, Massachusetts Institute of Technology, September 1989.

Piore, Michael, and Charles Sabel. *The Second Industrial Divide.* Basic Books, 1984.

Pizzorno, Alessandro, Emilio Reyneri, Mario Regini, and Ida Regalia. *Lotte operaie e sindaco: il ciclo 1968-1972 in Italia.* Bologna: Il Mulino, 1978.

_____. "Political Exchange and Collective Identity in Industrial Conflict." In *The Resurgence of Class Conflict in Western Europe Since 1968,* Vol. 2, C. Crouch and A. Pizzorno, eds. New York: Holmes & Meier, 1978.

_____. *I soggetti del pluralismo.* Bologna: Il Mulino, 1980.

Plosila, Walter H. "Developing Networking Relationships: The Experiences of Denmark, Germany, Italy, Sweden." Rockville, Md: Montgomery County High Technology Council, 1989.

Polanyi, Michael. *Personal Knowledge.* Chicago: University of Chicago Press, 1958.

Politca industriale, sevizi reali e opportunita di sviluppo a livello locale. Bologna: ERVEY, 1989.

Porter, Michael. *Competitive Strategy.* New York: The Free Press, 1980.

_____. *Competitive Advantage.* New York: The Free Press, 1985.

_____. *The Competitive Advantage of Nations.* New York: The Free Press, 1990.

Portes, A, and R. Bach. *Latin Journey, Cuban and Mexican Immigrants in the United States.* Berkeley, CA: University of California Press, 1985.

208

Powell, Walter. "Neither Master Nor Hierarchy: Network Forms of Organization," *Research In Organizational Behavior* 12 (1984) pp. 295-336.

_____. "Hybrid Organizational Arrangements: New Form or Transitional Developments," *California Management Review* (Fall 1987).

Prais, S., et al. *Productivity and Industrial Structure*. Cambridge: Cambridge University Press, 1981.

Przeworski, A., and M. Wallerstein. "Democratic Capitalism at the Crossroads," *Democracy* (July 1982): pp. 52-68.

Putnam, Robert, Robert Leonardi, and Raffaella Nanetti. *La pianta e le radici.* Bologna: Il Mulino, 1985.

Regini, Mario. *I dilemmi del sindacato.* Bologna: Il Mulino, 1981.

Regini, Mario, ed. *La sfida della flessibiliita.* Milan: Franco Angeli, 1988.

Regini, Mario, and Charles Sabel. *Strategie di riaggiustamento industriale.* Bologna: Il Mulino, 1989.

"Report VI: The Promotion of Small and Medium-Sized Enterprises." Report to the International Labour Conference, ILO, 1986.

Reynaud, J. *Les Syndicats en France.* Paris: Seuil, 1975.

Richards, Evelyn. "In Noyce's Passing, An Era Also Ends," *Washington Post,* June 5, 1990.

Richetto, J. "U.S. Industry: Decline and Fall?," *Long Range Planning* 21, 1 (February 1988) pp. 35-45.

Ridgeway, V. "Administration of Manufacturer-Dealer Systems," *Administrative Science Quarterly* 1 (1978) pp. 464-483.

Rodrik, Dani. "Disequilibrium Exchange Rates as Industrialization Policy," *Journal Of Development Economics* 23, 1, (September 1986) pp. 89-106.

Roehl, Thomas, and J. Frederick Truitt. "Japanese Industrial Policy in Aircraft Manufacturing," *International Marketing Review* 4, 2 (Summer 1987) pp. 21-32.

Roessner, J. David. "Prospects for a National Innovation Policy in the USA," *Futures* 17, 3 (June 1985) pp. 224-231.

Rogers, E., and J. Larsen. *Silicon Valley Fever: Growth of High Technology Culture.* New York: Basic Books, 1984.

Rogers, Joel. "Divide and Conquer: Further Reflections on the Distinctive Character of American Labor Laws," *Wisconsin Law Review* 1 (January-February 1990) pp. 1-147.

Romanagnoli, Umberto, and Tiziano Treu. *I sindacati in Italia dal'45 a oggi: storia di una strategia.* Bologna: Il Mulino, 1981.

_____. *La Question Syndicale.* Paris: Calmann-Levy, 1988.

Rosenfeldt, Martin. "U.S.-Mexico Borderland Industrialization Policies Revisited: The Need for Binational Strategies," *Akron Business and Economic Review* 16, 4 (Winter 1985) pp. 12-19.

Rosenthal, Paul C. "Industrial Policy and Competitiveness: The Emergence of the Escape Clause," *Law and Policy in International Business* 18, 4 (1986) pp. 749-793.

Rosenvallon, Pierre. "Participation et syndicats," *Management et Qualite* 25 (mars 1988) pp. 14-16.

Royo, Javier Perez, and Antonio Porras Nadales, eds. *El Parlamento de Andalucia: Analisis de la Primera Legislatura (1982-1986)*. Madrid: Tecnos, 1987.

Rubery, J. "Flexibility of Labour Costs in Non-Union Firms." In *Flexibility In Labour Markets*. London: Academic Press, 1987.

Runsten, D. "Mexican Immigrants and the California-Mexico Role in the U.S. Shoe Industry." University Of California, Berkeley, 1985.

Rutledge, John, and Deborah Allen. *Rust to Riches, The Coming of the Second Industrial Revolution*. New York: Harper & Row, 1989.

Sabel, Charles. *Work and Politics: The Division of Labor in Industry*. Cambridge: Cambridge University press, 1982.

_____. "Flexible Specialization and the Re-emergence of Regional Economies." In *Reversing Industrial Decline?*, P. Hirst and J. Zeitlin, eds. Oxford: Berg Publishers, 1989.

Sanchez de la Morena, Ricardo, and Jose M. Bueno. "El Instituto de Promocion Industrial de andalucia," *Boletin Economico de andalucia* 4 (1984) pp. 88-94.

Sapelli, Giulio., ed. *Il movimento cooperative in Italia*. Turin: Einaudi, 1989.

Sarathy, Ravi. "The Interplay of Industrial Policy and International Strategy: Japan's Machine Tool Industry," *California Management Review* 31, 3 (Spring 1989) pp. 132-160.

Saxenian, A. "Silicon Valley and Rte 128: Regional Prototypes or Historical Exceptions?" *Technology, Space and Society*, Vol. 28 of *Urban Affairs. Annual Review*. London: Sage, 1985.

Schlosstein, Steven. *Trade War: Greed, Power, and Industrial Policy on Opposite Sides of the Pacific*. New York: St. Martin's Press, 1984.

Schön, Donald A. *The Reflective Practitioner: How Professionals Think in Action*. New York: Basic Books, 1983.

Scott, Allen J., and Michael Storper. *Production, Work, Territory*. Boston: Allen and Unwin, 1986.

Scott, Bruce, and George C. Lodge, eds. *U.S. Competitiveness in the World Economy*. Boston: Harvard Business School Press, 1985.

Sekiguchi, Sueo, and Toshihiro Horiuchi. "Myth and Reality of Japan's Industrial Policies," *World Economy* 8, 4 (December 1985) pp. 373-391.

Sellier, Francois. *Strategie de la Lutte Sociale: 1936-1960*. Paris: Les Editions Ouvriers, 1961.

210

Seymour, L., ed. *Unions in Transition*. San Francisco: Institute for Contemporary Studies, 1986.

Shapira, Philip. "Modernizing Manufacturing." Economic Policy Institute, Washington, DC, 1990.

Shelp, Ronald K. "Redirecting North American Trade and Industrial Policy: Recognizing the Service Industry," *Vital Speeches* 52, 22 (September 1986) pp. 687-690.

Shepherd, James. "Manufacturing in Britain: Industrial Support Policies," *National Economic Review* 122 (November 1987) pp. 59- 71.

Shutt, J., and R. Whittington. "Large Firm Strategies and the Rise of Small Units: The Illusion of Small Firm Job Generation." Working Paper No. 15, University of Manchester, 1984.

Silver, Hilary, and Dudley Burton. "The Politics of State-Level Industrial Policy: Lessons from Rhode Island's Greenhouse Compact," *Journal of the American Planning Association* 52, 3 (Summer 1986) pp. 277-289.

Skidelsky, R. "The Decline of Keynesian Politics." In *State and Economy in Contemporary Capitalism* by C. Crouch. London: Croom Helm, 1979.

Smith, K. K., and D. Berg. *Paradoxes of Group Life: Understanding Conflict, Paralysis and Movement in Groups*. San Francisco: Jossey-Bass, 1987.

Smith, W. Rand. "Towards Autogestion in Socialist France? The Impact of Industrial Relations Reform," *West European Politics* 10, 1 (January 1987) pp. 46-62.

Sorge, Arndt, and Malcolm Warner. *Comparative Factory Organisation: An Anglo-German Comparison of Management and Manpower in Manufacturing*. UK: Gower, 1986.

Stableford, Joan. "Department of Defense Lacks a Strategy for 90's," *Fairfield County Business Journal*, June 11, 1990.

Starr, Martin K., ed. *Global Competitiveness: Getting the U.S. Back on the Track*. New York: W. W. Norton, 1988.

Steenbergen, Jacques. *Change and Adjustment: External Relations and Industrial Policy of the European Community*. Boston: Kluwer Law and Taxation Publishers, 1983.

Stone, Kathleen Van Wezel. "The Post-War Paradigm in American Labor Law," *Yale Law Journal*, 90, 7 (1981) pp. 1509-1580.

_____. "Labor Relations on the Airlines: The Railway Labor Act in the Era of Deregulation," *Stanford Law Review* 42 (1990) pp. 1485-1547.

Storey, D. J., and S. Johnson. "Small and Medium-Sized Enterprises and Employment Creation in the EEC Countries: Summary Report." Study No. 85, Commission of the European Communities, 1987.

211

Storper, Michael, and S. Christopherson. "Flexible Specialization and Regional Industrial Agglomerations: The Case of the U.S. Motion Picture Industry," Department of Graduate Architecture and Urban Planning, 1986.

Storper, Michael, and Bennett Harrison. "Flexibility, Hierarchy and Regional Development: The Changing Structure of Industrial Production Systems and their Forms of Governance in the 1990's." Paper presented at the International Conference on Industrial Policy, New Issues and New Models, the Regional Experience, Bologna, November 16-17, 1989.

Storper, Michael, and Allen Scott, eds. *Pathways to Industrialization and Regional Development in the 1990's.* Boston: Unwin and Hyman, 1991.

Streeck, Wolfgang. "On the Institutional Conditions of Diversified Quality Production." In *Beyond Keynesianism: The Socio- Economics of Production and Employment,* E. Matzner and W. Streeck, eds. London: Edward Elgar, 1991.

Streeck, Wolfgang, J. Hilbert, K.-H. van Kevelaer, F. Maier, and H. Weber. *The Role of the Social Partners in Vocational Training and Further Training in the Federal Republic of Germany.* European Centre for the Development of Vocational Training, 1987.

Succar, Patricia. "The Need for Industrial Policy in LDC's—A Re-Statement of the Infant Industry Argument," *International Economic Review* 28, 2 (June 1987) pp. 521-534.

Sugawara, Sandra. "Pentagon Plans to Aid Four Ailing Industries," *Washington Post,* January 2, 1990.

_____. "High and Dry in a Time of Peace," *Washington Post,* June 3, 1990.

Summer, Franz. *Das VOEST Debakel.* Vienna: Orac, 1987.

Tassinari, Giorgo. *Il sistema industriale dell'Emilia-Romagna.* Bologna: Il Mulino, 1986.

Taylor, Benjamin, and Fred Witney. *Labour Relations Law.* Englewood Cliffs, NJ: Prentice-Hall, 1983.

Teague, Paul. "Trade Unions and Extra-National Industrial Policies: A Case Study of the Response of the British NUM and ISTC to Membership of the European Coal and Steel Community," *Economic and Industrial Democracy* 10, 2 (May 1989) pp. 211-237.

Teitz, Michael, et al. "Small Business and Employment Growth in California." Working Paper No. 348, Institute of Urban and Regional Development, 1981.

Thakur, Manab, T. K. Das, and Wilke English. "Industrial Policy for the U.S. Steel Industry: An Empirical Study," *Southwest Journal of Business and Economics* 4, 3 (Spring 1987) pp. 1-17.

Thelen, Kathleen A. *Continuity in Crisis: Labor Politics and Industrial Adjustment in West Germany 1950-1987.* Ithaca, NY: Cornell University Press, 1991.

Thimm, Alfred L. "Codetermination and Industrial Policy: The Special Case of the German Steel Industry," *California Management Review* 29, 3 (Spring 1987) pp. 115-133.

Tilly, Charles. *An Urban Work.* Boston: Little Brown, 1974.

Tosi, Andrea, ed. *Il ruolo di una associazione sindacale artigiana nello sviluppo modenese:la CNA dal dopoquerra ad aggi,* Tesi di Laurea, Facolta di Economia e Commercio, Universita di Modena, 1986.

Tower, Edward. "Industrial Policy in Less Developed Countries," *Contemporary Policy Issues* 4, 1 (January 1986) pp. 23-35.

Trigilia, Carlo. *Grandi partiti e piccole imprese.* Bologna: Il Mulino, 1986.

_____. "Small Firm Development and Political Subcultures in Italy," *European Sociological Review* 2, 3 (1986).

Turk, Herman. "Comparative Urban Structure from an Interorganizational Perspective," *Administrative Science Quarterly* 18 (1973) pp. 37-55.

Turk, Herman, and M. Lefcowitz. "Toward Theory of Representation Between Groups," *Social Forces* 40 (1962) pp. 337-341.

Turner, Lowell. *Democracy at Work: Changing World Markets and the Future of Labor Unions.* Ithaca, NY: Cornell University Press, 1991.

Tyrus, Ober, and Lucy Martin. "Japan/U.S. Delegations Meet and Discuss Trade, Political, Economic and Security Relations as Three Day Symposium Kick Off," *Business Wire,* June 4, 1990.

Vaughan, Roger J., et al. "The Wealth of States: Policies for a Dynamic Economy." Council of State Planning Associations, 1985.

Vernon, R. "The Product Life Cycle Hypothesis in a New International Environment," *Oxford Bulletin Of Economics and Statistics* 41 (1979) pp. 255-267.

Veyssarat, Beatrice. "Industrial Flexibility in Switzerland: The Social and Institutional Aspects of Degeneration and Revivals." In *Worlds of Possibility: Flexibility and Mass Production in Western Industrialization,* C. Sabel and J. Zeitlin, eds. New York: Cambridge University Press, forthcoming.

Visser, Jelle. "In Search of Inclusive Unionism," *Bulletin of Comparative Labor Relations* 18 (Special Issue 1990) pp. 39-67.

Von Hippel, Eric. "Cooperation Between Competing Firms: Informal Know-How Trading." Mimeo, Sloan School of Management, Massachusetts Institute of Technology, 1986.

Vuilleumier, Mario. *Horlogers de l'Anarchisme, Emergence d'un Mouvement: La Federation Jurassienn.* Lausanne: Payot, 1988.

Waldinger, Roger. *Through the Eye of the Needle.* New York: Columbia University Press, 1986.

Warren R. "The Interorganizational Field as a Focus for Investigation," *Administrative Science Quarterly* 12 (1967) pp. 397-419.

Watanabe, Teresa. "Japan's Trying Hard to Catch U.S. in Software, *Los Angeles Times,* July 8, 1990.

Weaver, R. *The Politics of Industrial Change: Railway Policy in North America.* Washington, DC: Brookings Institution, 1985.

Weber, Henri. *Le parti des patrons.* Paris: Seuil, 1986.

White, Lawrence "Measuring the Importance of Small Business in the American Economy." No. 1981-4, Graduate School of New York University, no date.

Wilks, Stephen. "From Industrial Policy to Enterprise Policy in Britain," *Journal of General Management* 12, 4 (Summer 1987) pp. 5-20.

_____. *Industrial Policy and the Motor Industry.* Dover, NH: Manchester University Press, 1984.

Williams, Karel, J. Williams, and C. Haslam. *The Breakdown of Austin Rover: A Case Study in the Failure of Business Strategy and Industrial Policy.* New York: St. Martin's Press, 1987.

Wilson, John. *The New Ventures: Inside High-Stakes World Venture Capital.* Reading, PA: Addison-Wesley, 1985.

Wilson, Kenneth, and W. Martin. "Ethnic Enclaves: A Comparison of the Cuban and Black Economies in Miami," *American Journal of Sociology* 88 (1982) pp. 135-160.

Wood, Stephen. "The Transformation of Work." In *Transformation of Work?* London: Unwin and Hyman, 1989.

Wollmann, Helmut. "Stadtpolitik - Erosion oder Ernererung des Sozialstaats - von unten?" *Leviathan* 7 (1986).

Womack, James P., et al. *The Machine that Changed the World: The Story of Lean Production,* New York: Rawson Associates, 1990.

INDEX

Accornero, Aris, 34n3
Action plan
  coordination of, 61
  criteria for, 55-56
  implementation of, 59
  issue management by, 55-56
  negotiating, 47-48
  requirements for beginning
    negotiation, 4
  shared vision component of, 51
ACTWU. *See* Amalgamated Clothing
  and Textile Workers Union
  (ACTWU)
ADARO
  role in Macael Action Plan of, 49-50
  studies for Macael region by, 49, 52,
    56, 57
AFCERQ. *See* Association Française
  des Cercles de Qualité (AFCERQ)
Agricultural sector, Emilia-Romagna,
  23
Ahlen, Kristina, 164n18
Albrecht, Karl, 65n28
Amalgamated Clothing and Textile
  Workers Union (ACTWU), 95, 100
Angelini, Maurizio, 37n25
Antonelli, Gilberto, 35n9
Aoki, Masahiko, 164n13
Apparel and textile industry,
  Pennsylvania
  changes in, 96
  competition for, 95
  labor shortage in, 105-6
Armajani, Babak, 65n28
Association Française des Cercles de
  Qualité (AFCERQ), 70-71
Auroux laws, 70-71, 72
  effect of, 67-69, 73, 75-76
  experience of, 76
  fiat of, 6

participative structures created by,
  75, 69
Autogestion
  defined, 67, 68
  as ideal, 73
  as part of French Socialist program,
  75

Bagnasco, Arnaldo, 35n11
Baldissera, Alberto, 34n7
Balloni, Valeriano, 35n9
Bamford, Julia, 35n10
Barbagli, Marizio, 35n12
Bartel, Rainer, 163n6
Bartlett, Christopher, 163n7
Barzelay, Michael, 63nn2,3, 65nn27,28
Bassi, S., 38n35
Beauregard, Robert, 17n5
Becattini, Giacomo, 35n10
Becker, Gary S., 173
Behn, Robert, 5n35
Bennati, R., 38n35
Bennis, Warren, 65n38
Benya, Anton, 163n9
Berg, David, 65n36
Bernouz, Phillippe, 77n7
Biachi, Patrizio, 37n24
Biagi, Marco, 36n17
Bonazzi, Giuseppe, 34-35n7
Borzeix, Annie, 77n7
Bosworth, Brian, 107n2
Bounine-Cabalé, Jean, 164n13
Brödner, P., 173
Brown, Bernard E., 77n2
Brusco, Sebastiano, 35n11, 36n19,
  65n41
Bueno, José María, 63n7
Bunel, Jean, 77n7
Butera, Federico, 35n9
Buyers and marketing cooperative, 53-
  54, 58

Customized markets, 176
Cyert, Richard, 16n2

D'Angelillo, Massimo, 37n24
Demand-side economics, 170
Democratic Party of the Left (PdS), 22
De-skilling, 139, 168
Dispute resolution, 146, 151
Dluhy, Milan, 64n24
Dore, Ronald, 164n13
Downskilling, 177

Economic development organization, 93
Economic performance
in Michigan (in 1980s), 109
Economic structure
development of Almería/Andalusian, 57-58
diversification in, 134-35
response of firms to current, 138-43
transformation of Emilia-Romagna region, 4, 22-24
See also Demand-side economics; Supply-side economics
Economies of scale, 141-42
Economies of scope, 142
Edelman, Murray, 65n30
Education
in labor relations, 109-10
for metalworkers union members, 31
to stimulate modernization and innovation, 92
in technical assistance projects, 133
See also Training
Effective supply theory, 172
Eisinger, Peter, 16n3
Elden, Max, 90n3
Electric power development, Macael region, 52, 56
Emilia-Romagna region
economic transformation of, 4, 22-24

Employee participation. See Worker participation
Employers associations, 45
Enterprise committees
proposd role for French, 71-72
role in France of, 67-68
ERVET, 27-28
Execution reintegration, 139-43, 153
Expression groups
characteristic of successful, 70
creation and working of, 69, 72
perceived worker role in, 71
See also Quality circles

Fardin, G., 35n8
FIOM. See Metalworkers union (FIOM)
Firms
blurring of boundaries among, 153-54
patterns in structural transition, 105-6
reorganization of, 138-43
role of labor union in reorganization of, 143-53
strategies employed under MAIN project, 102-4
See also Clusters of firms; Subcontracting
Firms, large, 25
Firms, medium-sized, 31-34
Firms, small
definition in Pennsylvania of, 92
diversification, specialization, and networking among Emilian, 25
in marble mining industry, 52-54
perceived disadvantages of, 92
in small-and medium-sized firm sector, 112
See also Firms, small- and medium-sized
Firms, small- and medium-sized
in Emilia-Romagna region, 22, 24
goals of CAT for, 134-35

222

OTA (Office of Technology
Assessment), 177

Parker, Mike, 165n23
Participatory agreements, 31-32
PCI. *See* Democratic Party of the Left
(PdS); Italian Communist Party
(PCI)
PdS. *See* Democratic Party of the Left
(PdS)
Pennachi, Laura, 35n9
Perulli, Paolo, 37n26
Peters, Thomas J., 65n35
PEWS. *See* Programs for Employment
and Workplace Systems (PEWS)
Pinazzi, S., 38n35
Piore, Michael, 35n10, 163nn2,8,
164n20, 175, 184
Piro, Franco, 36n15
Pizzorno, Alessandro, 34nn4,5
Plant closing
decision to reverse plan for, 83-85,
88
proposed, 79
Plant restructuring
effect of SAT process on decision
for, 87-88
proposed, 79-80
Plosila, Walter, 107nn2,4
Polanyi, Michael, 64n23
Polese, Mario, 63n5
Political system
changes in French, 76-77
factions in Italian, 20-21, 22-23 role
in Andalusia's industrial
development, 42-43
use of demand side economics in,
170
Porter, Michael, 63nn4,6
Powell, Walter W., 163n4
Premio de Mármol, 58
Private sector, 151-52
Production
customized or small-batch, 174-76

firm response to costs of, 138-39
hybrid strategies for technological
change, 143
regionalization (clustering) of, 140-
41, 153
reintegration of conception and
execution of, 139
See also Flexible technologies;
Innovation, permanent
Production organization, 124
Product market fragmentation, 176
Programs for Employment and
Workplace Systems (PEWS), 7, 80
Przeworski, A., 170
Psdi. *See* Italian Social-Democratic
Party (Psdi)
PSI. *See* Italian Socialist Party (PSI)
Public sector, 151-52
Purchasing cooperative, Macael region,
52-53
Putnam, Robert, 37n24

Quality circles, France, 70-71, 75

Rebecchi, Emilio, 37n31
Regalia, Ida, 34n4
Regini, Marino, 34nn4,6, 35nn8,9,10,
37n26
Reich, Robert, 65nn32,37
Republican Party (UIL), Italy, 20, 21,
23
Reynaud, Jean-Daniel, 164n13
Reyneri, Emilio, 34n4
Rogers, Joel, 164n21
Role frame, 61
Romagnoli, Umberto, 34n2
Rosanvallon, Pierre, 74, 77n14, 164n12
Ross, George, 34n2
Royo, Javier Perez, 63n3
Rubini, Irene, 35n13
Ruffino, M., 38n35
Rumpeltes, Leslie, 90n4